# Sea and Sky

*A Life From the Navy*

# Sea and Sky

## *A Life From the Navy*

*David Howard*

First published 2011
by David Howard


Copyright © David Howard 2011, with the exception of the italicised
sections of Chapter 26 for which Copyright - REPRODUCED BY
PERMISSION - MARITIME BOOKS,
LISKEARD PL14 4EL.
Www.navybooks.com  January 2011

Printed in England by CPI Antony Rowe (Eastbourne) Ltd

*To my children*

# Sea and Sky

*A Life From the Navy*

# *Prologue*

THE Royal Navy I joined as a boy sailor in 1947 was required to support a British Empire, with a complement of ships or boats capable of meeting that worldwide commitment. Ships then in service ranged from battleships through submarines to gunboats. An extensive reserve fleet required maintenance from additional manpower. It was a large fleet overall with a large number of men. The Womens Royal Naval Service (WRNS) did not go to sea, and ships were all-male. Today's navy is much reduced. Ships are generally smaller, sleeker, more handsome, pack an infinitely more powerful punch, and are crewed by personnel more highly skilled, to meet the demands of more advanced technology. These personnel are both male and female. The Womens Royal Naval Service is now Royal Navy: women go to sea.

In my day sailors lived in 'messes', each a small compartment in a ship, in which a group of men lived, slept (in hammocks), ate, might prepare food, washed up the dishes and food trays, and took their recreation. Food was often mediocre, except in some smaller ships. Usually cooked in a central galley, it was served up and eaten in the mess.

Domestic activities outside the mess, apart from the heads (toilets), were showering and laundry – by hand; usually there were no ships' laundries. Fresh water was frequently rationed.

In today's ships, cafeteria dining halls offer excellent, multi-choice meals. Ships have laundries. Fresh water is rarely a problem. Personnel sleep in bunks.

Between 1947 and 1953 I graduated from Boy to Petty Officer Seaman.

The next two years were largely as an Upper Yardman under officer's training. From '55 to '70 I rose from Sub Lieutenant to Commander, my rank when I retired in '84. My time as a sailor was spent in small ships. They were happy ships. So were the aircraft carriers I later flew from, and my several squadrons during a full flying career. Back as a seaman I enjoyed total fulfilment as a frigate commander: in a happy ship. Life could not have better been.

I'm often asked: 'Don't you miss your flying?' or 'Don't you miss your ship?' No. These 'best' times have to end, and service life conditions you for it as you move on, roughly every two years. What I do miss is the camaraderie, the laugh round every corner. I'm sure it's still the same now.

What I hope has *changed* is the antipathy I sometimes found between the surface navy and its airborne side. They were not always comfortable bed-fellows...... As an aviator I called this anti-aviator-it-is.

My naval life was varied, challenging, always interesting and always rewarding. And it moulded me, throughout my life in the service, as well as after retirement. I'm proud of what the navy made of me, and what it did for me. It gave me a life.

Overall I had a ball – and I'd have it all over again.

# Chapter 1

## *Boy Sailor*

THERE was something utterly repulsive about this little man, as soon as he appeared in our home. I was fourteen, already a foot taller than him – didn't help! My sister was thirteen.

I couldn't put my finger on what disgusted me so forcibly. Couldn't ask my sister's opinion –my mother had hurriedly packed her off to boarding school.

It took another 40 years before she told me: the stepfather, by then long dead, had tried pestering her sexually as a girl, had then abused her daughters when they were four and five.

At last I understood. He'd been a paedophile.

In hindsight I'll bet I wasn't the only boy in 1947, knowingly, or unwittingly like me, to have used the navy to escape the nauseous canker of a paedophiliac stepfather. Didn't know why I was doing it, just knew I had to. I went along to the naval recruiting office in Brighton and was welcomed by a burly Chief Petty Officer. He wasn't the least interested in my educational qualifications. However my School Certificate proved up to the academic demands of the simple line drawing questionnaire the Chief slapped in front of me.

'Which of these would you use to drive a nail?' Outline drawing of a handsaw, a pair of pliers, a screwdriver and a hammer. Demanding stuff. There were a few more similar questions.

'Get your mother to sign 'ere, 'cos yer a minor, son. Bring it back to me and yer in'. That was it. Six months later I *was* in. In *HMS St Vincent*, Gosport.

The possibility of entering as an officer cadet had never been mentioned. Since I didn't know about officers anyway it wouldn't have made any difference. Getting away from home and that stepfather was the Number One priority.

From the very start it was going be a challenge. The first thing we saw as our coach brought us through the main gate of our boy's training establishment was the mast: 160 feet high.

'We've all got to climb that' someone said. 'At least once'.

It looked as tall as the Eiffel Tower! Felt like it too, the first time we went up it.

Boys' training at *St Vincent* was an eye opener to a boy who had led a relatively sheltered life to date. During our first month we had the option of 'walking'- leaving. There was no way I was going back. I no longer had a home as such. I would accept whatever the navy threw at me. Nothing would persuade me to chuck it and return – to the stepfather I had escaped – to our mutual relief and, on my part, utter loathing. That was probably mutual too.

My first meal in the navy was tea: two slices of bread, margarine, and disgusting tea. When I asked why, our newly self-appointed class know-all explained that it had bromide in it to counteract any homosexual tendencies we might have. Since I didn't know what homosexual tendencies were, let alone whether I had any, I decided to keep quiet. One of my mother's maxims had been 'It's better to keep your mouth shut and let people think you're a fool, than open it and let them know you really are'. In my strange new world it was sound advice.

'Know all' was one of the boys from *HMS Arethusa*, an old, long retired sail training ship which had given younger boys a home – many of them were orphans – until they were old enough to move on to *HMS St Vincent* or *Ganges*, the other boys' training establishment.

They'd lived a naval routine and thus knew a lot of 'navalese', which they willingly passed on to their new chums. This was an enormous help to most of us – green as grass. Only very few adopted the 'know all' role.

One 'know all' did manage to persuade some, at the initial clothing issue, that they should ask for a cap at least one size too small. This was considered 'tiddely', sailor speak (the know-all said) for smart. Not only was it neither smart, nor practical; with their caps perched precariously somewhere on top of their heads they soon became obvious candidates for the duty Petty Officer treatment, a painful thump across the cap with the flat of his hand, usually from behind, accompanied by the roar: 'In the navy, my son, yew wear your 'at, not walk along beside it'.

I soon learned that all that was required during working hours was to be in the right place at the right time in the right dress. Every morning we had instruction, which I enjoyed, especially seamanship, none of which I've forgotten. Afternoons were mostly sports or boatwork. I started on the rugger I'd played so much at school but soon found out that naval scrums were all free-for-all punch-ups and stuck to soccer.

Three mornings out of four (the fourth was an earlier call for laundry) we were turned out at 6 am by a duty petty officer. Depending which petty officer it was depended on how quickly you turned out. Some of them carried 'stonachies'. A stonachy was a short length of flexible rubber hose about a foot long and an inch and a half in diameter. Thumped across the backside it hurt. We soon got to recognise the voices of each petty officer as he came round shouting 'Wakey, wakey', going through the dormitory to check we really were turning out. Stonachy users got us all turned out pretty quickly but some brave souls would leave it to the last second. If their feet snarled up in the blankets they were instant victims.

Food was a shock to me: even worse than at a Roman Catholic boarding college during the war. That had been bad. This was awful. I'd become used to my mother's cooking, and having her pander to all my boyhood likes and dislikes, even with rationing. I disliked fish intensely. Every fourth morning the smell of 'yellow peril' (smoked haddock) permeated up through our multi-storey block from the ground floor dining hall and galley to our third floor dormitory. Before we'd turned out I knew I'd be eating only bread and margarine for breakfast that day.

Other fourth day breakfast regulars were 'train smash': tinned tomatoes, and soggy bacon (swimming in the watery tomato juice), pretty revolting scrambled egg (the wartime dried variety) with I don't know what, and our only favourite: baked beans on fried bread (thick wedges of golden brown, stomach-filling heaven There may have been a banger thrown in now and then, I don't remember, but it would have been popular. Even a naval banger was just about edible. I don't remember a thing about the other meals of the day.

My abiding memory was of being hungry all the time. NAAFI cake saved us. The NAAFI produced large trays of cake about two feet by two feet and two inches thick, cut into four inch square slices. Each slice cost us one old penny but provided enough of a filler to keep a permanently hungry boy going for a while.

In the latter half of our first year, 1947, naval teams were chosen to take part in the Festival of Remembrance. *St Vincent* and *Ganges* (the other boys' training establishment) were to do a Hornpipe demonstration. There were 49 of us and we practised and practised until we had a pretty good demonstration, and off we went to London and the Albert Hall.

On the evening of the show we danced the Hornpipe. It was rapturously received and we all trooped off, to come back on later for the final hymn singing, the 'They shall grow not old' dedication and the two minutes silence, when the poppies started to fall from great nets in the overhead. That was the only sound: poppies, fluttering down in a whisper, before they settled on and around us, until we seemed to be ankle deep in them. We were bareheaded until they started to fall. When they stopped, after one of the most memorable silences I've ever experienced, we all wore a crown of poppies.

As we left the floor, outside in the passages running around the auditorium were crowds of the audience. This was 1947, not long after World War 2, and a lot of them were in tears, grieving for relatives who hadn't made it back, others simply so moved by the scene they'd just witnessed, as were we the participants. Many of them asked us to go back into the auditorium and get some poppies for them. We went back several times and filled our caps. Every one of our poppies was gratefully collected.

We managed one short run ashore in London. Since our cap ribbons read *HMS St.Vincent* or *Ganges* it was obvious where we were from, but that didn't stop one budding old seadog shooting a line about his sea time. He soon got his come-uppance, from an ex-*St Vincent* boy, now a policeman: 'Yes son. I went there', he came back. 'Fell over the side and got gravel rash'.

After a year's initial training I was drafted to *HMS Sirius*, a World War 2 *Dido* class light cruiser and, of her time, a beautiful ship, with three for'ard and two after 5.25" gun turrets, and twin masts and twin raked funnels. I was on a steep learning curve but the knowledge I picked up about life at sea stuck. Many memories still stand out. *Sirius* had wooden decks and wooden decks had to be scrubbed daily. We scrubbed and scrubbed – winter and summer – in bare feet.

Another vivid recall is the upper deck wash-house. Men returning from shore leave drunk and incapable were locked in the wash-house until morning when a salt water hose was turned on them to clean up the mess. No Health and Safety in those days. It was salutary.

Health and Safety now would certainly have a lot to say about cleaning the ship's double bottom, the rusty honey-comb of little more than over-sized coffins running almost the length and breadth of the hull. Not only were they rusty, but often wet, and all had to be dried out, wire-brushed and painted. The only access was by interconnecting body-sized openings. It was a filthy job and the paint was lead oxide, unpleasant anywhere, but in the confines of our workspace, almost lethal. The only naval acknowledgement to the health hazard, from dust and paint fumes, was a free pint of fresh milk a day. We survived.

We also survived painting the ship's side in harbour in Montego Bay, Jamaica. Nobody risked falling off our paint stages (platforms) and joining the sharks we could see investigating the rope ends dangling in the water from the stages.

Happier memories were swimming over the ship's side in mid-Atlantic, eerie but enjoyable; and the affair of the drunken seagull, again in mid-Atlantic.

When the unfortunate bird arrived on deck, exhausted and covered in oil, many of the ship's company immediately formed a seagull support team. The shipwright went below and built a palatial cage. Puttee (in charge of the paint store) produced about a gallon of white spirit. Tankee (the butcher) found some choice fillet steak and chopped it into pieces considered a suitable size for a seagull's gullet and enough for a banquet. Meanwhile a formidable body of 'swabbers down' had grabbed the white spirit and started swabbing down what appeared to be black oil on much of the bird's plumage. Finally an almost pristine passenger, now promoted to Able Seaman Gull, was lovingly introduced to the shipwright's palace and placed on the perch running the full length of its new home. The ship rolled slightly and A.B. Gull tottered all the way downhill. The ship rolled back and Gull tottered back. It looked a bit unhappy. Only after several repeat performances was it realised that perhaps a gallon of spirit had been a bit over the top.

Under the influence of white spirit fumes, Able Seaman Gull was blind drunk.

I look back on the completion of my time in *Sirius* as the end of my 'joining the navy' period. When I finally left her I was about to become an able seaman; I was no longer 'wet behind the ears'. I'd made just about all the mistakes makee-learnee sailors can make, and learned. And I'd been lucky enough to see quite a lot of the world.

A footnote: latterly in this period I managed to acquire what was then probably the most prized possession in any sailor's kit – a bucket! Up to that time dhobying had to be done either in that dual purpose, small upper deck wash-house, or in a hand basin in your allocated bathroom. A dhoby bucket meant you had your own receptacle for your dhobying, usually done in the bathroom, for carrying your clean wet dhobying along to a drying area, bringing it, dry, back to your mess deck, and for stowing your dirty dhobying in until you could wash it. The bucket was sacrosanct and it was unacceptable to ask to borrow someone's bucket; such a favour was rarely sought – or satisfied. A dhoby bucket was one of the most valued items you could acquire and its pride of place amongst a sailor's gear was invariably honoured by your messmates. It was also the hallmark of a mature sailor.

Since abandoning home I'd been free of that stepfather. The navy had given me what I had left home for, food, shelter, clothes and independence. And the navy became mother and father to me. I wasn't going to get to university. That boyhood ambition was dead.

I'd grown up. I was a loner, but could live with myself, and was at last good at being a sailor.

# Chapter 2

## *Jan*

IN 1949, now an able seaman, I was drafted to *HMS Trafalgar*, one of countless ships in reserve and a late World War 2 *Battle* class destroyer. She was moored in mid-stream at the northern end of Portsmouth harbour, which meant you had to get ashore and back by boat. This could make a run ashore a little ponderous but at least we were afloat and living in a ship rather than a barracks, and preferred it that way. The job of the skeleton crews in the reserve fleet was maintenance, not very exciting and no seatime.

*Trafalgar* used a system of catering called 'canteen messing'. Each man was credited with a daily messing allowance and food was 'bought', on credit, either from the canteen or from the ship's stores, prepared by the sailors themselves, and then cooked in the galley by the ship's chefs. We ate well, and any messing allowance not spent at the end of each month was shared out among the members of each mess. The system was popular, and was my first experience of on board cooking.

I had a chum in *Trafalgar* nicknamed Darkie. He managed, once a week, to get up to London to see a girl friend who, he confided to me, was a prostitute. Initially I was horrified; and I couldn't understand how he could afford it on our very meagre pay. He explained to me that she was incredibly kind to him, never charged him anything and always paid his train fare back to Portsmouth. Apparently all 'the girls' were equally kind, according to Darkie who often spoke glowingly to me about them. Darkie was a good looking chap and must have had a way with women. Obviously his charm worked wonders, especially with his own personal Suzie Wong.

I didn't stay long in *Trafalgar*. I had to specialise and get myself some professional sub-specialist qualification (my first specialisation was as a seaman). I'd filled in the usual required form to get me on my way, hopefully as a Hydrographic Surveyor; second preference had been for Quarters Armourer; don't ask me why; you had to put something and I didn't know what else to put on the form. I got my second preference. I moved to Whale Island for my training. Whale Island, proper title *HMS Excellent*, is also in Portsmouth harbour, on the eastern side just north of what is now a cross channel ferry terminal. In those days it was the Gunnery school for the navy and everyone went around in boots and gaiters, routine gunnery dress. If you were a sailor you also 'doubled' (jogged) everywhere. The parade ground wasn't the usual tarmac, it was gravel, and if you doubled or even marched on it on a dry day you created your own mini dust storm. Needless to say, being the gunnery school meant a lot of parade ground drill and we regularly practised manoeuvres that must have been current at Waterloo, and, given the right weather, marched around knee-deep in a cloud of dust.

This gave rise to a story, possibly apocryphal, to illustrate the Whale Island gunnery mentality. Serried ranks of sailors were drawn up on the parade ground when a messenger reported to the parade commander: a gunnery officer. This was long before mobile phones arrived so it was a note which read: 'Much regret Able Seaman Smith's mother passed away. Please have him report to the Admin. Office for compassionate leave asap'

The parade commander ordered the Chief Gunnery Instructor (aka God to sailors) to report to him, told him the problem and to get Smith away.

'Aye, aye, sir' said the Chief and saluted.

He then called the parade to attention and ordered: 'Able Seaman Smith: one pace forward march' to which Smith smartly responded.

'Your mother's dead'.

Smith collapsed in a dead faint – and was carried off.

After the parade finished the commander drew the Chief aside and told him his treatment had been a little hard on Smith. God forbid it should happen again but, should it, the Chief must demonstrate more compassion.

'Aye, aye, sir' said the Chief and saluted.

A month later, at a similar parade, another message arrived for the parade commander: 'Much regret Able Seaman Smith's father died of a broken heart. Please release Smith again'.

The Chief was ordered to report and the parade commander told him the sad news, reminded him of the need for some compassion, and to release Smith.

'Aye, aye, sir', said the Chief and saluted.

The parade was called to attention.

'All those wiv' a mother or a father still alive, one pace forward march… Where d'you fink you're going Smith?'

\*\*\*

My Quarters Armourer's training is only memorable in that I can't remember anything about it, except that it was supposed to teach me how to maintain minor gun mountings and small arms. It must have done that because I qualified and even, subsequently, worked as an armourer when I went back to sea, though for only a short time.

Whale Island was more memorable in that period because I met my first, steady girlfriend at a NAAFI dance there. Her name was Jan – Janet. She was tall, attractive, and caught my eye instantly. I knew she'd seen me and seemed interested, but I was much too shy, and green, to make any sort of approach to her.

Quite soon I found this attractive girl behind me in the queue for tea. She broke the ice and said Hello. Over a cup of tea and some NAAFI cake we chatted until I was brave enough to ask her to dance (I was hopeless on the dance floor), and she tolerated my staggering around massacring her toes. Eventually I plucked up more courage and asked her for a date. Jan had been wondering whether I would ever get round to it since that was what she'd been angling for ever since she first spotted me. She told me this a while later when I was a little less wet behind the ears. I had a lot to learn about the wiles of women! We went on from there.

Janet had two sisters and three brothers. All the brothers had left home, two of them married, but they all often visited their mother and father, so that I met the whole family regularly. Jan's parents made me very welcome, as did all her brothers and sisters. They were a really charming family, wonderfully supportive of each other, and this was my first experience of what a family really meant. I was even rather envious of the togetherness that permeated the whole family, and the fondness and respect they showed for their parents. They were happy to share all this with me whenever Jan took me home, which was often.

I revelled in it. It was completely new to me and I began to understand how I'd become the loner I was, and what I'd missed because of the circumstances of my childhood.

Jan taught me to dance. She was infinitely patient and eventually I could stagger through a waltz. Then she moved me on to a foxtrot, and so we went on, until I could dance quite passably, and without crippling her long-suffering feet.

This was the era of the big band, Ted Heath style, with a team of vocalists like Dickie Valentine, Dennis Lotis and Lita Rosa, playing in large dance halls. There were several in Portsmouth. Money was always scarce but, for two shillings entrance per person, you could have a wonderful evening and maybe afford one fairly meagre drink, or a cup of tea and some cake.

Jan and I danced a lot for a few days after my fortnightly payday. When my money ran short we lived on tea, before our routine Goodnight snog on her front door step. I had to miss out on that once. Just after a payday dance evening, when I was temporarily in funds, Jan had a gin and tonic and I had a large black velvet: cider and Guinness. I'm no beer drinker but was stupid enough to accept Jan's challenge to drink another. Halfway back to Jan's home I was so woozy I had to leave her on the bus to get home on her own - livid. She issued no further challenges.

I need to digress slightly and describe what had passed for sex education up to that point in my life. There had been no sex education at home, not one mention of the subject. At school the only knowledge gleaned had been from my friends, and, in hindsight, most of that had been idle boasting of the crudest kind, and based on boys' lurid imagination rather than experience.

Thus I joined the navy absolutely ignorant of even the basic elements of sex. On the lower deck, sex was a major topic of conversation and from this I gleaned some rudimentary aspects. It seemed to me that sex for men in my situation was simply 'getting one's end away' (a polite version of what the average sailor said he went ashore for), and there was never any mention of how the girl might feel about it, either the psychological or the physiological side of a sexual relationship. In other words, for your average sailor, self-gratification was what it was all about, wherever and whenever it was available. Armed with this totally inadequate and unsuitable introduction to the world of sex, I sallied forth into my early, serious boy/girl relationships.

Jan was my first lover. She was gentle, tolerant and loving and with her I learned a lot about what made each of us tick as far as sex was concerned. These were the days when most girls simply wanted to get married and start a family. Career women hadn't been heard of as such. Jan was no exception and perhaps we shouldn't have pursued the sexual side of our relationship to the extent we did, but she was a very attractive girl, and, for my part, what man would not want to make love to someone so attractive? I had a lot to learn too and with her I started on a natural learning curve.

I managed once to take Jan back to Peacehaven to meet my mother, aunt and uncle. This was a period when I was staying with my aunt and uncle who were absolutely charming towards Jan. Having come over from Hove for the day, my mother was just the opposite, in fact she was so frigid towards Jan that it verged on outright rudeness. This was another of many indications I'd had that my mother was an out and out snob. I was terribly hurt, and afterwards apologised to Jan for my mother's behaviour. She was kind enough to tell me not to worry, some mothers tended to be that way about their sons, but I guessed the air was pretty blue when she described the visit to her family back in Portsmouth.

Jan got much too fond of me, and she and her family wanted us to get engaged. Nothing was ever mentioned but I would have been crass not to have felt the 'vibes' coming my way whenever I went home with Jan. I was fond of her and we had some wonderful times together but I didn't want to get engaged, although I'd never expressed this viewpoint. Neither did I give any other indication of feelings of any sort, not being prepared to take on any commitment that I would be too immature and inexperienced to be able to live up to. I knew I was much too young and what I'd seen at home about marriage did not encourage me in any way. In any case, when I'd finished my gunnery training I was to go out to the Mediterranean to join another ship. That meant being separated, a long separation too, and even then I knew that that would be hard on a relationship. I was going to stay unattached until I was capable of supporting a relationship in terms of being home-based, as well as psychologically and financially. I had no idea when that might be but it definitely wasn't then.

I had to say farewell to Jan before I left England for the Mediterranean. I was aware that some kind of deputation of Jan's women relations, mother, two sisters and a sister-in-law, would be gathering together at Jan's home for my last evening before I went away. I guessed that they'd be hoping I'd ask Jan to marry me before I left. Before I entered that lioness' den I spent a lot of my not too generous leave pay on a bottle of gin, one of port, and some orange. As usual I was made very welcome and I soon started offering the booze around as a 'going away' drink, or drinks rather. The levels of gin and port went down quite quickly until, by the finish, all the women were incapable, and Jan had had to go upstairs to bed. I left quietly, stone cold sober. I don't drink port or gin. Six months into my scheduled two and a half years in the Mediterranean I got a 'Dear John' letter from Jan.

Through the years I kept in touch with the family. They always welcomed me and gave me news about Jan, and I even saw her a couple of times when she was down visiting her relatives. She and her husband had gone to live in Liverpool but, in true close-knit family fashion, she came down to Portsmouth regularly, a port I often visited when I commanded *Lincoln*. The whole family had followed my career with great interest and, when *Lincoln* hit the press with her Cod War activities off Iceland, Jan commissioned a painting of *Lincoln* on patrol among the trawlers.

Jan came down to Portsmouth especially to present the painting to me. She explained that the artist was an old gentleman in the Isle of Wight. He'd apologised if some of the detail was wrong – he was too old to remain fully conversant with changes to ships' equipment – but anything that was wrong he'd willingly change for Jan. Jan wouldn't have known if any of the detail was wrong and she gave it to me as it came to her. I was so touched by this gift and the fact that she'd followed my career all the way, I wouldn't have had anything altered for worlds. The painting is one of my most treasured possessions.

# Chapter 3

## *Armada*

HAVING said goodbye to that alcoholic gathering of Jan's womenfolk, I had an uncomfortable passage out to the Med. in a crowded troopship, one of the Empire class. We had sailed from Liverpool on New Year's Eve, 1950. The ship was overcrowded, short of fresh water and had only salt-water showers. In those days salt-water soap was more like carborundum! Possibly it still is.

Once in Malta I joined another *Battle* class destroyer – the *Armada*. They were handsome ships and *Armada* had an extra 10,000hp over her sister ships in the class to boot. In speed trials she could outrun her sisters effortlessly. The other ships in the squadron were *Saintes* - the leader, *Vigo*, and *Gravelines*, and our usual billet in Malta was moored in line ahead down Sliema Creek.

Malta was our base port and my new shipmates quickly inducted me into the dubious attractions of the island. Runs ashore inevitably lead to 'The Gut', a notorious street full of bars, each bar staffed by even more notorious girls, none of whom were, to me, in the slightest way attractive, just the opposite in fact. Many of the sailors used to rave about them though and, presumably, they represented the 'end away' goal for a lot of them. One woman in particular was notorious throughout the fleet. Her nickname was Sparrow (I believe because of her looks!) and she worked in a bar called the New Life in the Gut. I never ever saw her because I never went into the New Life.

In my next ship, a minesweeper also based in Malta, a chum of mine couldn't get ashore soon enough to see her. Uncharacteristically he had come back aboard early one evening, and very glum. It was his first night ashore after we'd returned from the minefields. Sparrow had been killed in an accident while we'd been at sea: thrown down the stairs in the New Life by a marine. It broke her neck! My friend, a pragmatist, soon got over her demise. I suppose when he'd got keen on a Fleet bicycle he had accepted that the competition could be fierce, and the association had to have its drawbacks.

The local beer was ghastly but preferable to the wine, Ambit, which could be deadly! The beer was all we could afford to drink safely; ambit had got many sailors into a lot of trouble. We used to round off the evening with the Maltese version of steak, eggs and chips at one of the several restaurants in the Gut, standard price three shillings and sixpence old money. The steak was probably 'shoat', a cross between a sheep and a goat. I don't remember seeing a cow on the island. After an evening on Maltese beer it still tasted pretty good to us.

The chap in charge of my new mess in *Armada* was known as 'Hooky' (traditional, because of the leading seaman's anchor badge or 'hook' on his arm). He was a stolid, taciturn rather dour Yorkshireman and, I soon discovered, a sound professional seaman, highly respected in the ship. In the mess his word was law and, to us, he was God.

Like many small ships the *Armada* used Canteen messing, which I'd first experienced during my reserve fleet time in another *Battle* class, the *Trafalgar*. Two cooks were detailed each day by Hooky, and were responsible for the preparation and serving up of all meals, and for clearing away afterwards. Hooky planned our weekly menus and issued the roster for cook duties.

Shortly after joining the ship my turn for duty cook came round. My fellow cook told me, nervously, that the menu for the day decreed steak and kidney pie for dinner (lunch). Pie meant pastry, or 'clacker' in naval terms, (it also means a pretty girl to a sailor, as in 'a nice bit of clacker'). Unexpectedly, my new messmates joshed me about this, and told me, with a laugh, they were really looking forward to it. Apparently quality was vital and the clacker all-important.

Keen to prove myself, I volunteered to make it. This was the rash leap-before-you-look courage of teenage youth. I had very little on-board cooking experience. Despite my earlier service in *Trafalgar*, the knowledge gained could barely be described as much more than limited. At home I was a dab hand at beans on toast or boiled eggs. My pastry-making skill, such as it was, stemmed from a few shaky attempts supervised by my mother. Her most important tip had been always to mix your dough with a cold spoon or knife, never with warm hands. It made the pastry tough. Loftily I passed this pearl of culinary wisdom on to my fellow cook as if I'd invented it. It immediately won me his admiration and confidence. Plainly he was relieved not to have to put himself to the test! Inspired by what he gratefully assumed were my culinary 'skills', he was confident that his cook's tour this time around would be hallmarked by quality clacker. In my youthful arrogance I assumed that his evident delight and relief that his team-mate cook knew what he was doing was due entirely to a lack of self-confidence. It simply never penetrated my conceit that there could be another reason, or that my cocky self-confidence might be dangerously misplaced.

Most ship's food then was cooked in large aluminium trays about 50 cms long, 30 cms wide and 8 cms deep. It took quite a lot of hard labour, not only in mixing the dough, but also with the rolling pin, to produce sufficient dough to line two of the trays, with enough left over for the covering. We loaded the trays with mountains of fresh steak and kidney – canteen messing meant you usually ate like kings! I then laid a blanket of dough over each, trimmed and crimped the edges with what I fondly imagined to be professional flourishes, and used the trimmings to decorate the tops: anchors and hawsers, sailor's stuff. The two enormous pies were, I thought, absolute perfection. So did the other cook. Proudly I ferried the dishes up to the galley; my fellow cook wasn't going to get the kudos for such culinary masterpieces. En route the pies attracted many admiring glances. At midday I went and fetched them, now cooked a beautiful golden brown and giving off an aroma that generated pure envy along the passages back to the mess.

With blatant false modesty I set the pies down on the mess table alongside the other trays of vegetables my fellow cook had collected. With self-conscious nonchalance I pretended not to notice the buzz of approval from my messmates, eyeing, and sniffing, their dinner as they queued for their rum issue at the other end of the mess table.

Rum issue complete, the sailors sat down at the rectangular, well-scrubbed deal table, Hooky at the head, the rest in a rough pecking order of seniority along each side of the table. We two cooks served up the meal, sharing out the food as fairly as possible until everyone had, before him, a generous, steaming-hot meal of which, I thought, the star item, the literally crowning glory, was the beautiful golden clacker.

I had assumed that the almost tangible air of expectancy was from hungry sailors about to tuck into a feast. My supreme conceit was shattered by the other cook when he passed Hooky his plate, referring to it as his 'favourite meal'. Only then did I realise why there had been the mysterious concern about who should make the clacker, and why quality was so important. Hooky was keen on his clacker and, to us sailors, as I said, Hooky was God!

In that mess, presided over by God Hooky, there was an old-world etiquette among the sailors. No one would have dreamed of picking up their knife and fork until Hooky had done so. Nor would he until he saw that everyone had their meal in front of him. And no one would start their meal until Hooky had taken his first mouthful. He did, and began chewing slowly, sampling the food, much in the manner of a professional wine taster. All eyes were on him, awaiting his verdict. How did the new arrival rate on his first cook's duty? Painfully it penetrated: my clacker and I were in the dock.

The clacker was good, even though I say it myself. I had put a great deal of care into its preparation. Although there had been an awful lot to mix I had managed to minimise using my hands in the mixing, as my mother had advised. After my first mouthful I assessed she would have been proud of her sailor son.

Recognition of talent by sailors is instantaneous. Acknowledgement of such talent is hard to come by and begrudging. There was no acknowledgement of the quality of my clacker in any way. Except for the sounds of chewing – they were at least eating it – there was complete silence. We all waited for a verdict from Hooky, and it appeared to be de rigueur not to pre-empt him.

As Hooky chewed on endlessly my earlier over-confidence evaporated. Serious qualms set in. Was the clacker as good as I had assessed it to be? Well, I would have thought that anyway, wouldn't I? Had I been too hasty in volunteering to make it, and on the strength of such limited experience? Positively 'Yes'.

Sailors are small-c conservative and Hooky was an extreme example. Rapturous praise would have been uncharacteristic. Faint praise was more his style, and probably more likely, if at all! I can't remember whether I was ever asked to make clacker again; I only recall the suspense of a situation entirely of my own making. I had broken the golden rule of service life: never volunteer for anything. My inflated opinion of myself as a first-class clacker maker could be on the point of rapid deflation. Would it be thumbs up or thumbs down?

At last Hooky finished. He would never have spoken until his mouth was empty, certainly not centre-stage as well he appreciated he was. I realised that, besides my clacker, he was savouring the new boy's evident discomfort. This, I accepted sadly, was well deserved: pride and a big head both fall heavily.

The last morsel swallowed, Hooky gazed portentously, and slowly, around the expectant group, spinning my agony out. Finally he pronounced.

"'oo made the clacker?'

***

About this time I discovered a peculiar and surprising habit some of the sailors affected. We wore 'white fronts' under our sailor suits ashore. This was simply a white shirt with a rectangular opening for your head, the opening edged with blue denim. It saved a lot of dhobying if, instead of the white front, you wore what we called a 'dicky' front. This was simply two small rectangles of white cloth, joined at the top to provide the same rectangular opening for your head. At the bottom there were tapes that you tied round your waist at the sides so that, under a blue serge suit, it looked just like a regulation full white front. This was normal practice for many of us, not least because it was a lot cooler than the heavy white front. What made it a bit peculiar was that some sailors had managed to buy, from the less reputable sailors' tailors, a dicky front with false hair glued on the inside of the front. The hair was readily visible above the blue denim, so that the wearer looked as if he had a very hairy chest. I never found out whether a 'hairy' impostor ever managed to pull, or, if he did, what the girl said if and when she found out. Neither did I ever discover whether you could buy different colour hair adornments, to match your own hair!

In this period I tried growing a beard. In the navy you can only 'discontinue shaving'. You can't have a 'goatee' or any other part-shaved style. It's all or nothing at all. I thought I did quite well, and even waxed my moustaches when they were long enough. The hair on my head is dark and straight. My beard was auburn and curly. When I considered myself sufficiently hirsute I went ashore to get my photo taken to send home to mum. In those days photographic 'studios' were plentiful enough but most of them, including the one I chose, were simply a room with one bare light bulb overhead. Knowing nothing about photography I dutifully sat under the light bulb as requested and had several photos taken. It would be a week before they'd be ready.

Back I went after a week, keen to see what I hoped would really impress mum. On every photo the bottom half of my face was in shadow, under the overhead bulb, and you couldn't see anything of a beard. In disgust I tore them up and threw them all in the creek. The next day I applied to start shaving again.

By this time I had taken and passed the examination for Leading Seaman, and after a short wait had been promoted.

# Chapter 4

## *Fierce*

AFTER I'd been in the *Armada* a year the ship sailed for the UK – without me. In those days you usually did two and a half years on station and I'd joined her less than half way through my allotted time.

So I'd had to say Goodbye to all my chums, and I then joined *Fierce*, an *Algerine* class minesweeper, also based in Malta. *Fierce* was the leader of a four-ship minesweeper squadron. These were very comfortable ships because we had two messdecks. In a lower messdeck we had our kit lockers and slung our hammocks. This was closed down for safety while we were in the minefields, when we used an upper (above the waterline) messdeck where we ate and spent our off-duty time. Once we'd finished the day's minesweeping we'd leave the minefields and the lower messes were opened up.

*Fierce* was another canteen messing ship.

It was traditional in those days for canteen messing ships to prepare an enormous spread in preparation for Captain's 'rounds' (inspection) on Christmas day, when the Captain toured the messes on a goodwill basis rather than a pukka inspection. We used to lay it on, with large joints of cold roast beef, pork, and ham, Christmas cake, mince pies and many other attractions. One Christmas the unique item for our mess was to be four roast chickens. They weren't too big; you didn't find big chickens in Malta, and you were very fortunate to find a chicken at all. So we were very proud of our chickens and looked forward to them gracing our spread for the Captain. They were duly roasted on Christmas Eve, along with all the other dishes, and were stowed carefully in the galley all ready for the big day.

That evening a messmate chum, Shiner Wright (all Wrights in the navy are called Shiner) went ashore, got drunk, had no money left to buy himself a meal before he came back, arrived back on board ravenous, and raided the galley for something to eat! Shiner found our four roast chickens. He ate every leg and wing, eight of each, and as much of the breasts as he could tear from these rather spare birds, before climbing into his hammock and falling asleep, sated. When the four skeletons were discovered on Christmas day, there was uproar and Shiner was pretty unpopular. He readily confessed to having devoured the chickens but, well oiled, had forgotten what they were for – or what day it was!

*\*\**

Once during a spell in Malta, the squadron was about to sail for a minesweeping patrol in the Zante channel off southwestern Greece, where we were to continue sweeping for and destroying World War 2 mines left by the Germans. Three or four days before we sailed a young sailor from another sweeper, on a swimming party, dived into the sea and ripped himself open on a rusty underwater metal bar. He was taken straight to the naval hospital at Bighi. We never understood why, but he was returned to his ship, still dreadfully ill, in time for our sailing. As we progressed towards the minefields we got regular reports about his condition, which was worsening, and the whole squadron was pretty glum. He died a few days out at sea. The entire squadron, about 550 officers and men, grieved. We were a close-knit squadron.

His burial was arranged for us, in some haste, at a little Greek fishing village on the mainland but not too far from the minefields. Like so much of Greece ravaged by the Germans, in those years (this was 1952) so soon after WW2, that area was desperately poor. Nowadays tourism has improved their lot. Zante has become the popular resort of Zakynthos.

As we approached the tiny harbour, really only a dent in the coastline to give a bit of shelter to its fishing boats, we could see a huddle of typically Mediterranean buildings at the foot of a sheer mountain, one of many rising from the coastal ribbon, some just straight out of the water, all of them thickly forested with pine.

As we berthed on the harbour wall we eyed the all too evident poverty ashore, wondering how such a run-down looking place could possibly lay on a funeral for us. The minefields were an urgent commitment and time was short. We were already dressed to go ashore: best blue-jacket uniforms, white shirts and caps. Four ships' companies filed over the gangways and silently formed up to march – somewhere.

Suddenly we heard music, funeral music, and round a corner came the most ragtag and bobtail band we'd ever clapped eyes on; but they'd managed a kind of uniform and they played enthusiastically, if a little erratically. They followed a flat-bed truck – the hearse – which, somehow from this arid, rocky ledge by the sea, was a colourful riot of fresh flowers. We warmed to the Greek locals. We were welcome and they were going to do us, and our dead sailor, proud.

We moved in behind the hearse with our guard of honour, and the cortege moved off along a rough track winding up the mountain immediately at the back of the village. After some initial difficulty our pace approximated to the band's approximation of a slow march. As we marched away the pine forest closed in around us and we soon lost sight of the village, the harbour below, and the open sea beyond. The track became steeper, traversing the mountainside through the forest. The route continued zig-zagging upwards, the sound of the band now quite muffled by the trees crowding in on us. Then suddenly, around yet another bend, the pine trees fell away. We were in a clearing, graves and headstones: the cemetery. The band stopped playing, the lashings holding the coffin from sliding off the hearse on the steep climb, were cast off, and we gathered around the open grave, on either side of our naval guard of honour. The cemetery must have been at the end of the track. The clearing seemed to be completely enclosed by thick, lush, green pine forest, appropriately contrasting with the navy blue and white of our uniforms. The delicate perfume of the pines was fragrant, the sky azure, the sunlight golden, and the view across the pine tree tops up to the nearby mountains, breathtaking. We all knew we'd come to the right place, a suitable haven, to leave our shipmate.

Our squadron padre conducted the service and, without the band, among other hymns, in that quiet peace we sang Abide with Me – which has always choked me up ever since. Finally the guard raised their rifles to their shoulders and fired three ceremonial bursts, the sound crashing around the stillness and echoing back off the mountains. Then abrupt and utter silence.

The hearse, with the band now riding on the flat top, had gone down ahead of us. We filed back down the mountain, sadly and silently, more moved than a bunch of fairly hardened matelots could ever have imagined.

Back at the harbour there was the band, and the flat top driver, with all the villagers, waiting to welcome us, offer condolences, and to say Goodbye. We met a lot of wonderful people in those few minutes. With sadness somehow mingled with happiness, we sailed for the minefields. I doubt any man there will ever forget that occasion, or what the Greeks did for us that day.

***

Minesweeping was a daytime task. In the evenings we would take over one of the many uninhabited small islands in the vicinity. In turn, each ship would ferry in a boatload of beer and set up a bar ashore. Since each ship had a dog, four dogs attendance was a given.

*Fierce's* dog, Alf, was a big Labrador type animal. He got ten for initiative when he managed to copulate with a Dachsund from another ship. Her name was Dinky. He got another ten when, a few weeks later, *Fierce* got a signal from Dinky's ship:

> *Every dog must have his day.*
> *Dinky's in the family way.*
> *Alf's the father – what a spree!*
> *Wonder what the result will be.*

Life wasn't all roses for Alf. *Fierce* had embarked a Fleet Clearance Diving Team for shallow water sweeping and they also had a dog - another Dachsund. Alf was overjoyed to have another dog on board (shades of Dinky?) and they soon became great chums, skylarking on the upper deck and generally spending a lot of time together.

One day in the minefields all four ships were in company, sweep wires streamed out on either side, when Alf accidentally knocked his chum over the side. There was no way we could stop and recover the animal and we had to leave him. Alf was heartbroken. He went below and, except for coming up for a pee, stayed below for six weeks.

Soon after I'd joined *Fierce*, fed up about having to leave all my chums in *Armada*, I'd read an Admiralty notice asking for volunteers for aircrew. I had all the educational qualifications and had applied earlier in *Sirius* (for a slightly different scheme), with no luck because that scheme was being closed down. I applied again.

I had been a trifle apprehensive about my shipmates' attitude: would they resent my trying to better myself? Not a bit of it. They all wished me well and were confident I'd succeed.

After endless interview boards, and nine more months, I was sent home to go before an Aircrew Selection Board.

# Chapter 5

## *Towards a Commission*

THE Board sat at the naval air station at Lee-on-Solent and I went to the naval barracks in Portsmouth to wait for the next board. My stay there was hall-marked firstly by the food. It was now 1953 and the barracks was the first naval establishment to try cafeteria messing. It was a tremendous success. I'd stayed in the barracks briefly before when the food under the old messing system had been virtually inedible, and always cold by the time it got to us, dispersed in our barrack block messes. This new system was quickly adopted by all naval establishments and then by ships afloat. I rarely ate a poor meal thereafter.

The other memorable thing about the barracks was the very good chums I had. We were usually broke but often managed to have some wonderful runs ashore on just enough money for a cup of tea in the NAAFI, where we played snooker and table tennis, which were free. When we were briefly in the money, immediately after our fortnightly payday, we'd go out with our various girlfriends, all wrens who had to be back at their barracks by 11pm. There was a cut and dried ritual about returning the girls to the barracks.

The barracks was surrounded by a long high fence, panelled in to hide the wrens from prying eyes, and having steel spikes on top, either to discourage intruders or to stop the girls from unauthorised exit, we were never sure. From about 1030 pm every inch of the very long section of fence up to the main gate was occupied by couples locked in desperate clinches until a few seconds before 11pm. Then the girls would all disengage and rush for the gate. I never got into this situation and it took me several evenings to appreciate why my friends always wanted to get to the fence early – there was no room on the fence if you left it too late!

I steered clear of romance at this stage because I didn't know what my future held for me. Might I actually be accepted for aircrew and have to leave the area to go off for flying training? If I eventually got a commission I certainly wouldn't be locked in a clinch with a wren outside her main gate. With all this uncertainty I'd decided to avoid any attachment. My chums, however, had decided otherwise, and produced partners for me with monotonous regularity. I'd not made it known that I didn't want a girl friend – I'd thought it might sound rather overconfident and getting above myself, but they assumed that I simply couldn't find one –'pull' as it's now commonly called. As a result I was once paired off with quite an attractive girl; we danced and had a few drinks, and then I took her back to the barracks where we arrived at 10.55 pm. No room on the fence by that time, had I wanted it. I simply thanked her for a pleasant evening and said goodbye. She seemed quite surprised; I only realised much later that she'd lost a lot of brownie points in the eyes of her friends, all lined up along the fence as she arrived with her 'new' boyfriend. They were all snogging madly. She didn't get the chance.

The following evening we all went ashore again and, to my surprise, there was the same girl, hovering with the group. She moved in to pair off with me. Unknown to me she'd conferred with my chums as to why I hadn't kissed her goodnight the previous evening. They'd spun her some yarn about me not being the sort of chap to kiss a girl on his first few dates. So, after a rather awkward evening, I got her back to the main gate at 10.55pm and you could hear the snogging it was so intense.

Notwithstanding any embarrassment the girl might feel about not being part of it, I was just about to say thank you and goodnight when she thanked me, grabbed my hand and shook it vigorously – a sight probably never before seen outside the wrens' barracks.

When the rest of my chums had disengaged and said goodnight to their respective girlfriends we all started back towards our own barracks. I told them what had happened and they weren't in the least surprised, just fell about laughing and explained: 'We told her that's what you preferred. You'd much rather just shake hands for the first few times'. I can't print what I called them. Worse still, I had quite a bit of trouble getting rid of that girl, and I've never put it down to what little personal charm I may have had.

Eventually my name came up for the Aircrew Selection Board. Come the day I was extremely nervous. We'd been briefed on what newspapers to read, the Telegraph being thought the most suitable, and had swotted up on current affairs as much as we could. The board consisted of the headmaster of Eton, a captain, commander and a lieutenant commander. I was doing quite well until I got into a furious argument with the lieutenant commander about South African politics. Apartheid was rife at that time and I was violently anti. He, of course, stoked me up and I responded rather more strongly than a lowerdecker seeking to become an officer should have done. Not only that, I only managed a miserable attempt at a five-minute lecture we were told to prepare (in two minutes) and give to the board as a finale to the interview. I failed the interview.

'I want you to try it again' my Divisional Officer told me when I reported to him that I'd failed miserably at the selection board. I protested that I'd had enough. Since I'd first applied for a commission it had taken a year, several local interview boards in the Mediterranean in *Fierce*, the dreariest military charter flight home, and months of waiting in the RN barracks at Portsmouth.

'Shut up and do what you're told' my Divisional Officer said. It sounded abrupt but, I realised immediately, it was a firm indication that he believed I could do it. 'Reapply, and do the Petty Officers' course while you're waiting'. I did what I was told.

While I was doing what I was told I had plenty of time to consider what had gone wrong when I failed. I was nervous, hesitant, inappropriately prepared with what I had thought were the right tools for the interview and, blackest of black marks, I'd lost my temper during that white-heat exchange with one of the interviewing officers over apartheid. Only afterwards did it dawn on me that he'd deliberately set me up. I had allowed myself to be goaded, there was no other word for it, into justified but over-heated support for black South Africans. My only consolation from the incident had been that the officer in question had also lost his temper. All these years later I get a vicious satisfaction from the probability that he must afterwards have had a roasting from the president of the board.

In passing my Petty Officer's exams a rebellious element surfaced. I appreciated my Divisional Officer's faith in ordering me to retake the board, but a bolshie streak took over. I'd do all that he had said, go through the motions at the interview board, fail again – they couldn't possibly want me after the last shambles – and come back to report another failure, thank him for his support, not say 'I told you so', and go away and be a non-commissioned Petty Officer instead of an officer. In short, I couldn't have cared less about the next interview board. My mind, in hindsight about as wide open as a hair-line crack, was made up. End of story.

Came the day of the interview. I set out to walk the three quarters of a mile from the barracks to the harbour to get a boat across the water, thence by naval transport to the naval air station at Lee-on-Solent, since this was a selection board for officer aircrew. Being the sort of person who would rather be one hour early than one second late, I had plenty of time. I decided to take a slightly longer route to the harbour than the most direct. This took me to a crossroads over which trolley buses ran regularly, quietly and quickly.

Beyond the junction, along the nearside kerb for about 30 yards, was what looked like strawberry jam. It was, in fact, blood. Horrified, I asked an equally horrified fellow pedestrian what had happened.

'Motor cycle', he told me. 'Going much too fast, tried to jump the crossroads. A trolley bus had the right of way but had no chance – just smashed right into him. That's half of him painting the kerb. The other half is on its way to hospital'.

I'd always had a loathing for motor bikes, never been tempted to indulge, as had so many of my contemporaries, and considered them the most dangerous things on the road. They were dangerous because of their attraction, often fatal, to young men who couldn't resist showing off, and because the rider had virtually no protection in any sort of accident. This ghastly disaster seemed to prove both my points.

I continued my journey, finally arriving at the air station in a fairly thoughtful mood after what I'd just seen, and still with a deal of time to spare before the interview. I could hear a lot of aircraft activity on the airfield so I went along to see what was happening. Dozens of aircraft were taxi-ing out for take off and a rehearsal of the flypast for the coronation celebrations. I watched for a while and then went back to the interview building, the scene of my previous debacle.

Nothing had changed. There were the same faces, including the officer I'd had such a furious argument with. As I sat down in front of the interview panel we glowered at each other in recognition. But I was no longer nervous or hesitant. I'd given up the idea of preparing myself, reading the 'right' newspapers; if my interest in current affairs, and my ability to articulate that interest, wasn't good enough for them, to hell with it. I was going to be my own man whether they liked it or not.

The glowering one got first shot at me.

'What have you done to improve yourself and your knowledge of aviation affairs since we last saw you?' I told him I'd taken and passed the Petty Officer's examinations. Then I started to tell him about watching the aircraft just before the interview. Cutting me short, with a sneer he asked: 'So you think you could do that do you?'

Instantly I knew I had the bastard by the short hairs. I wouldn't have been sitting there before an Aircrew Selection Board if I didn't think I could do it. It was a damn fool question, he immediately realised it, he knew that I knew it, and both of us knew that the rest of the Board knew it. My 'Yes, Sir' was deliberately insolent, just a degree short of contempt. He never said another word throughout the interview.

One down, three to go. My insolence had guaranteed I was going to fail again. But I enjoyed talking to the rest of the Board. Even if I was doomed I might as well get some pleasure out of the experience, and we had a lively, pleasant conversation.

After every candidate had been interviewed we were all given three cards, each printed with a different subject. We were to leave the interview room, choose one of the three subjects, and take two minutes to prepare a five-minute talk to the interview board on it. One of my subjects was motorcycles. I didn't need two minutes. My mind was still on the strawberry jam.

When it was my turn I came barnstorming back into the interview room. As the saying goes, I hit the ground running, or talking to be more precise. They were all so startled, if I'd called them to attention I'm sure they would have jumped to their feet. I commanded their interest, and continued to command it while I let them have five plus torrid minutes on what I thought of motorcycles and why. And if they wanted an endorsement of my views, I was sure the strawberry jam was going to take a long time to clean up. There was plenty of time for them to go and see for themselves.

I passed.

# Chapter 6

## *Upper Yardman*

NOT too long after that interview I travelled down by train to Portland sharing a carriage with a group of other chaps, all destined for officers' training in the carrier training squadron, three retired carriers anchored in Portland harbour. One of the guys was really well up on what we were going to do and where we'd be going after we'd passed out of the training squadron. I remember listening to him and wondering how he knew so much and I knew so little about our future. How could he be so confident, almost cocksure, about his becoming an officer? I remembered my mother's advice about keeping my mouth shut. Subsequently I passed; he didn't. In fact he only lasted a few weeks.

We spent six months in the carrier training squadron and it was hard work. We had become 'Upper Yardmen', the term used in the navy to denote a lowerdecker under officers' training. We wore the same lower deck uniform but we had a white band around our caps in lieu of a cap ribbon and white flashes on each shoulder to show the rest of the navy we were 'unclean' in their eyes i.e. we were undergoing training to become an officer.

In contrast, all my shipmates in *Fierce* had wished me the best of luck and held me in a lot of respect for having made it through the countless interviews I'd had before I left the ship. They seemed to expect that I would eventually become an officer but showed no resentment. It was only once we'd got the white stigmata up back at home that any antipathy showed. It was only minor. By this time we were allowed to wear plain clothes ashore so we weren't too much in evidence publicly.

My class in our training carrier, the *Implacable*, had three seaman Petty Officers (one of them myself, having recently been promoted), three leading hands, two from the air branch, and a Chief Artificer. The third leading hand was a seaman whose father was a Group Captain and had apparently pulled strings to get his son on what was now his third attempt at officers' training. The three Petty Officer seamen naturally thought we didn't stand a chance against the two from the air branch and the Chief Artificer, but we kept our doubts to ourselves and got on with it. We were the only ones who eventually made it all the way, got commissioned and became pilots.

We were taught the rudiments of how to become an officer, and a variety of academic subjects. This was where the hard work was required. It was several years since I'd left school and my mind hadn't exactly been challenged in the interval. It took me a lot of effort to get back into academic gear. A lot of work was also necessary in writing up our journals, commenting on topical affairs in general, naval, civilian, and political, and furnishing them with sketches. Several of my sketches were highly commended and one has since become something of a family heirloom. I produced it during the period covered below: a pen and ink silhouette of a native boy climbing a palm tree.

Political trouble had brewed up in British Guiana and we took on personnel, stores and equipment for a battalion of the Argyll and Sutherland Highlanders. We stowed their transport and heavy equipment on the flight deck and the soldiers set up their accommodation in one of the hangars. They played the bagpipes incessantly. Their regimental tune was something called the Black Bear and at some stage they used to whoop loudly and jump in the air whenever they got to it. It didn't matter where they were or what they were doing, if they could hear the pipes they'd whoop and leap about. This regimental custom could be quite disconcerting on board ship until you got used to it.

We took the Highlanders across the Atlantic to the West Indies and eventually down to Georgetown, in what is now Guyana, where we offloaded them and their stores. We didn't spend much time there but this was my second time in the area and I was beginning to feel like an old salt.

On passage back across the Atlantic we ran into some foul weather and took a large wave over the bow of the carrier. It partially stove in the for'ard lift and did a lot of damage flooding the upper hangar deck which was part rigged with jury (temporary) class rooms. Had we run into this weather on the way out the Argylls would have suffered. Although they were billeted down in the lower hangar, their transport and heavy equipment on the flight deck would really have taken a hammering.

Back home in Portland we finished that stage of our training and to my surprise I got a first class pass: the only one. My prize was a big, rather uninspiring book. I can't remember what it was about but I didn't keep it long. I gave it a float test: it didn't float. Not all of us passed. One of the leading airmen didn't make it.

After the passing out ceremony the senior instructor officer came to see me. We'd always got on quite well but I should have been a bit sharper and wary when he started calling me David. I fell for his line: those of us who'd passed were to go down to the naval college at Dartmouth 'as a trial' since the navy was considering sending future Upper Yardmen (Air) courses there, a money saving scheme. It would be a rest period for us after all our hard work and we could 'browse in the library', go sailing on the river and generally relax. The college would have no jurisdiction over us as far as our future was concerned. We were just an experiment. Enjoy!

When we arrived we were issued with two armloads of textbooks, together with a syllabus that took up most of each working day and half the evening. This rather upset me. I had worked hard in the carrier training squadron and had swallowed the senior instructor officer's story hook, line and sinker. The rest and relaxation he'd mentioned never materialised and, because we were Upper Yardmen (Air) rather than just plain Upper Yardmen and, in the college's eyes unclean, we were leant on hard. Looking back on it I suppose this was my first encounter with the anti-aviator attitude I was to meet with a vengeance too often, covered in later chapters.

I had the temerity to ask how all this study fitted in with what our senior instructor officer had promised would be a 'rest period'. Needless to say I was slapped down hard and was a marked man from Day 1. Worse was to come.

The college's pride and joy, a luxury sailing boat, had just been moored in the river after a refit and a repaint. She was gleaming. The group captain's son managed to ram her only minutes after she'd left the slipway. He was in only a 14ft dinghy but stove a hole clean through her bow timbers. Only he could have managed a disaster on that scale. I happened to notice him report the accident to the college Boats' officer, who turned purple. Further minor incidents occurred during the six weeks of our 'rest period' trial and we were generally as unpopular as it was possible to be.

I started playing rugger again while we were there. It was expected of us. Soccer was beneath contempt for the college. I managed to avoid too much roughing up although I did get my nose kicked repeatedly when we scrummed down in one match against Greenwich College. After several belts in the face I eventually located the source of the kicks: a chap in the second row of the opposing scrum. Having found my man, all my wicked intentions of fixing him up with a good 'seeing to' evaporated. He looked such a nice bloke and I don't think he even realised where his boot was landing. I packed down for the remaining scrums a bit further back but spent the rest of the match with a cracked nose. It turned out later my assailant was a Royal Marine. Try and avoid them if you're playing rugger. I think I would have been the one who got a 'good seeing to'. The Royals get too much training in 'roughing' it, and they don't wear their badges of rank on their rugger shirts.

Rugger collected me a few more black marks. Photos of a recent match appeared on the wardroom notice board. I was looking at them when the Commanding Officer came in for a drink. He asked me what I thought of the photos and I told him: rubbish. He'd taken them.

We never managed to score any brownie points during our time at the college and were considered quite unclean and unsuitable as officer material. The only thing our senior instructor officer in *Implacable* had got right was that the college had no jurisdiction over our future; otherwise this story might never have been told. We were very glad to leave and the college was no less glad to see us go.

We were through another hoop on our way to a short service commission.

# Chapter 7

## *Flying Training*

AFTER that short experimental spell at Dartmouth we upper yardmen went on to the next phase of our training: pre-flight training at Fort Rowner in Gosport. Here we joined up with the officer section of our course, four lieutenants and two sub-lieutenants. We learned about meteorology, the principles of flight and a few other flying-associated subjects. After the naval college the pace was more leisurely and the subjects more interesting, not least because they related to aviation. The subjects in the overloaded syllabus at the college had had nothing to interest us, either naval, or, even less, aviation.

The upper yardmen lived in their own mess in *HMS Siskin*, then a naval air station, just down the road from Fort Rowner, and had a pensioner steward to look after us, quite a luxury for sailors used to making do for themselves.

Our commanding officer at Rowner insisted on taking each of us up for a flight in a Harvard trainer aircraft. Things were going well for me until he announced he was going to do a slow roll. I didn't like this manoeuvre one bit. When he asked me if I'd liked it my "No sir" was emphatic. He went straight back and landed. I think he thought I was going to be airsick. So did I; but I managed to contain myself.

From Rowner we went to an RAF training airfield, Syerston, near Newark in Nottinghamshire. It was 1954. There we at last started flying. Our initial training aircraft was a Piston Provost. We quickly discarded the Chief Petty Officer artificer and the son of the Group Captain. They both found landing the aircraft too difficult and left to return to normal naval duties. I understand the Group Captain subsequently managed to get his son out of the service and the last I saw of him he was an 'up-market' interior design consultant in Pimlico, probably faring rather better than he could ever have done in the navy.

One novelty for the upper yardmen, still in lower deck uniform, was that, as part of our officers' training, we were now members of the officers' mess. It was strange to be rubbing shoulders with officers socially, especially at mess dinners when the officers would all be wearing their mess undress, informal evening wear, or even full mess dress with stiff fronted shirts at the more important functions. All we could wear was our best uniforms so we felt a little obvious and the officers did their best to make us feel reasonably at home, even if we did stand out like sore thumbs.

This practice was stopped not too long afterwards. Thereafter upper yardmen discarded their lower deck uniforms and became acting sub-lieutenants as soon as they started training. If they failed they didn't return to the navy. They left the service.

We enjoyed Syerston, and those that were left passed out and then went on to RAF Valley in Anglesey for jet flying training. We started on twin-seat Vampire trainers before going solo in the single seat version, the Vampire 5.

Again we lived in the officers' mess, still in our lower deck uniform, and mixed socially with the officers. It was still strange. I'd been in sailor's rig for eight years, it was now 1955, and found it difficult to shake off the 'us and them' attitude developed on the lower deck.

Jet flying training was great fun. The Vampire wasn't exactly the fastest thing with wings but it was exciting for us and we all enjoyed it, especially the single-seat trainer, which was the first single-seater we'd flown.

The day we finished jet flying training was the day we were commissioned and were awarded our 'Wings', the flying badge on our sleeves to indicate we were qualified naval pilots. The run-up to the great day had involved getting measured up for our officers' uniforms by the Gieves representative, and being issued with all the other officers' kit, shirts, shoes, and caps. This included the formal stiff-fronted evening shirt, winged collars and bow ties. Our first attempts to don this lot weren't too far away, in fact, there'd be a celebratory mess dinner the day we passed out.

Our passing out parade was particularly special for the upper yardmen. Not only were we getting our 'wings'. We put on our officers' uniform for the first time, and I was commissioned as a Sub Lieutenant with seniority backdated to the time we'd started our officers' training. Thus I became a Supplementary List officer on a twelve-year short service commission. My mother came up for the ceremony.

For the party that night getting into full mess dress for the first time was a struggle. Somehow we managed. Bow ties ranged from ten to four to five past seven. It took me a long time to get mine to stay at a quarter to three.

Our next stage was Operational Flying training, wherever our flying aptitudes took us. Some went off to fly helicopters. One of the ex seaman Petty Officers went to fly Gannets, an anti-submarine aircraft. I and the other ex-Petty Officer plus some of the other officers on the course, went to the naval air station at Lossiemouth to start our operational flying training on Seahawks, the aircraft we would eventually fly operationally. It was here I started to come seriously unstuck.

Eight years living as a sailor had ingrained in me many inappropriate attitudes that I found difficult to lose as a very new and junior officer. I could not slough the 'us and them' syndrome. To make matters worse I found some of the flying instructors very awkward to get on with. A lot of them were Korean War veterans and considered themselves the bee's knees, in the air as well as on the ground. I hadn't the experience to realise that some of them were mediocre at their jobs. For me they were senior, and I was trying to learn what they were supposed to be trying to teach me. My flying suffered badly and with it my confidence. Eventually I had to fly with the Commanding Officer on what we called a 'scrub' check: the last chance saloon.

The C.O., or boss as we called him, Don Morrison, must have appreciated what my problems were because he had me into his office for the flight briefing. I was to lead a four aircraft formation and the boss had me write down on my flight kneepad everything he wanted me to do on the flight. He put it across in such a way that I managed to fly the trip faultlessly; I could stay.

Don Morrison died a few years ago now but I met up with him once after both of us had long retired. I reminded him of that trip, so many years before. Not unnaturally he didn't remember it (I was just another of many students) but I told him what he'd done for me, and thanked him. And I never forgot his insight into my problems, and his faith in me. It influenced me a great deal during the many years that I was a flying instructor and subsequently a Commanding Officer.

When we passed out we were given a Flying Assessment, which graded you from one to nine. One to three was below average. Four to six was average, and anything higher, above average. I got a four, together with a report that I'd 'struggled hard to achieve a low average standard'. It was well deserved. I kept that report in my flying logbook for nearly 15 years, the intention being that if I ever improved I could look back on it as a great leveller and not get big-headed. At that stage I doubted I'd ever fly well enough to warrant getting big-headed.

Somehow I got to be the squadron Line Book officer and had managed to produce a fairly creditable cartoon illustration of our course progress through our Operational Flying training. I mention this here because such talent as I had got to the ears of someone in my next squadron. It was to cost me dear.

We'd now completed our flying training.

While we waited for our next appointments a group of us were sent to a holding squadron at the naval air station at Ford in Sussex. We hoped to get some deck landing practice on any carrier that might be around and could spare the time. *Bulwark* was around and we managed to get four touch and go landings, without putting the arrestor hook down and landing on. I was a long way off being fully deck qualified but was on my way.

This was really the end of my formal flying training. My next appointment would be a front line operational squadron.

# Chapter 8

## *Front Line*

IN January 1956 I joined 804 Squadron, a front line operational Seahawk squadron, parented at Lossiemouth. We had 16 pilots. The 14 Seahawks we had were Fighter/Ground Attack aircraft. They were armed with 20mm cannon, bombs or rockets.

As about the most junior sub-lieutenant, and one of the most inexperienced, fresh out of Operational Flying Training i.e. the end of the training pipeline, I was assigned as wingman to the Senior Pilot (the number two in the squadron hierarchy).

One of the several non-flying duties I was landed with was that of Line Book officer. I only collected this job because someone had heard about my Line Book cartoons in the training squadron. As a junior officer you learned through the many necessary miscellaneous non-flying duties. Somehow every other junior officer had managed to convince the boss that they had no artistic merit whatsoever. Ergo, Howard became the Line Book officer. The book was about eighteen by fifteen inches. In it I was responsible for keeping a record of the squadron's activities, pictorially with appropriate captions, and hopefully with a humorous side to them. Entries could be cartoons or whatever could be cut out of a variety of magazines and pasted in, with appropriate captions. I usually inclined towards cartoons, as colourful as I could make them.

This line book still exists, in the Fleet Air Arm museum at Yeovilton, and recently Tricia persuaded me to take her down there and show her some of my efforts. She was quite impressed and the museum staff very kindly produced copies of some of the cartoons which we now have framed.

I hadn't helped myself in collecting the line book duty. The squadron crest was the head of a tiger with a dagger clenched between its teeth, and was supposed to be painted on both sides of the nose of every aircraft. It wasn't, and the only copy of the squadron crest I could find was so badly painted that I was rash enough to comment on it. I was immediately ordered to redesign it. Resolving to learn to keep my opinions to myself in future, I set about redesigning the crest, but, knowing it would have to be painted twice on each of the fourteen aircraft, I simplified it and kept it to black and white. The boss was delighted and ordered the crest to be painted on each aircraft (twice) as soon as possible, and assumed it would be me doing all fourteen aircraft. Twenty-eight crests were just over the top for me and I persuaded him that it would encourage pilots' interest in their aircraft if they did the job themselves (fourteen of the sixteen pilots had their names painted on an assigned aircraft; I was too junior). This idea appealed to the boss and he decreed that the paint job go ahead

It quickly became apparent that several of the aircrew who'd declared they had no artistic merit weren't wrong, or were out to give that impression anyway: there was a junior sub who'd let them in for the work; let him get on with it. And if my crest wasn't to become an object of ridicule, I had to help them out. After some marathon sessions with a paintbrush the entire squadron complement of aircraft was finished. And I was a much wiser young officer. But I remained the Line Book Officer for my whole tour, in addition to the several other duties that a junior officer inevitably collects.

This first front line squadron was more notable for me for several things. I started to slough the 'us and them' attitude that had held me back in Operational Flying training. I also discovered I had very long range eyes and could spot anything , ship or aircraft,  and report it to whoever was leading the flight, long before anyone else. This was particularly useful if we were practising air-to-air interceptions, or when coming home to the carrier.

I developed a love of formation aerobatics and was a regular member of the squadron aeros team in air displays all over the country. My usual position was in 'the box', the rear aircraft in a diamond formation of four aircraft. I did my first deck landings and catapult launches. I also started depressingly regular visits to Lossiemouth's boot hill – the cemetery where local naval personnel were buried, in the woods between Lossiemouth and Milltown, a few miles to the east. Of the sixteen pilots we started the tour with nine pilots were killed either whilst in the squadron or soon after they left. I can't remember how many died during my time in the squadron but I can think of at least four. Two of them were killed in the Mediterranean; more on this later. These two were very good chums of mine and shared a cabin with me and another pilot (sadly killed soon after in another squadron). Although these were not the first losses the squadron had suffered, as cabin mates they were close to us and we felt quite bereft when they went.

Our initial flying from the deck was again in *Bulwark*, now our parent carrier. Because I was about the most junior pilot and we had two more pilots than aircraft, I was one of the two who walked aboard, rather fed up. I learned a bit more though. I had gone up into the flying control position, FLYCO for short, to watch the squadron land on. The officer in charge of flying was the ship's Commander (Air), known as "Wings". He was the 'feet up on the desk' type and knew who I was, the junior sub in 804. As the aircraft started to land on he asked me: 'So you think you could do that, Sub?' That same question again, but in a much more friendly manner than at the aircrew selection interview. I gave him the only answer anyone can give in that situation: the same 'Yes, sir', emphatically, but in a much friendlier way.

I must have impressed him. He supported me later on, in an incident in which incompetent radar control directed me and my flight of three other aircraft away from, instead of towards, the carrier. We got back aboard dangerously short of fuel. I was only leading because my leader's radio had failed and he passed the lead to me. It ended up as my word against a lieutenant commander in the radar control team. Wings accepted my word. At the time I didn't know that the lieutenant commander was useless anyway, something Wings knew, but I was too inexperienced to appreciate. Wings and I got on pretty well after that. I'd got my flight back aboard without any panic, just tightly crossed fingers!

This occurred in the summer of 1956 before we actually started attacking Egypt in the Suez affair. We had gone out to the Mediterranean in quite a hurry after the Egyptian president, Nasser, had nationalised the Suez canal, and we were 'working up' for an offensive operation against Egypt, practising with bombs, rockets and cannon on targets in the Malta area.

Finally, in the following October, in company with two other carriers and supporting ships, we went off to Suez and bombed, rocketted and shot up every Egyptian airfield we could find, our objective being to neutralize the Egyptian airforce. My most satisfying attack was against a line of parked Mig 15 fighters, using 20mm cannon. They went up in flames.

The two chums I lost were killed during this period. One had had to eject off Malta before we got to the Suez area. His parachute fouled with his ejection seat and the chute never deployed. We buried him at sea. The other, my closest buddy, Chris, early in the actual Suez operation, landed on, his arrestor hook pulled out and he went over the side of the carrier. He and his aircraft never surfaced.

Chris' parents later asked my Squadron Commanding Officer if we could produce some memento of the squadron. I came up with a large squadron crest in colour for them and it was presented when we got home. They were so pleased with it they had it made into a stained glass window in their local church. Until recently I'd never managed to see it. I at last got to see it in 2003 in the United Reform Church, Otley, Yorkshire. It was a moving experience, 47 years on. As a result I met Chris' brother for the second time (the first was briefly before Suez). We've been close friends ever since.

I must have done pretty well in 804. My first flying assessment had gone from four when I joined to seven, above average, and I was the only junior pilot to reach these dizzy heights. I seemed to have put the 'us and them' bit behind me and appeared to have settled down to being a reasonable pilot, and officer.

We arrived back home from the Suez operation in December 1956 and shortly afterwards I married Jo. The occasion has its own chapter.

Early in 1957 the squadron re-embarked, this time in *Ark Royal*, and off we went to the Med again. But for me, not for long; I soon left *Ark* to come home. I was appointed to a Lossiemouth Seahawk training squadron, 736, as a tactical instructor. Good news. It was a feather in my cap to be given an instructor's job so early in my flying career, and it meant I would be shore-based for quite a spell.

My new wife and I would have a chance to settle down to married life.

# Chapter 9

## *Marriage*

GENERALLY known as the Range Assessing section, the Weapons Analysis team attached to 804 squadron in our hangar at Lossiemouth, was staffed by wrens. One was a girl called Jo Severs. She was extremely attractive, even in a wren's uniform (which didn't always flatter!), and she stood out with her elfin, short-styled haircut, very attractive features and figure. We started going out together and by the early summer of 1956 I had become seriously keen on her and she seemed to feel the same way about me to the extent that I was considering asking her to marry me. I never got to pop the question personally. Towards the end of July Jo was sent down to Lee-on-Solent where she and the rest of the wrens detachment were to be billeted while they rehearsed for and then took part in a big parade in Portsmouth.

Almost as Jo left on the train from Elgin to come south, 804 Squadron was suddenly posted back to *HMS Bulwark*, our parent light fleet carrier. This was what the navy call a 'pier-head jump'. The Suez crisis was brewing up, Egypt's Colonel Nasser had nationalised the Suez Canal, and we had to embark as quickly as possible and sail for the Mediterranean.

I had no idea how long we'd be away. I thought Jo was much too attractive to be left unattached, and I imagined she'd be fighting off a horde of hopeful young officers after I'd disappeared from the scene. I still had fears that some good-looking young lothario would somehow sweep her off her feet. She was the most attractive girl on the air station.

I left a letter for Jo, proposed to her and enclosed a cheque for an engagement ring. I was still a practising catholic and in a later letter I explained that we'd have to marry in a Roman Catholic church, and that I'd need to apply for a Papal dispensation to marry a Church of England girl. I'd ask the Fleet RC padre to fix it. Not knowing when we'd be home I also had to ask Jo to arrange the wedding as best she could. This was quite a tall order. Jo had to find a Roman Catholic church, assume that the Papal dispensation would be no problem (I wrote to her later, as soon as I'd seen the RC padre), and, once she had a date for our arrival back home, fix the date of the wedding.

On our way out to the eastern Mediterranean the Fleet assembled in Grand Harbour, Malta, and I had a chance to visit the Fleet RC padre in *Eagle*, another carrier in the group.

I took a boat over to *Eagle* quite early, mid-morning. The padre, broad Irish, assured me that the dispensation would be no problem at all and that he would make the application straight away. I wrote to let Jo know.

Suez over, the Fleet started home and I could write Jo and tell her the date I'd be back, and please to allow a few days for me to get down to Derby and let her parents see that I didn't have two heads, or any other ogre-like tendencies, before I married their daughter. There was still the problem of the Papal dispensation. I hadn't heard a word from the RC padre.

En route home the Fleet reassembled in Grand Harbour, Malta, and I got the first boat across to *Eagle* to see the padre. I got to his cabin at 2.30 pm. He was blind drunk and fast asleep, completely comatose in an absolute fug of gin vapour. I made a few enquiries and learned that the padre was a bottle of gin a day man: at least one bottle. In those days duty-free gin cost one old penny a tot. At 26 tots to the bottle it didn't cost a lot to get stoned if you'd a mind to, and he had a mind to, every day in fact. I had to assume that somehow I'd be able to sort out the dispensation problem when I got home. Roman Catholicism and I really started drifting apart from then on. Nothing has made me change my mind since.

I arrived at Jo's home in Littleover, Derby, on a Tuesday, and met her parents for the first time. Jo's father was fully as charming as Jo had given me to believe. I wasn't so sure about her mother but she was welcoming and kind and I gave her the benefit of the doubt.

They, and Jo, were just a bit anxious. There'd been trouble about the church. I then discovered that my problems with the Roman Catholic Church were nothing compared to what Jo had had to endure. Although her home was literally just a few hundred yards away from the nearest

Catholic church, it was the wrong side of the RC parish boundary. The church wasn't inclined to bend the rules and allow the wedding there.

The nearest Catholic church inside the parish boundary was miles away. Because of the Suez crisis this was a period of petrol rationing. It would have been frantically expensive to have held the wedding there. Provisionally Jo had arranged the wedding in a Church of England church just up the road. Even more disenchanted with Catholicism, and to hell with the dispensation; I gave her ten out ten. I was only too happy to agree with this, and Jo and her parents were very relieved. It must have been a dreadful worry for them, waiting to see my reaction.

We were married the following Saturday, 26 December 1956. Naturally Jo looked wonderful and I felt that my naval uniform and sword was the only suitable accompaniment for her in her gorgeous wedding dress. My mother managed to come up for the wedding and met Jo for the first time, and her parents of course. Jo was only the second girlfriend of mine that my mother had met, Jan being the first. My mother's reaction was somewhat warmer than for Jan. There was no comment on us being married in a Church of England church either.

Limited by the petrol rationing and the fact that I had no car anyway, we went by train to Buxton for a brief honeymoon. We stayed at the Buxton Spa hotel, a very imposing looking place and straight out of one of those black and white World War 2 movies like Brief Encounter. The restaurant was large, with a stage on which a trio of WW2 ladies clutched a violin under several quivering chins, a cello between two determined thighs, and a piano not quite so grand in front of its prop forward sized player.

They 'entertained' us at lunch and dinner. Perhaps 'entertain' is not quite the word. When they first started playing Jo and I couldn't believe it. We quickly learned not to sit too close to the stage because we got the giggles. Giving their all amid a cluster of potted ferns, and on instruments that were sufficiently off tune for us to notice but for no-one to complain, all accompanied by theatrical flourishes and gestures with every movement, these three old dears were too much. We couldn't keep a straight face. We usually managed to contain ourselves to a smile, but it was always difficult not to lose our self-control. Meals were got through as quickly as we could decently contrive and we would disappear out of the dining room giggling furiously.

I don't remember much of Buxton itself. Having no car, we would have had to get around on foot, bus or by taxi, and this was in the days long before service pay went up to a respectable level, so I presume taxis were out. I can't remember now how long we spent at the hotel, certainly not long because I do remember it had to be a short honeymoon; I only had a total of a fortnight's leave before I was due back at Lossiemouth to rejoin my squadron. Even though my leave, and my money, were short, we had a lot of fun,

Once back at Lossiemouth I applied for a married quarter but, because there was a waiting list, we set up our first home in rented accommodation close to the airfield while we waited. Eventually we were allocated 66, MacDonald Drive in the married patch at Lossiemouth.

# Chapter 10

## *Tactical Flying Instructor*

IN my Seahawk time a tactical flying instructor was a pilot with no instructor qualification but who, nevertheless, was considered capable of general flying instruction in Seahawk Flying Training.

The only instructor 'training' I'd had was the example shown by my instructors when I myself went through operational flying training. Though I didn't realise it until somewhat later, this example was often not as sound as it should have been, so now not only was I teaching; I was on a steep learning curve myself.

Perhaps the most important part of my first job as an instructor was learning to give a really thorough briefing. Most of what happens in the air, and how it happens, stems from the briefing, and if you're teaching student pilots then that briefing becomes vital. Sometimes their lives may depend on it. This grounding in briefing was to stand me in very good stead throughout my flying career, as well as giving me the confidence to stand up and talk, brief, lecture, whatever, to countless audiences in a variety of situations and different countries through the rest of my naval service.

In my own operational flying training I'd been on the receiving end of too much destructive criticism. Whilst the criticism might have been justified it was delivered in a manner that often made me resentful. I now felt strongly that there had to be a better way, and that, given the chance, I could develop a more effective method of instruction. I like to think that the problems I'd had as a student, with the same exercises I was now teaching, helped me in showing my students what to do, and, just as important, what not to do. Only much later did I realise how much I had myself learned in this my first job as a flying instructor.

Those early years as a flying instructor were blighted by the policy of the higher echelons in the flying training command that pilots were expendable. There was a shortage of operational pilots and every student had to be passed, regardless of his ability. Time and again our training squadron would recommend that a pilot be withdrawn from training because he wasn't up to it, only to have this recommendation turned down. Some student pilots never even made it out of the training squadron; others got to their front line squadron before they too were killed. Several of these unfortunates are buried in Lossiemouth's boot hill. I visit there regularly and it's no less depressing now than when I stood in that graveyard attending the funerals of these young men.

If anything it's even more depressing: in those days a Seahawk cost £59,000 and the pilot's training possibly a little more. The total loss when the student crashed thus amounted to not much over £120,000. Only when the navy introduced the Buccaneer, cost £1,000,000 plus, and two aircrew, training costs about £500,000, did the authorities start to heed their training squadron commanders, and accept their recommendations. Not to do so might prove expensive. In my experience latterly this happened only once. The pilot was subsequently killed. This sad accident is discussed further in Chapter 22.

From such depressing incidents I developed a conviction that instruction had to be absolutely first class, in the air as well as on the ground.

# Chapter 11

## *Flying Qualifications*

DURING my time as a tactical instructor I was 'trapped', the naval expression for being examined by the Flying Standards flight on instrument flying and flight principles. I was rubbish; and I was rubbished by the flight commander, a miserable lieutenant commander who could only be destructively critical. I was so fed up I decided if I couldn't beat them I'd join them.

At the end of my tour I went down to Yeovilton to do the Instrument Rating Instructor's course. There I learned how to fly on instruments accurately, how those instruments worked, and about principles of flight, especially flying for range and endurance. Thus I became an IRI, Instrument Rating Instructor, and each squadron had at least one to examine pilots annually for their Instrument Rating card which qualified them to fly in various levels of bad weather. More about this qualification later.

Immediately after that I went on to Portsmouth, to the Gunnery school (where I'd trained as a sailor and where I'd met my first steady girlfriend, Jan), to do the ground syllabus for the Air Warfare Instructor's course. Being terrible at Maths I nearly failed this part but they squeezed me through and I went back to Lossiemouth, with the other five students, to do the flying part. This was in Seahawks again, at the Advanced Flying Training unit, 764 Squadron.

Right from the start we were encouraged to be aggressive. We bombed, rocketted, strafed air-to-ground and air-to-air, and practised air-to-air combat. We also learned how to brief weaponry exercises, and how to lead, and to fight aircraft we were leading under simulated combat situations. Flying was intense and sometimes we flew three or even four tough sorties a day. Although it was tiring, it was satisfying, especially as we saw our skills in the various exercises improve steadily. Finally we all passed and became qualified Air Warfare Instructors. Together with my IRI qualification I was going to be busy.

I would say that while aggression is the right approach for air warfare, or for any confrontation situation as long as you keep your cool, it can be difficult to keep it out of domestic or social matters. I think this was a fault of mine and probably did not sit comfortably with Jo. It made me much too assertive, perhaps to the point of outright chauvinism at times.

Even so, aggression at the right time and in the right situation was to stand me in excellent stead later on when I became a squadron commander, and subsequently a frigate commanding officer.

# Chapter 12

## *Squadron Air Warfare Instructor*

AFTER the Air Warfare Instructor's course I was appointed to a front line Seahawk squadron again, as the AWI. It was 1958 and Jo was pregnant by this time. The squadron was 806 in *Eagle* which was in the Med. My new boss was 'Hoagy' Carmichael. I flew out to Luqa, Malta, to join 806. To my surprise I was met at the airport by no less than the squadron senior pilot who drove me back to the air station at Halfar where the squadron was disembarked. *Eagle* was in Grand Harbour.

I soon discovered why I'd been accorded the unexpected 'honour' of being met by the senior pilot. He was the squadron aeros team leader and one of the team had gone sick. They had a display that afternoon and needed a fourth man. Could I do it? I was only too happy, and so my first flight in the squadron was that same afternoon, back in the box, the rear man in a diamond formation. It was quite an initiation into the squadron but enjoyable, and successful.

After the Air Display, Hoagy Carmichael decided on the spur of the moment – Hoagy was nothing if not impetuous – that we should have a squadron beach barbecue. An aircraft lighter was organised – a flat topped craft that would take the whole squadron, up to about 250 officers and sailors, and enough beer to supply the whole of the Mediterranean fleet. Off we went across a bay towards some cliffs with just a thin ribbon of sandy beach below them.

Hoagy then made another of his decisions and chose the closest beach. This happened to be the one with the thinnest strip of sand, and not a vestige of shade anywhere. It was hot, with a clear blue sky and even the sea was lukewarm. In or out of the water I burned. I can take a lot of sun but this was over the top. This was my first day back in hot weather and I wasn't acclimatized. My rather small towel did nothing to protect me but I just had to stick it out. We were miles from anywhere and the only way back was the way we'd come.

Eventually we started back and halfway across the bay Hoagy had another brainwave. The officers, Chief Petty Officers, and Petty Officers would all have a run ashore together down the 'Gut', that street, then of ill-repute, in Valetta. Since this was my first day in the squadron I felt that I couldn't let the boss down, sunburn or not, so off I went. We all duly met up in the Gut and drank the awful beer until 1 o'clock in the morning when Hoagy declared himself starving, knew of a good restaurant in Rabat and called up some taxis. By this time the party had thinned down to about two taxi loads.

Away we went again, found the restaurant, drank a lot more, had an indifferent meal and looked for a taxi. We were now down to one taxi load. Our leader, the indomitable Hoagy, now fully in his cups and staggering, but still vaguely in command, asked the first taxi he flagged down the fare back to Halfar. A very fair quote of 30 bob was refused indignantly by Hoagy who declared the driver a robbing bastard. We all sat down on a public bench to await the next taxi. Meanwhile the taxi driver went back to the taxi rank in the main square, told his chums about the drunken English pig on the bench around the corner, and asked them to ignore us.

They ignored us for another two hours. It was 4.30 am when a taxi happened along. Hoagy had been snoring loudly for those two hours so I shook him and told him there was a taxi. He lumbered to his feet and lurched across to the taxi.

'How much to take us back to Halfar?

'Thirty bob'.

'You're the only honest taxi driver in Malta. Take us back'.

I turned in at about 5.30 am, vowing never to 'follow my leader' again.

In passing it's worth noting that Hoagy had the reputation of being the ugliest man in the Fleet Air Arm. He was.

He had also become famous for having shot down a Mig 15 during the Korean war and got the DFC for this. As Hoagy's Air Warfare Instructor I know in my time he never hit anything, whether with bombs, rockets or cannon, so perhaps his gong was well-deserved if only for the uniqueness of the occasion.

*Eagle* had an interesting itinerary during my time in 806 and we ranged from Brest, down through Gibraltar, Naples, Istanbul and several other ports, disembarkations to Halfar, Malta, and enjoyed a deal of flying, both embarked and from ashore at Halfar.

While I was out in the Med Trevor was born, September 29th. It had felt very strange not being home for the birth of my first child but Jo appeared to be coping very well and it was quite common for a naval husband to be away at such a time. You only qualified for compassionate leave if there were complications. So I got a telegram: I had a son, and mother and baby were doing fine. We had quite a celebration on board that evening.

I had discussed my service future with Hoagy who wanted me to apply for the Empire Test Pilots course. I felt that my school weakness in Maths (shown up so badly on the AWI's course) would let me down and, also, were I to pass, an ETP's job would take me out of mainstream flying. Despite Hoagy's entreaties, I decided to stay with the mainstream and to apply for a transfer from my Supplementary List engagement to the permanent General List.

The carrier visited Istanbul and, while we there, as some preparation for a General List interview, Hoagy arranged for me to go and do a few days sea time in an accompanying destroyer as soon as we sailed. Coincidentally the destroyer was the *Trafalgar*, the ship I'd served in as an Able Seaman when she was in the Reserve Fleet in Portsmouth. Since I'd had a lot of experience of seamanship as a sailor I knew my way around as well as many of the officers, so my few days in her were fairly painless. As I first stepped aboard, immediately prior to sailing, I was told I had the middle watch that night. That's midnight to 4am. We'd had quite a hard last run ashore in Istanbul the previous night so the sleep I'd been looking forward to was curtailed.

Once back in home waters we prepared to fly off to our various parent airfields and I was offered a chance to get home a little early. I was asked to fly another squadron's aircraft off to Abbotsinch, later Glasgow airport. I jumped at the chance. I'd get home earlier, to see my new son.

At the time both of *Eagle's* catapults were out of action and we had to do a free take-off. We defuelled the aircraft down to about a quarter fuel to lighten them, and another carrier, *Victorious*, stationed herself just ahead of *Eagle* after the carrier had worked up to full speed and turned into wind to give the maximum wind over the deck. In turn we all lined up as far aft as we could get, wound up to maximum throttle, released the brakes and hoped for the best. We got airborne in about two thirds of the deck length, very comfortably, but none of us had done it before and it was quite an anxious few moments until the wheels lifted off. We then landed on in *Victorious*, spent the night, and were launched with full fuel from *Victorious'* catapults next morning for the flight to Abbotsinch. I can't remember how we got from Abbotsinch to Lossie but I got home early and saw my baby son for the first time. It was quite a moment.

Soon after getting home the squadron was re-parented to the naval air station at Brawdy in south west Wales. As one of the married officers I elected to go by road. Jo and I decided to drive the journey in one, with baby Trevor of course, and our large Labrador retriever, Glen, named after Glen Grant whisky to which I was rather partial. What little effects we had went with us in the car. We didn't have much since the married quarters at either end were fully furnished.

En route to Brawdy we stopped somewhere in the middle of nowhere at a 24 hour café that would now be termed a service station. Trevor was wearing a blue jump suit, and was wide-awake at 2 am, happily talking scribble and grinning at the few people around. He absolutely enchanted the waitress and, as she went through the door into the kitchen, I heard her say to someone inside: 'Gorgeous child'. He was. And he took the marathon journey in his stride.

Glen soon became accepted by all the children in the married patch, and was allowed to go to the front of the queue when the ice-cream van arrived. With his front paws up on the counter Glen was always given an ice cream. Additionally, since a child's hand-held ice was about eye level for Glen he often managed to scrump a few more. The children seemed to accept this without too much grief. Glen was one of the gang.

Brawdy was uneventful. I did a lot of airborne instruction there. Not only did I have my IRI commitment, but, as the Air Warfare Instructor, I also used to fly a Meteor target towing aircraft so that I could see how my squadron pilots were performing at shooting at the banner target I towed, and correct them as required. A lot was required. It was a very useful teaching medium and we did manage to improve our hitting percentages.

I'd never been quite happy about letting squadron pilots shoot in roughly my direction but it sharpened up my instruction technique in trying to ensure that there was an adequate safety angle off.

The target banner was a white nylon flag, about 6 ft deep and 30 ft long. The tips of our cannon bullets were painted, a different colour for each pilot. If a round went through the white nylon it left a telltale colour.

On return to the airfield I dropped the banner over the grass and it was taken across to the squadron where we counted the holes, scoring the various colours to each pilot.

While at Brawdy I finally applied to transfer to the navy's General List, which meant that, if accepted, I'd have a full career in the service, rather than the twelve-year short service commission that I'd started with as an officer. I sat the interview before a board convened at Brawdy. The President of the board was Doug Parker and one of the questions he asked me was didn't I think the Field Gun run at Earl's Court each year was a bit dated and not representative of current service life?

Once again at an interview I'd been handed on a plate a subject I felt very strongly about. My experience with the field gun at *St Vincent* all came back to me. Enthusiastically, I let Doug have a few minutes of how the field gun run was a classic example of what team work could produce and how necessary it was during the run to stop people getting hurt. I'd had personal experience, and there couldn't be a finer example of the sort of team work that was vital in the service.

I passed, this time with no difficulty, and was accepted for the General List. This meant getting a bridge watch keeping certificate, and that meant at least six months more sea time, and more separation.

# Chapter 13

## *Bridge Watchkeeping Ticket*

IT was now November 1959. For my six months' bridge watch keeping training I had been appointed to the Dartmouth Training Squadron (DTS) and a destroyer, *HMS Carron*. We subsequently switched to *HMS Vigilant*, a frigate, and *Carron* went into reserve.

Since the squadron tended to operate from Plymouth or Dartmouth Jo and I moved down to Slapton Sands, within reasonable commuting distance of either and somewhere away from the hurly-burly of a semi-suburban existence and married quarters. Jo was pregnant again. I didn't yet know the programme for the DTS and how much I'd be away at sea. Slapton was a quiet attractive spot down by the sea, so Slapton it was. The village was also not too far, but not too close either, from my mother's cottage and that stepfather, near Kilkhampton.

Almost immediately after joining *Carron* we sailed for Hamburg where we tied up on a floating pontoon opposite a luxury cruiser in harbour for the winter. One evening all the wardroom officers were invited on board as guests and enjoyed free drinks, and as much as we wanted, all evening. There was a small band, a dance floor, several young hostesses, and we danced and drank a lot.

The event was marred only by our senior lieutenant, an officer inclined towards self-importance. This tendency was to the fore when he suddenly appeared in front of the band with a microphone in his hand. Absolutely horrified, we sat there and listened to 'True Love' rendered in a cracked, badly off-key tenor.

The affair was squirmingly embarrassing; there we were, guests of some very generous hosts who were polite enough to applaud as the fiasco ground to an end. None of us suspected the senior lieutenant even fancied himself as a latter day Bing Crosby; even less that he would make such a complete ass of himself in public. We were appalled. Our hosts were the only ones to applaud.

Revenge was quick and absolute. Breakfast was a meal at which the senior lieutenant, also inclined to affectation, had always insisted he did not like talking or even being spoken to, and to remind us all of this fact always displayed a miniature skull on the table in front of him. The following morning the skull was missing. Nobody wanted to talk to him anyway but eventually someone asked why no skull. He spoke. He had not known that singing with the band in Germany had to be paid for, and he'd been charged 100 Deutschmarks. Would we help him out with the cost? We wouldn't. He got an emphatic, loud, and unanimous NO.

Not much later we sailed for the West Indies, for my third time. With our second child due Jo couldn't stay at Slapton on her own so we had moved in with my mother and stepfather, in their cottage in Cornwall. I was to be away yet again when one of our children was born.

Being an aviator I wasn't the Captain's favourite officer. Additionally, with my seamanship knowledge I was at least as knowledgeable as most of the other officers, if not more so, and since our job was training Dartmouth cadets, and instruction by now second nature to me, I could do the job with my eyes closed.

The Captain decided to get rid of me for a week prior to a visit to St Lucia. I was put ashore, a week before the ship arrived, as the ship's liaison officer. To go ashore I had to wear a formal uniform white suit, with sword and medal, and was on my way in to Port Castries, the capital, in our scruffy little ship's boat. I took with me a signalman who would radio back to the ship the social functions I hoped to arrange for the ship's company when the ship eventually arrived in St Lucia a week hence.

Halfway across the harbour a gleaming white motor cruiser came creaming out from the jetty towards us and eased down close alongside. Standing in the stern was the smartest officer I'd ever seen. He was dressed in khaki shirt and shorts, creases like knife-edges, major rank badges on his shoulders, and he was black. He shouted across to me: 'Your boat or mine?' There was no contest. The signalman and I willingly climbed aboard this spotless cruiser, and said goodbye to the ship's boat's crew.

We set off for the jetty and on the way, after we'd introduced ourselves, I thought I'd better explain to this black chap what I'd come in for – to arrange outings, cocktail parties, banyans, and sports matches for the ship's company. He simply pulled out a large sheet of paper covered from top to bottom with functions for the officers and the sailors and said: 'Will this do?' All my work was done before I'd even set foot ashore; and much better than I could ever have done it. The major had done it all before, many times, for many ships' visits.

The major's name was Yorke and he was the police chief on St Lucia. He took us to a pre-booked hotel and we changed into plain clothes. An escort was arranged for the signalman, who was keen to find the best location from which to radio back to the ship. Major Yorke and I had our first drink together and then he drove me all over the island, pointing out the badhats and introducing me to all the good guys. I think Major Yorke knew where and when every crime on the island would be committed almost before it happened. He seemed to be several jumps ahead of trouble and was obviously very popular, and very good at his job.

During that idle week I now had nothing to do; we became firm friends, not least because our drinking habits were alike, except that he started at nine o'clock each morning. I managed some time for the navy, my signalman had found his optimum spot for transmitting and we quickly radioed back the complete programme Major Yorke had arranged. Thereafter the entire week was our own.

Once the ship arived in Port Castries I found the First Lieutenant (second in command) had obviously been impressed with the social programme and was more than satisfied. I admitted to having had some help from Major Yorke but thought it prudent not to mention that, in fact, he'd done the lot and I'd spent the entire week on a jolly. As an aviator among fishheads my standing wasn't too high and I didn't want to diminish it further.

Major Yorke always turned up at the ship at nine o'clock in the morning sharp. I met him and took him along to the wardroom where he invariably had a couple of whiskies and soda, and expected me to join him. He was a hard man to keep up with but I did my best, morning, noon and night. In the entire week I got a total of roughly eight hours sleep. The major must have had much less but he was always immaculately turned out, and in very good spirits, much of them naval.

We only had one slight misunderstanding. On the last night of our visit there was a ship's company dance, to which most of the officers and Major Yorke went. At about 2am, after a great evening, the major appeared with two very attractive black girls, explaining that they were mine 'for the night'. I would have been gobsmacked with one, but two! Not only that, the major had been thoughtful enough to provide me with some variety: one girl was tall, slender and gorgeous, and the other was shorter, only slightly plump, and gorgeous. I had to explain that I was married and couldn't accept his generous offer. For the one and only moment in our whole relationship, I felt that he thought I might be racist and had a colour hang-up about black girls. Presumably some ships' liaison officers before me had jumped at the chance! I did not have a hang-up about black girls and have always wondered, ever since, what pleasures I passed on.

The band didn't stop playing at the end of the dance. They simply got up with their instruments and carried on playing, down the stairs and along the street. We all carried on dancing behind them and eventually I finished up at the water's edge where someone was waving to me to come up a gangplank and on board a very large cabin cruiser. I went, and found unlimited champagne and glasses standing around and several of the other officers, already on board while I'd been sorting out my small problem with the two black girls. I don't know who the boat belonged to but assumed this was Major Yorke's parting gift to us. We set off across a moonlight bay, awash with champagne.

Only one small note jarred on that cruise across the bay. The senior lieutenant, the one who'd fancied himself as a crooner in Hamburg, had taken a girl up on the top deck and was singing to this unfortunate woman in his dreadful off-key, cracked tenor. Needless to say it was 'True Love' again. Now all too familiar with the voice and his tendency to inflict it on whoever was his luckless victim, we shouted him down, and quite ruined his night, and his chances. I suspect he might already have done that with his crooning.

The next morning at nine o'clock we sailed. Major Yorke came to see us off and I left behind a very good friend, and one who'd made my time in St Lucia memorable. I've never forgotten the island, Major Yorke, or the two black girls.

We called at several other ports, all extremely welcoming and hospitable, especially Barbados, where an ex-naval officer and his wife invited a chum and myself to be their guests and stay overnight. We had a fabulous evening at a nightclub and then went home with them. We woke up to humming birds in the hibiscus bushes.

On passage back to Plymouth and some deep maintenance, Jenni was born. I still regret being unable to be at the birth of either of our children. Fortunately Plymouth wasn't far from my mother's cottage and I got up there pretty fast to go and see Jenni for the first time. I was now firmly a family man with two very attractive babes and my very attractive, and proud, wife.

In Plymouth we changed captains and the new chap was a very pleasant Commander Sandy McCarthy. One day he came into the wardroom when I was duty officer and the only other officer on board at the time. When I offered him a drink he told me he'd like to celebrate: his wife had just given birth. When I told him mine had too he insisted on splitting a bottle of champagne. So we wet both our babies' heads, naval fashion.

At the end of my six months in the squadron I was awarded my watch keeping ticket and left. I hadn't taken any exam for the ticket; it was just awarded on the strength of the bridge watches I'd kept, usually under supervision. Furthermore the only ship handling I'd been allowed had been minor alterations of course in mid-Atlantic. I note this because a few years later I found myself in command of a frigate, and the only naval craft I'd handled before had been a ship's boat. The service operates in peculiar ways.

I was reappointed to 738 Squadron, back at Lossiemouth, as the Air Warfare Instructor of the Seahawk Operational Flying Training squadron, where I'd been a student five years earlier. I now had a son, baby daughter and my wife to get back up to Scotland. We drove up, and moved back into married quarters.

# Chapter 14

## *AWI in the Operational Flying Training Squadron*

AFTER my seatime for my Bridge Watchkeeping ticket, I had a short flying refresher course. I then went to my next appointment as the Air Warfare Instructor in the Seahawk Operational Flying Training squadron, 738, at Lossiemouth. Derek Monsell was the boss and James Moore the Senior Pilot. I joined in June, 1960.

I had developed some pretty strong views on flying instruction and could now put them into practice. The rough time I'd had in operational flying training still rankled with me, as had the gunnery results, then viewed as acceptable. Now they were unacceptable to me and I had a chance to try and prove that students could turn in much better results.

I took each of my students up in a Vampire twin-seat training aircraft to demonstrate how to handle the gyro gun sight properly when tracking a target aircraft. They then took film of these airborne exercises in their Seahawks and these films were analysed back in the squadron by the Wrens weapons assessing section. The results for each pilot, given in hitting percentages, were debriefed carefully. Pretty soon student pilots caught on and their results started to improve spectacularly.

The effect on the students was marked. Like everything else in this world, if you can prove to a student that not only can he do it, but he can do it well, then he goes from strength to strength. They did, and I was proud of the results my students achieved.

Six months later I was reappointed to be the Air Warfare Instructor's instructor in the Advanced Flying Training Squadron, 764, across the airfield at Lossiemouth. The squadron flew Hunters, my first swept wing aircraft, and very exciting. Nevertheless I left 738 Squadron with some regret. I'd proved a point. I'd shown that flying instruction properly applied could produce excellent results, and, of course, better pilots.

But I wasn't only instructing, I was learning. James Moore, my Senior Pilot, was the finest senior pilot I ever served under. He ran a tight ship and I picked up a great deal watching him operate. When I eventually became a senior pilot myself I was eternally grateful for everything from him that had rubbed off on me. James was my first 'role model' officer.

# Chapter 15

## *Air Warfare Instructors' Instructor*

WITH one training and two full front line squadron tours under my belt, two of them as the AWI, I was appointed to the Advanced Flying Training squadron, 764, at Lossiemouth, as the Air Warfare Instructor's instructor. We were flying Hunters and they were great fun to fly after the Seahawk, which I always regarded as the Tiger Moth of the naval jet world.

The Hunter was the first swept wing aircraft the navy had. It was sleek, fast and spacious, important for my tall frame. It handled beautifully and was far more representative in air combat training at that time than the old Seahawk had been, as well as being a very stable weapons platform for air-to-ground attack. I welcomed the leg room. The Seahawk's foot pedals had to wind in and out depending on pilot's leg length. It had always been just my luck to jump into a Seahawk's cockpit immediately after the shortest squadron pilot had been flying it.

I enjoyed the instruction as well as the flying, especially when the Instrument Trappers flight descended on us with almost visible, vicious anticipation. Air warfare Instructors were traditionally considered fine for their professed specialisation but, compared to Qualified Flying Instructors (QFIs), were held to be mediocre on the finer points of pure flying, like instrument flying. Thus Air Warfare Instructors were considered fair game for the trappers; there was a mutual dislike, and the trappers obviously looked forward to telling us what rubbish they thought we were after their flying and ground examinations.

With some bitterness I recalled how, as a tactical instructor, I'd been rubbished by the chief trapper. Now I was a qualified Instrument Rating Instructor (IRI) although latterly my AWI work had had to take priority.

I flew the airborne test and then retired to a briefing room with the examiner, the trapper's new Commanding Officer. He asked me what I knew about range and endurance flying – a standard (and important) subject for pilots. It was a subject I was keen on, and had been since my active IRI days, although the trapper plainly didn't know that.

The large briefing room had a wall-to-wall blackboard and I started at the left-hand side, chalking the board with appropriate range and endurance speak to support my patter. When I'd got about 12ft across the board the examiner, who hadn't said a word so far, stopped me and asked if I'd given this lecture before.

Only then did I tell him that I'd been an Instrument Rating Instructor but had had to give it up to spend more time on my Air Warfare instruction. He was miffed and stopped the examination there and then. I'd excelled in both the air and ground tests. I felt I'd at last redeemed myself with a vengeance after my poor showing a few years earlier. I got an almost vicious kick out of this 'victory': plainly the trappers hadn't checked their records before they came or they wouldn't have wasted time on checking out a former IRI. I was never 'trapped' again.

For some reason my boss never told me the results of my examination. I think he must have felt embarrassed that one of his pilots, his senior AWI, had done so well. He wasn't too keen on instrument flying himself. I only found out later from 'Wings' the head of the Air Department, when he congratulated me.

My tour in 764 Squadron was marred by a dreadful accident involving two of my students. In the calmest of situations and under no stress whatsoever one of them flew into the other, coming up directly underneath him. The impact ejected the top pilot involuntarily. He was lucky and survived. He never flew jets again. The other pilot was killed.

They were both good friends of mine and I was asked to escort the body of the fatality down to his home town for the funeral. Draped in the White Ensign, the coffin was given an entire railway guard's wagon on its own and I'd never had such good service from British Rail, as it then was. We travelled from Elgin to Bedfordshire and I never once had any worry about the coffin. Its carriage was always transferred to the next train without any action on my part. Eventually we arrived and I met and comforted the parents as best I good. They were charming and hospitable. I stayed with them that night, and went with them to the funeral the next day as the naval representative, and their son's friend and instructor.

My boss flew down to take me back to Lossiemouth the same afternoon. He let me fly the aircraft back and it was a relief to concentrate on something else. I was getting to be all too familiar with burying naval pilots, most of them friends of mine, and 35,000 feet in a clear blue sky for the return flight helped considerably.

Soon after that I was re-appointed as the Air Warfare Instructor of a Scimitar squadron, 800, boss Danny Norman, an ace aviator, Empire Test Pilot and a pilot renowned throughout the Fleet Air Arm for his flying ability, his charm, and the fact that he was one of the service's gentlemen. I looked forward to him being my new boss, and to getting my hands on the Scimitar.

# Chapter 16

## *Scimitars*

THE Scimitar was the first 'heavyweight' aircraft I was to fly, and the first twin-engined type. It was a big, single-seat beast powered by two Rolls Royce engines each producing about 10,000 lbs thrust. On my first familiarisation sortie I lined up on the runway and settled back firmly in the ejection seat: I'd been advised that the acceleration would surprise me. It did. You really felt pushed back into the seat as you screamed down the runway, lifted off and climbed away. The speed build up was like nothing I'd ever experienced before: really exhilarating. In no time at all I was shooting through 20,000 feet on my way to 35,000 faster than I'd ever done.

And there the problems started. The Scimitar wasn't an aircraft for altitude. True it could get up there really fast but once there its manoeuvre capability was severely limited. Turning was almost a joke, the aircraft being 'on the burble' of the high speed stall most of the time. The only thing to do was to ease the turn and wander round it slowly as best you could.

But come down to low level in the Scimitar and then the fun really began. Here the aircraft was in its element, fast, fairly manoeuvrable and very pleasant to handle. Its only problem down at that level was its fuel consumption. You could almost see the fuel gauges unwinding. Thumbing through my logbook I see that many of the Scimitar sorties are less than an hour. On a lot of the longer sorties I was able to in-flight refuel. Nevertheless, enjoy what you've got while it lasts, and I did. The Scimitar was a fun aircraft to fly at the time I was flying it. Latterly it got terribly tired: it was only meant to be in service for four years as an interim aircraft between the Seahawk and the Buccaneer but it eventually stayed for eleven.

After my familiarisation flights in the training squadron I crossed the airfield to join my operational outfit, 800 Squadron. I soon bumped into my new boss, Danny Norman. Danny had recently led the very successful Scimitar aeros team at the Farnborough Air Show. He immediately suggested we go up for some flying practice. No briefing; we simply strolled out to the aircraft and got airborne, Danny leading. We did a formation take-off, my first in the Scimitar, and we stayed in close formation throughout the trip. Low level over the Moray Firth, Danny went through a series of steep turns usually with me on the lower side between him and the water, which, you always felt in that position, was uncomfortably close. Occasionally he reversed the turn so that I was on the top, just to let me see how low we really were. I had no option but to stick with him, and I wouldn't have wanted to do anything else anyway. He was a very smooth leader and I had no qualms about staying with him, but very close!

We returned to the airfield and, as we walked back to the hangar, Danny debriefed me: 'That was OK Dave!'

Soon after that sortie Danny was relieved by a new boss: Jock Mancais, who I'd heard of and knew by sight. Jock had a reputation for being a hard man to follow, especially in the bar, and he certainly appeared to live up to it, although I soon discovered that the amount he actually put away was but a fraction of what we all thought he'd drunk. He was a leader all the way, in the air and on the ground, and the latter was to cause me a few problems. I was now one of the senior pilots in the squadron and became Jock's natural companion on many hilarious escapades ashore.

We duly embarked in *Ark Royal* and sailed for the Mediterranean. Jo and the children were in our married quarter at Lossiemouth and life must have seemed one dreary separation after another. I'd been away in *Eagle* for almost a year, during which time Trevor was born. Almost immediately after that I'd gone to sea again for another six months for my bridge watch-keeping ticket when Jenni was born. This time we were going to be away for over a year, the longest separation so far. It was now September 1961 and we'd been married less than five years.

Not too long after we'd embarked I discovered that, at the usual squadron gathering in the bar after dinner (we were a day fighter outfit, no night flying) Jock was never there. It took me a long time to run him to earth. He was always down in our hangar. The squadron had the lower hangar in *Ark*. It was directly over the boiler rooms and, in the tropics, just one large sauna. To add to the discomfort for the maintenance crews, the Scimitar was a dirty aircraft. It had 'wet' wings i.e. some fuel tanks in the wings themselves, and these seeped fuel regularly. On top of this the aircraft leaked hydraulic fluid copiously. This entailed each aircraft requiring several large drip trays underneath it to catch this involuntary seepage; and this meant that the maintenance crews were often sloshing around in the stuff. Thus maintaining the Scimitar, and getting sufficient numbers serviceable for the following day's flying could be an unpleasant task.

But there was Jock, down in the hangar. He knew everyone's name, and he jollied them along; and too often they really needed jollying. He chatted with them, discussed the problems they were trying to remedy on their aircraft, their personal problems, and really encouraged them. It paid off handsomely. Any of those maintenance ratings would have died for Jock.

I began to learn what was really required of a commanding officer there and then. I started visiting the hangar each evening, got to know those names I hadn't yet learned and soon knew everyone's name. Thereafter this was an absolute must and, in every squadron and latterly my frigate, I knew every man's name within days of joining the outfit. It was to pay off dividends. I was also fanatical about knowing my aircraft inside out and could chat to the maintainers from a pilot's point of view – something they valued, not only because they were interested in what their aircraft were doing when they were launched from the carrier, but also because it helped them understand why they were doing whatever was necessary for maintenance and rectification. It goes without saying that a pilot should know his aircraft inside out. Too often they didn't.

How Jock lead the squadron and how he handled the men became the way ahead for me. He was a Scot with a penetrating sense of humour which always went down well; he didn't pull his punches if he thought something was amiss, but I never saw him lose his cool, and there must have been many times when he could reasonably have let off steam. Jock became another of my role model officers.

In May 1962 we were operating around the Philippines and I had to take a Scimitar ashore for a bombing trial. The ship was to go into Manila harbour shortly after that and Jock was keen to get as many of our sailors out of the ship and away to a US rest and recreation centre up in the mountains and the cool. The centre was at Baguio. He asked me, when

I got ashore, to organise transport for up to 180 men up to Baguio. I immediately started thinking along British lines about welfare coaches and some sort of organisation that could take care of it. The US navy had nothing like that.

Each time I walked around the base looking for help and inspiration, I had to pass a squadron of US Marine Corps helicopters, dozens of them, which seemed to be doing nothing. *Ark* was due in Manila shortly and I was getting desperate. These helos could do the job. Dare I ask?

I'd seen the helicopters crews often enough down at the officers' pool and they were a good bunch. Their Commanding Officer, a colonel, in red baseball cap (in the water and out) with his badge of rank, was something of a character and very popular. I thought if I didn't try I'd never get anywhere so I called at the squadron and asked to see the boss. I was told he was in his room up at the Bachelor Officer Quarters if I'd care to try there. I did. And there he was, on his bunk in a pair of shorts, and the baseball cap. It was about 1030 am. I introduced myself and explained I was from *Ark Royal*, made what I considered to be an outrageous request for an airlift, and apologised profusely.

The colonel didn't bat an eyelid. He said: 'One moment, lootenant. I have to buzz my Operations Officer'. He put his cigar back in the corner of his mouth and Ops came in. The boss explained who I was, what I wanted and when I wanted it, ending with: 'we doin' anything that day Ops?' Ops consulted the inevitable clipboard and then said: Sir, we're embarking in the USS... (a carrier) at 0830'. My heart sank. These guys were going back to Vietnam on that day (two days hence). A UK squadron would have been running around like madmen. I didn't have a prayer. Ops continued, talking to me now: 'Sir if you could have your men ready to go in sticks of eight on the flight deck at 7am tomorrow we could ferry them up to Baguio then. Would that be OK?'

Darned right it would. I thanked them and got out of there fast.

I sent a signal to Jock asking him to have the 180 men on the flight deck at 7 am, ready in sticks of eight, for a helicopter lift up to the rest and recreation centre. It went like clockwork and the sailors got their R & R. They'd earned it and really appreciated it. Jock never commented on what I'd managed to do but I knew that, in his eyes, I'd graduated to miracle worker.

I sent a couple of bottles of Malt whisky up to the colonel's cabin in the BOQ.

One time we were anchored off the Philippines again one Sunday morning when there was a banging on my cabin door with Jock outside shouting: 'Dave, get down in the bar. We've got some US marines to host'. I got changed into a clean set of whites and went down. Although it was a Sunday, bar normally not open until midday, Jock had managed to persuade the mess president to get the bar open early, to entertain the marines. We started drinking at 11.30 am.

The bar closed at 1 pm and we were still drinking. Jock then asked these two marines, one medium height, normal looking chap, the other as tall as me and twice as broad at the shoulders, with a pencil sharpener haircut and a Bronx accent, if they'd like to stay for lunch. Yes please.

I shuddered. Unusually, the food in *Ark* at that time was terrible. Worse still, at 1 pm steward service stopped and the mess went to cafeteria service. You queued up and got whatever was available, from a steward serving behind the counter. The menu was roast beef, roast potatoes, cabbage, Yorkshire pud and gravy. Dessert was suet pud with custard. Each of our guests grabbed a tray and a dinner plate and asked for, and got, an enormous helping of the roast dish generously topped out with gravy. They then had the suet pudding plonked on top of it all and topped that out with custard. I could hardly believe anyone could eat that much, let alone that mix, but eat it they did, smacked their lips and both declared: 'Gee. That was deeelicious!' Worse was to come.

After what the US marines obviously considered a feast, Jock, who had recovered his composure after watching these guys demolish their meal, declared we should all go ashore to the local officers' club. I protested feebly, anticipating what was coming. That evening I and two other officers had invited the senior US army general in the islands, and his wife, to supper on board and then a cinema show on the quarterdeck: standard naval hospitality on a foreign visit. We three had met this couple at the cocktail party the ship always gave first evening of the visit, and thought them charming. They had been delighted to have been invited and were looking forward to the occasion.

Jock was not impressed with this excuse. 'Howard, you are coming ashore'. Up to my cabin, into plain clothes and out to the gangway. Off we went in a ship's boat. After the lunchtime drinking session I was already three sheets in the wind and was not looking forward to an afternoon's continued drinking one bit. I needed sleep.

The walk from the landing jetty to the officers' club wasn't far but I noticed that the earth was almost orange, and dusty.

In the club we drank. The conversation descended from the ridiculous to the totally ridiculous. Limp jokes like 'Why are all the waitresses wearing such funny little shoes; because they've got such funny little feet' reduced us to incredible fits of laughter, needless to say raucous, but the two marines were obviously regulars and we were tolerated.

At 5 pm I got up to go, explaining that I had to catch the next boat – 5.30 – so as to be ready for my guests who were catching the 6.30 boat. Enter Jock, well into his cups, as was I. 'Sit down Howard, you can catch the next boat, and keep your guests company on the boat trip'. Another direct order which I couldn't pass on. I sat down, had more drinks and, at 6 pm, Jock gave me permission to go.

It had rained while we were in the club. The orange earth had turned into an orange quagmire and somehow it splashed halfway up my flannels. Although I didn't know it, my tie had worked its way round to the side of my neck as well. And there on the landing jetty were the general and his wife. Mrs General was not amused. The general managed a wry smile.

We chatted as we progressed towards the carrier, heaven knows what about. As we came alongside I saw the other two hosts, both senior to me, glaring down over the guardrails, as un-amused as Mrs General. Once on deck I was almost thrown through the door from the quarterdeck and told to get into mess undress. I got a shower, changed and back on deck just as the party was going down to the mess for supper. I managed this quite well, even getting a moment to explain privately to the senior host what had happened. He remained un-amused.

Supper over, we all trooped back up to the quarterdeck where chairs had been set out for us to watch the film. By this time I was sober enough to remember that the general asked specifically for me to sit beside him, and I thought maybe he wanted to ease my embarrassment. The film started. I fell asleep on his shoulder!

As we bid our guests Goodbye before they went down to the boat, Mrs General gave me the kiss of death. 'Goodbye' she said, icily, 'I hope you had a good sleep'.

Mrs General must have forgiven me because later the general invited all three of us hosts to be his guests for dinner. A car would take us to his house and from there we'd all go on to one of several officers' clubs. Needless to say, this club was the best and I only realised how important the general was when we arrived outside the club. A retinue was waiting for us and everyone anywhere near the general seemed to be washing their hands.

The general gave us a fabulous meal and the wine was wonderful. However, we'd had a martini at the general's house, American strength, and that much gin doesn't mix with wine for me. I was almost temperate, much to the relief of the senior RN guest, but possibly to the disappointment of the general who appeared to think I might be something of a wine buff. I daren't try and prove any credentials, which were virtually non-existent anyway.

While we were in the Philippines we embarked some VIPs and the ship put to sea for a display of bombing, rocketing and strafing on a target we towed astern, and then, as a grand finale, an aerobatics display with our Scimitars. We had a box four, diamond formation and, because the Scimitar took up so much sky, to fill in the intervals before they got back in front of the audience, a singleton to do solo aeros: me. The final act in this show was Jock leading the box four up into a loop while I thundered low and fast past the VIPs. This was very impressive. The Scimitar, low and fast in high temperature and high humidity, was just a blur of vapour. I was then to pull up and pass through the centre of the box as they split and peeled away. Jock timed his split on his sighting of the blur. My positioning was simply by mark 1 eyeball. I was early.

I radioed him: 'Break early please boss'. By this time Jock was coming over the top of the loop at about 300 knots and I was pulling up at roughly 620 knots: closing speed over 900 knots. Jock radioed back: 'Say again!'

It crossed my mind, the way things do in fraught situations like that, that this could be a spectacular finish to an aeros display. To my relief I saw the box split like magic and I was clear through them as they peeled away.

Back in the carrier at the debriefing I asked Jock how come he hadn't heard my desperate 'Break early please boss'? He said he'd heard it clearly but, seeing my vapour trail and knowing I was early, he'd frozen up and hadn't been able to think clearly. The other three laughed and told me; 'We heard you, Dave, and knew what you meant. We just went'.

It was the one and only time I ever knew Jock short of a word.

At about this time I was given the dubious honour of trial firing the first naval Bullpup missile. The Bullpup was a pilot guided missile which you fired in a shallow dive and then followed on down behind, guiding it, by means of radio signals, hopefully on to the target. I think we'd bought it cheap from the US who'd quickly realised that what surface-to-air defences really liked was an aircraft coming straight at them in a long, shallow dive; it gave them plenty of time to take it out. Anyway, I hit the target, a rock, landed back in the carrier and was given another missile to fire next sortie. Good fun, but of no operational use whatsoever. The navy didn't keep the missile long, but I did later experiment with it at night, low level, in a Buccaneer.

Shortly after this exercise, again in the Philippines, we sailed for Australia. The carrier went into Fremantle, near Perth and we disembarked six Scimitars to Pearce airfield close by.

Perth was one of the most beautiful places I'd seen. It still is as far as I know. It's the home of Swan lager and we saw a lot of that. Jock disappeared, with another Commanding Officer, having managed to persuade the Captain that being a Commanding Officer was so stressful that they needed to get away for a complete break. I think they rented a villa and, as far as I know, they de-stressed themselves probably sitting by the pool with a gallon or two of Swan lager every day.

Those of us who'd flown ashore stayed in an hotel which was straight out of a John Wayne movie. We ate steak, eggs and chips, standard Aussie breakfast, drank a lot of Swan, and de-stressed that way. It was a good break for us but we didn't fly a lot, in fact I think, in hindsight, taking the aircraft ashore was simply an excuse to get us out of the ship. Jock had invented it for our benefit.

From Oz we worked our way back west via Singapore, Aden and Mombasa, eventually getting home to Lossiemouth for Christmas 1962.

We stayed ashore until May 1963 when we re-embarked in *Ark*, this time flying direct from Lossiemouth to the Mediterranean. This was a long trip for a Scimitar and involved in-flight refuelling over France. I logged 2½ hours for that flight which ended with us landing on in *Ark* off Majorca.

We'd had a change of Commanding Officer in March, Pete Newman taking over from Jock. Pete had a bad back though, post ejection seat trouble I think, and had to leave the squadron very soon. By this time Don Mills had taken over as senior pilot. He moved up to be the new Commanding Officer when Pete had to leave, and I then moved up from Air Warfare Instructor to be Senior Pilot.

Again we made our way out to the Far East via Aden, Singapore and Hong Kong where I got off. I'd been re-appointed to a shore job: the Gunnery school, *HMS Excellent*, Whale Island, Portsmouth. I flew to the UK in a British Airways Britannia. It took 28 hours flying time, involved a refuelling stop in Colombo at 2.30 a.m. in the height of summer, and I was very glad to get home. I managed to cadge a much-needed bath at a friend's house and then made my way up to Lossiemouth.

# Chapter 17

## *Whale Island*

FOR an aviator, Whale Island, *HMS Excellent*, to give it its correct name, was quite a culture shock even though I'd had experienced it before as a sailor. Everyone wore boots and gaiters and, being the gunnery school of the navy, everyone was expected to be 'pusser' at all times. Pusser is the naval term for correct in every detail: caps on dead straight, boots and gaiters gleaming, march or 'double' everywhere, swing your arms, salute whoever you were supposed to salute (heaven help anyone who didn't) and generally behave like an automaton. And gunnery officers, fishheads all, without exception thought aviators were all barking mad, and totally incapable of conforming to their strict code of dress and bearing.

My job at Whale Island was the ground syllabus training of Air Warfare Instructor student pilots, and new entry wrens destined to become Range Assessors (as Jo had been). Additionally there were countless briefings and lectures to give to any number of people requiring some degree of familiarisation with naval air weapons. Perhaps the most important of the latter group were the Long Gunnery Course students who would eventually qualify as gunnery officers when they completed their two-year course.

These officers would come up to Lossiemouth each year for the air familiarisation part of their course. This entailed them actually flying and I and the other aviator on the island were given a flight of Vampire trainer aircraft for the purpose. We were supposed to give them an introduction to the various aspects of air warfare but it was rare for any of them to withstand the "g" forces necessary when pulling out of dive attacks without feeling, and even being, airsick. Most of the sorties we flew with them were fairly gentle. To make them concentrate on something other than their stomach, I even persuaded some of my students to take off and land (my hand never far from the control column). This worked pretty well and those that had a go were agreeably surprised that they could make a reasonable fist of it, and that they could remain airborne without feeling sick.

There were always a few for whom even the thought of having to fly was anathema. They were obvious from their lack of interest; they didn't want to attempt to handle the aircraft and refused point blank to try a take off, even less a landing. All you could do for these unfortunates was to fly them around gently, show them the countryside, and do something innocuous and gentle like a Ground Controlled Approach (GCA). I felt very sorry for these students but fly they had to, and fly they did, albeit in a very antiseptic manner.

Needless to say we two pilots welcomed our annual two weeks flying. The shore based job would have been very boring for us without getting our hands back in, and introducing the Long Gunners to some of the delights of Scotland, mainly malt whisky. They all used to party quite well, and the malt was very successful in releasing what we considered were the inhibitions that appeared to be part of the Whale Island mentality. The flying part of their course always took place in the summer, when the weather factor could guarantee good flying conditions. It also enabled plenty of beach parties where, given enough malt, you could tolerate the Lossiemouth summer temperatures without getting frostbite.

In early January 1965, it had become obvious that Winston Churchill had not long to live. A full state funeral had long been planned for him and it was traditional for the naval gunnery school to provide the gun carriage crew and guard of honour for any state funeral. Apparently the tradition dated back to Queen Victoria's time when, at Prince Albert's state funeral, the horses then pulling the hearse took fright and attempted to bolt. Sailors from the street lining contingent broke ranks and quickly calmed the frightened animals, Queen Victoria was duly impressed, and the navy was accorded the honour of pulling the gun carriage thereafter. The privilege had naturally fallen to the gunnery school, *HMS Excellent*, prestigious for its meticulous parade ground drill and immaculate ceremonial guards.

It had to be a 'boots and gaiters' job, with every sailor and officer being of good upright bearing. The captain of the school always led the gun carriage crew. Since he had to have someone else beside him to balance things up, and since he was six feet three inches tall, and since the navy always has to have people of the same height beside each other on ceremonial parade, the only other officer available who fitted the bill was a junior lieutenant commander, me, and an aviator to boot (no pun intended).

This selection caused an absolute uproar on the island: not only had they to put up with this aviator in their midst, bad enough, but the bounder had been chosen to be out front with the captain for the only state funeral they were likely to see in their careers, let alone have a chance of taking part in. It was just too much for some of them to bear. One in particular, who had been chosen to march but towards the rear of the contingent, would sometimes sidle up to me when we'd fallen in for one of our early rehearsals and say: 'You're at the back today Dave'.

I thought it might ease the pain of having an aviator out front, (or possibly the fact that it wasn't him) and he was quite a bit senior to me, so back I would go. Each time without fail, a few minutes after we'd started marching, the captain would snarl 'get Howard back up here'. Crestfallen, the officer in question, short, dumpy and with a tendency to waddle, would come back and explain that the captain wanted me up at the front again. And there I stayed for most of the rehearsals and, of course, the actual state funeral. Teeth, 'fishhead' teeth, were gnashing all over the island.

After my bridge watch keeping ticket experience this was my next exposure in the service to serious prejudice against aviators, anti-aviator-itis as I now call it. There was much more to come.

We rehearsed on the island for several days before Churchill finally died. Since the island is actually an island and there were always security guards on the bridge across, the press never managed to get at us. The paparazzi today would have had a ball, but at that time the gun carriage crew rehearsals weren't bothered, although some outside agencies must surely have known what was going on. Perhaps a 'D' notice had been issued.

The gun carriage had been given a set time to get from Old Palace Yard at Westminster to St Paul's Cathedral. Dividing the distance by the time gave a marching speed of 68 paces to the minute: only just faster than the normal 60/minute. Therefore 'chanters', senior Chief Petty Officers dressed as sailors, were stationed at various points in the crew and quietly called the correct beat, 68/minute, until we got to the stage where the band deliberately played a different time but the chanters kept us at the required pace.

Once up in London the entire contingent of street lining personnel, the rest of the navy, and all the army and the RAF, wore greatcoats. There is nothing smarter than a blue-jacket (sailor) guard, and the gun carriage officers thought greatcoats would ruin the effect. We decided to try letting everyone, sailors and officers, put on as much warm clothing as they could and still get their blue jackets and white shirt fronts on without anything untoward showing. A dress rehearsal in the barracks gym was a great success; the sailors were keen. I managed to get on a couple of warm vests and a cardigan under my white uniform shirt. So the gun carriage crew, officers and sailors, were the only personnel that day to appear without greatcoats. It was a terrific one-up for Whale Island and the navy. The sailors had wanted to stand out, look smarter. They did.

When we started off for the first rehearsal in London, three sleepy guards bandsmen with big bass drums were the only band that the army could produce at 4.30 on a very cold January morning. They appeared to have forgotten to wind their metronomes and what they were banging out was certainly not 68/minute. The captain endured this around Parliament Square and up into Parliament Street.

Guards colonels were sprinkled along the pavements all the way up Whitehall, their bearskins glinting in the lamplight. When the captain couldn't stand the drummers nonsense any longer he adopted his parade ground voice and roared: 'If that's 68 to the minute I'll eat my b---- hat'.

Every bearskin on the pavement swivelled about and started back down Whitehall towards the gun carriage crew and the very angry, very senior captain. They stopped when the drummers shut up, silenced by the captain's roar, which may have shaken Nelson on his column. The bearskins stopped when the drummers shut up, for good. The gun carriage crew carried on, the chanters keeping us on time, and got to St Paul's on the second.

Marching on either side of the gun carriage crew was a line of army officers, in their greatcoats and bearskins, the line nearest to me led by a very young looking captain. On the first rehearsal the whole assembly came to a halt outside St Paul's, as ordered by the gunnery commander who marched besides the coffin. Immediately the crew clumped to a halt, up from a basement flight of steps to our left there appeared a Regimental Sergeant Major (RSM) carrying a pot of whitewash. He marched up to the young guards captain to my left, pushed him back a pace and then painted a white cross on the pavement where he'd just come to a halt. The RSM then pulled the captain, by his belt, back on to the white cross, and told him: 'You stand there sir. That's your spot'. The captain appeared quite relieved to know where he had to stand. The RSM disappeared back down the steps.

On the next rehearsal the gun carriage crew again came to a halt outside St Paul's. The Guards captain was 6 ft short of his spot. Up from the basement came the RSM, looked at his white cross, and glared at the young guards captain. He was visibly upset. So was the Guards captain. The RSM marched in front of me on his way across to Captain Power as the officer in charge of the whole gun carriage crew. Now the captain was not only very senior; in the chilly twilight he looked pretty 'chokker' (navy for 'fed up'), very fierce, and disinclined to talk to an RSM at this early hour on a bitingly cold January morning. He was also, of course, carrying his sword: drawn. The RSM wisely chickened out. He came back to me, clumped to attention and chopped me off a salute. I returned the salute and asked what his problem might be.

Patronising tone: 'You've stopped in the wrong place sir'.

'What on earth do you mean RSM?'

'Well sir' the RSM explained, even more patronising, 'Yesterday you stopped further forward, by that white cross I painted for my captain. Now he doesn't know where to stand'.

The poor young captain did look rather distressed. I only learned later that his distress stemmed from his not being able to do what his RSM had told him, rather than any belief he might have had that the gun carriage crew were at fault and had got it wrong.

'I think you'd better speak to the officer in charge of the body, RSM. He's back there with the coffin, a commander'.

The RSM was never seen again. The gunnery commander I referred the RSM to was even fiercer than the captain, and could eat RSMs for breakfast. He'd called the crew to a halt on the first rehearsal directly beside the red carpet up the steps of the cathedral. The carpet had had to be moved a few paces back for the second rehearsal. There may still be traces of the RSM stamped into the tarmac outside the cathedral. The gunnery commander took no prisoners.

For the state funeral itself an overcast London was unnaturally quiet. From any of the thousands of mourners crowding the pavements, even an occasional lone cough barked out clearly. In this eerie, memorable silence the gun-carriage crew waited, stock still, for the service to finish. Winston's coffin would then be returned to the bier.

Every man jack of the gun-carriage crew, some 140 sailors and 10 officers, shivered silently outside the cathedral, wishing poor old Winston could have hung on beyond this bitingly cold January. Each one, officers and sailors, in our summer rig white shirts, but with all those extra layers underneath, still felt the penetrating wind whistling up from Cannon Street. Ye Gods it was cold.

Possibly even more frigid had been Captain Power's responses to army nonsense. On the first rehearsal the rest of the cortege had dropped well behind the gun carriage. Having heard this at the debriefing, the captain, by now completely fed up with the army, especially the Master of the Queen's Musik to whom the sleepy bass drummers belonged, asked his only question: 'Who keeps station on whom?'

'Why, we keep up with you of course, sir' answered one of the many colonels.

'That's all I have to say' replied the captain. He picked up his cap and gloves and left the debriefing session.

The state funeral itself went absolutely as planned and as we'd rehearsed so many times. It was a moving occasion, not least because of the thousands of mourners, the general public, lining the streets. Of the many enduring memories of that day, one that still stands out strongly was the silence as the gun carriage crew waited outside the cathedral during the service. In the heart of a city as big as London it was almost eerie.

At last the service ended and the gun-carriage crew was called to attention for the coffin to be returned to the bier. We marched off, thankful to get our frozen limbs moving again on the shorter stretch along to Tower Hill, where the coffin would be transferred to a bearer party, down to the launch, the naval guard of honour, and the passage upriver, beneath the salutes of all those dockside cranes, their jibs lowered in respect for Winston.

The Master of the Queen's musik never got it right for the captain. He was a small, dumpy, eager-to-please major, but he never managed to please the captain. Getting his band to play a 68/minute tempo was, apparently, impossible, and infuriating for the captain. The chanters were our saviours. The final straw was when the crew and the coffin parted company at the top of the slope down to Tower Pier.

The band carried on towards where the Royal Mint was in those days and we all heaved a sigh of relief to see them go. Then they countermarched and came back.

Afterwards back in the mess, drink in hand, the major came bouncing up to Captain Power, craving a compliment at last: 'Well, how was that sir?'

'Bloody awful' said the captain. 'Just when we thought we'd got rid of you, you countermarched and came back to join us again'. The major's face crumpled. He may have gone away and fallen on his sword!

I doubt Whale Island ever forgave me for being in the limelight at the expense of one of their gunnery specialisation. What galled the fishheads particularly were the pilots' wings on my sleeve, evident in many of the photos. That really hurt.

After the funeral I was surprised that my father, no contact for many, many years, got in touch with me. He had several friends in Fleet Street and had managed to get hold of some wonderful press photos of the gun carriage crew at various points along the funeral procession's route. Out in front, alongside the captain, was his son. Apparently his elder brother Tom had somehow discovered I was involved, had done quite a lot of research on my naval career, decided that I was the family's blue-eyed boy, and that I'd 'done the family a great honour by being chosen to take part in the funeral'. Coming from my father's side of the family, that had shown not the slightest interest in me for 30 years, this was the height of hypocrisy. I vented my anger when told. I did keep the photos though, and regularly bore anyone polite enough to look at them, and listen to my account of the whole funeral affair.

For my 75th birthday my younger son enlarged two of the best of those photos and they now have pride of place in our hall.

I left Whale Island for a new appointment shortly after the state funeral. The family moved back up to Lossiemouth, and I came back to the air world, and my introduction to the Buccaneer.

# Chapter 18

*Buccaneer Senior Pilot*

BACK at Lossiemouth, Jo and I decided we'd had enough of married quarters and opted for a small cottage at Llanbryde, a village out on the Aberdeen road and about eight miles from the air station using the back lanes.

I went to 764 Squadron, the Hunter training outfit. Besides training AWIs they also gave refresher courses for pilots out of flying practice (I'd been away from operational flying for the 18 months at Whale Island) and courses for Commanding Officers and Senior Pilots designate. My next appointment was to 800 Squadron, a Buccaneer squadron, as the Senior Pilot. I had to get back into flying practice, and refresh on the finer points: weaponry, leading, air combat, and low level navigation. Having done this I then went across the airfield to the Buccaneer training squadron, 736, for my Buccaneer conversion, which was enjoyable and uneventful.

It was also an eye opener for me. The Buccaneer was the first time I'd had the benefit of an observer: the other half of the aircrew. The only time I'd flown with someone else was in a training aircraft, either being taught or examined by, or myself teaching or examining, another pilot. The pilot/observer crew gave a whole new dimension to my flying – I could concentrate on flying the aircraft to its limits while the observer handled the navigation (never my long suit), a lot of the weapon system, and the variety of checks required during different phases of flight. I wasn't to realise how much benefit I'd gained until I had more experience on type but I knew I was going to enjoy operating the Buccaneer, and was looking forward to the front line squadron.

My conversion to type complete, it was back across the airfield to join my front line Buccaneer outfit. The boss was my old Commanding Officer from 764 when I'd been the AWI's instructor.

I crossed the airfield in my little Messerscmitt three wheeler, had my first flight in the squadron with the Senior Observer, and then drove him up to the wardroom for lunch, sitting behind me in the tandem seater.

The flight had been pretty routine; not so the trip in the Messerschmitt. Having just sat behind me for the very first time in a Buccaneer, Bob must have been distinctly unimpressed sitting behind me in the three-wheeler.

I turned it on its side!.

The Messerschmitt's canopy opened sideways – to the right. So there we were, quite unharmed, lying on our right side, wheels still spinning, like a beetle flipped on its back, unable to get out. To make matters worse, the petrol filler cap was immediately outside, under Bob's right ear - and leaking. Bob was un-amused.

The sailor passengers of a passing naval van came running back and peered down at us lying on our side in our horizontal cockpit. They knew my vehicle.

'Are you alright, sirs?'

'Yes thank you' I replied in as dignified manner as was possible, looking up from a very undignified position. 'I wonder if you'd mind tilting us upright, please?'

They kindly did, and we continued on up to the wardroom with no further mishap. I believe Bob got back to the squadron another way.

I knew my new boss had a dislike of night and instrument flying; the two are really synonymous. The Seahawk and the Scimitar were essentially day fighter/strike aircraft and both were single seat; the Buccaneer was an all weather strike aircraft and all weather meant night as well. My new squadron was dreadfully short of night flying hours.

The boss' dislike of night flying had not gone unnoticed by the staff at naval air command headquarters at Yeovilton. Almost the first event after I joined was that the Flag Officer Naval Air Command (FONAC) came up to visit the squadron in person and ordered the boss to get each pilot 40 hours night flying before we embarked. This was a very tall order; it was July and there wasn't much night at that time of the year so far north, and we were due to embark in *Eagle* the following month. On top of that the Buccaneer Mk1 wasn't too hot on serviceability, so aircraft availability wasn't really up to the requirement. Additionally, all the aircraft had to have pre-embarkation checks before we went to the deck, which would further reduce aircraft availability.

We tried. We took off from Lossiemouth late in the evening, let down to low level (200ft) in the Moray Firth where it was almost dark and you had to fly on instruments. We then flew east to Fraserburgh, turned right into the North Sea, all the way down to the Dover straits and into the English Channel. By this time it was well and truly dark. We then flew down to the Isle of Wight area and coasted in to land at Yeovilton at about 2 am. After a quick turn round we took off again, climbed to altitude until we had to let down again to remain in the dark, and landed back at Lossiemouth, usually as dawn was about to break, at around 5am. This was pretty tiring stuff but was the best we could do to meet FONAC's order. I did seven trips like that but still clocked up less than half the 40-hour requirement. Even so, we'd done more night flying in that short period than the squadron had done in the previous year.

The next event of some importance just after I joined the squadron was that I had the father and mother of all rows with my new boss. Lossiemouth's annual air day was due and the squadron wasn't taking part. Anathema to me; we were the only front line squadron disembarked at the time and I thought we should make some sort of show as the 'pointed end' of the air station. We didn't. The boss was adamant that, with embarkation looming, we couldn't possibly participate. I got really angry and pushed my luck to the extreme. The boss listened to all my arguments, some of them pretty strong, but he wouldn't budge.

So off we went to sea, and to the third notable event in my new outfit. Whenever a carrier embarked its air group there was always a tremendous party in the mess; old buddies from other squadrons, other air stations and specialisations, welcomed each other and a good time was generally had by all: except 800 Squadron.

I had been looking forward to this thrash but every other outfit seemed to be taking the Mick out of the Buccaneers, and me, as their senior pilot. The boss wasn't around, being teetotal, but, as I was soon to discover, he knew better than to join the party. As the senior 800 man present, I was taking a lot of stick, and couldn't understand why. To make matters much worse, most of the other 800 aircrew were taking it all on the chin.

Eventually I took a friend, one of our observers who'd been on the previous embarked tour, outside and asked what was going on. I'd never seen a squadron take stick like this, and so much of it. It was something uncharacteristic in any Air Group and it was coming from many of my old chums in other squadrons.

Steve explained to me that the previous embarked tour had been an absolute disaster for the Buccaneers. Our Mk1 aircraft had the Gyron junior engines, an expedient imposition on the navy. The Gyron was preferred to the Spey which the Mk2 Buccaneers were to have. The Gyron was underpowered, subject to catastrophic failures, and every engine had had to be lifted and modified during the tour. The amount of flying the Buccs got was very limited and, worse still, the carrier appeared to have lost interest in operating them. If there was the slightest hiccup with a Bucc preparing for launch, and who could blame the aircrew for being cautious, the flight was cancelled, and the aircraft immediately taken out of the programme. Hence the opinion of the rest of the air group about us, and the stick they were giving us at that party.

The boss had given me no warning what to expect. I realised I had a job on my hands. I had to turn the ship's attitude around, turn the attitude of the rest of the air group around, and lift the squadron morale up off the deck: aircrew and groundcrew. I started right there and then.

The loudest mouth in the mess, and the most unpleasant in terms of what he thought of 800, belonged to the Senior Pilot of a helicopter squadron. I went back into the mess, got a loud jeer from him, grabbed him by the lapels and lifted him almost clear of the deck. As I held him up I snarled at him: 'in 6 months' time I'm going to piss all over you'. He stopped laughing and I put him down. 800's recovery started right then.

Word got around that the new Buccaneer Senior Pilot was a stroppy bastard. It was true, and I threw my weight around shamelessly to get what I needed in the ship to support the squadron – getting aircraft up from the hangar as a matter of priority for engine runs, tolerance from Flyco when a Bucc was a bit slow in the launching procedure, anything that would facilitate Buccaneer operations.

I also firmly believed that if I'd gone to the trouble of briefing, strapping into an aircraft, and going through all the pre-take off checks with the observer, the only thing that would stop me getting airborne would be if the wings fell off. Groundcrew and aircrew quickly got to know that I was determined to fly Buccaneers come what may.

I spent hours down in the hangar talking to the maintenance crews and the squadron technical officers, jollying them along, and supporting them. It became squadron policy (I wrote the flying programme) that we would fly the junior aircrew early in the day when serviceability was good, and bring on the more senior of us when the aircraft had started to wilt later, especially by the evening. By that time aircraft had often developed minor faults which, provided the aircrew were willing, could be flown in safety, but might require careful monitoring by an experienced crew. The fault could easily be rectified overnight but another sortie could be got out of the aircraft that day, or night.

After an embarkation a carrier usually had three work-up periods, successive work ups becoming more intense in terms of the exercises flown. The all weather fighters flew at night during these early work ups, which was part of their role. Because we had no Buccaneer night deck experience yet, night deck operations for us started in the third work up.

The more senior of us merely required a few dusk refresher deck landings (touch and goes with the arrestor hook up until the final land on in the dark) but a handful of junior pilots had to be selected with some care to make up the night flying team. To start with they were given dusk deck landing practice. When they were considered proficient they were then launched at dusk, flew an undemanding sortie and came back for some demanding fully dark night touch and goes before being recovered. We had about six crews in the night flying team. Naturally the boss and I were part of the team but I was discreetly aware he detested night flying from the deck. To his credit he stuck it out. We'd come a long way from when FONAC had ordered an intensive night flying programme back at Lossiemouth.

And the more we flew the better we got, the better the aircraft serviceability became, the better the morale, and 800 started smiling. We flew by day, we flew by night, and we flew quite a lot. We were now fully a part of the air group.

By the completion of the third work up the squadron had flown more hours than it had done during the whole of the previous tour. I never actually pissed (other than metaphorically) over that unpleasant Senior Pilot. But it would have been fully justified.

The first two work ups had been in the Mediterranean. By the start of the third work up we were operating in the Indian Ocean and up into the Arabian Sea. We did a lot of flying overland in what is now the Yemen, using Khormaksar (Aden) as a diversion field.

One of my sorties over the mountains north-east of Aden was with a journalist. He had managed to get MOD approval for a carrier-based flight and 800 was the outfit which got the job. I tried to be gentle with him. He stood up to the catapult launch quite well, and the flight across to the mountains, but flying low level in the mountains can be a bumpy ride even in a Buccaneer. Chasing up and down wadis and around mountains was what he asked to do but it soon got to him. Suddenly he wasn't answering me on the intercom. I checked in my rear view mirror. I could see he was still with me but he appeared to have taken his flying helmet off, which was why he wasn't talking or listening to me any longer (the microphone is in the oxygen mask and the receiver in the inner helmet). I returned to the carrier taking things very gently and we landed on uneventfully.

The groundcrew came up the ladders to put our ejection seat top pins in and help us unstrap. I asked the pilot's mate who'd helped me unstrap if my passenger was OK. He told me the journalist had been sick: in his flying helmet. This was pretty cool thinking on the journalist's part. Had he not used his helmet the whole cockpit would have had to be cleaned up by the maintenance crew, and this would have meant lifting the ejection seat. The aircraft would have been out of the flying programme for at least the rest of the day and probably the night too, and the maintenance personnel who had to clean everything up would have had a very unpleasant job. My passenger was quite cheerful about the affair and I thanked him for his forethought. I didn't tell him what trouble he might have been in if, in an emergency, I'd tried to order him to eject.

On completion of the third work up we went to Mombasa for a rest, recuperation and self-maintenance spell, which the ship well deserved. The harbour couldn't accommodate us alongside because of our draft and we had to anchor out in mid-stream. As usual we threw a cocktail party on the first evening: a standard routine to enable the locals to meet the officers and vice versa. I call it a standard routine because there is always a local contingent of professional cocktail party goers for whom a ship's cocktail party is standard; you can usually tell them straight away, they're fully at ease on board, usually have pretty well-worn party dresses, and have seen it all before. It's the naval version of the clichéd situation: same faces, different wallpaper, or, in this case, a different ship.

One person who didn't fit into this group was Mary. The first time I saw her I knew she wasn't used to the seething crowd in the wardroom, and that somebody had been fixing her drink. There is always at least one slob in a group of men. I could only see her, looking very lost on the other side of the mess across a sea of heads, but I knew she was in trouble and didn't know how to get herself out of it. I fought my way over to her, introduced myself and said I thought she looked as if she might have a bit of a problem. She asked me if I could get her drink diluted; it was supposed to be a whisky and dry ginger. I sniffed it and guessed that there was barely a dash of ginger and far too much whisky. I took it over to the bar to the senior steward and asked him who had ordered it. He knew the problem immediately and told me: it was the 'officer' I knew was the wardroom slob. I asked the steward to see it never happened again and took a plain dry ginger back to Mary. I never bothered with the slob. He'd been watching me since I'd first spoken to Mary. I knew that he knew that I knew what he'd done. I also knew that he wouldn't try it on again with any other unfortunate girl, not in that mess anyway.

I saw quite a lot of Mary during that visit; we went out to dinner and danced, and she showed me Mombasa: the interesting parts, rather than the junk side with thousands of carved impala, elephants, whatever. I'd told her straight away that I was married, and the friendship stayed platonic. I met her uncle, who lived on a small yacht at the Mombasa yacht club, and we went sailing in the harbour. It was then that I discovered that her uncle should never have left the sanctuary of his mooring at the club. He was quite the most dangerous element on the water.

Mary was a nurse, had nursed her way around the world once, going west about, had come home, been unable to settle, and had started to nurse her way around the world again, this time going east about. Mombasa was her first stop and, unlike all the other European nurses, she had passed over the popular, mostly white, European hospital (Catherine Bibby?) and gone to work in an African hospital. They were always desperately short of drugs and dressings and too many Kenyan children died too regularly. But she loved them.

The friendship was still platonic when we sailed but I started a correspondence with Mary which was initially pretty random because of the movements of the carrier. Later it became less random because Mombasa became the ship's shore link for mail and supplies when we started our stint on the Beira patrol.

Late in 1965 *Eagle* was somewhere off Singapore and the squadron had just re-embarked from Changi. My re-embarkation sortie had been a nightmare and I was turned in with jaundice when I got back aboard. This is covered in the next chapter.

About this time the squadron got a new Commanding Officer. My old boss had been very complimentary about my time as his senior pilot and had recommended me for squadron command, a very nice thank you, because, between us the squadron had turned around completely since the disastrous earlier tour in the carrier. The new boss had a great outfit to take over.

The ship was off Singapore when we were ordered to relieve *Ark Royal* on the Beira patrol. This was the operation set up by Harold Wilson after Ian Smith, the prime minister of what was then Rhodesia and a British colony, made a Unilateral Declaration of Independence (UDI). After unsuccessful attempts to resolve the problem politically, the Labour government had decided to blockade oil supplies to the errant colony. Because Rhodesia (now Zimbabwe) is landlocked and has no natural oil, her only access to oil is by overland supply or by sea through the port of Beira, in Mozambique. Our job would be to intercept oil tankers approaching Beira to try and prevent any of them carrying oil for Rhodesia going into harbour. I never discovered how we were supposed to stop them, but presumed that Lloyds would know where they were from and where their cargo was bound. What happened after that I don't know; presumably any ship known to be carrying oil bound for Rhodesia would be blackballed. We wouldn't have the right to stop them, just report them. I think some sort of political pressure must have been exerted on the ship's owners.

Our passage from Singapore across the Indian Ocean was to be discreet, and we avoided other shipping completely, making detours as necessary to keep out of sight. We were also to make as fast a passage as possible so there was no flying en route. Turning into wind to launch and recover aircraft slows a ship's advance considerably and, for some reason we had to get over to relieve *Ark* quickly. I believe she may have had mechanical problems.

Our patrol was to cover as much as we could of the Mozambique channel. The carrier was supported by our Royal Fleet Auxiliaries (RFAs) operating from Mombasa. A tanker brought us fuel (ship's and aircraft) and a supply RFA brought us food and dry stores. Both supply ships brought mail. We met up with one or other of them roughly every four days so that we were well looked after. It meant that the carrier tended to operate in the northern part of the Mozambique channel, closer to Mombasa, to reduce the RFAs' passage time in keeping us supplied. This was to have an important effect on how we flew our patrol sorties. Beira is a long way down the Mozambique channel and we were extended to maximum range most of the time.

There was no shore diversion airfield for us to use so we always had to be back at the carrier with a set minimum fuel state, calculated to give us some waiting allowance should the deck be unable to accept us straightaway because of some emergency, or a pilot did a 'bolter', meaning he missed the arrestor wires and had to go round for another try. To minimise any problems the carrier kept the deck 'open' i.e. available for landing whenever we requested it. This meant we had to calculate the fuel and time required to get back to the ship no matter how far away we might be, so that we could give the ship as much notice as possible of our required recovery time (known as Charlie time). This requirement sharpened up our attention to range and endurance flying and we really had to put into practice the lessons we were supposed to have learned for our instrument flying examinations. I was thankful for having been an Instrument Rating Instructor all those years ago and could squeeze quite a lot of extra miles out of a Buccaneer by applying the principles I'd learned then.

Because the Buccaneer Mk 1 had such a mediocre pair of engines, those Gyron Juniors, the fuel consumption, and therefore the range, were poor and we used Scimitars modified for the flight refuelling tanker role. We would rendezvous with the tanker some 100 miles out from the carrier, having used an enormous amount of fuel staggering up to 35,000 ft where fuel consumption was much more economical. We would then refuel to full from the Scimitar and carry on to our intended patrol area, to investigate contacts the observer had picked up on his radar, and let down to low level to identify them.

After a little practice all pilots became adept at calculating exactly how much fuel they would need for the climb back to altitude, and how much would be required for the high level run back to the top of the descent to the carrier. There was the small amount of fuel used in the descent, throttled back, to make up the total fuel needed to get home with the minimum state required. The difference between that amount and what you had left in the tanks gave you the time and the distance you could run at low level for any visual sighting necessary on tankers suspected of running oil into Beira. If we found any likely tanker we would photograph it, making sure we got the ship's name prominent in the photo. The photographic officer back in the carrier would then pass the photo to the intelligence officers for checking.

One tanker we were all looking for was proving elusive. She'd been reported coming up from the southern end of the channel, absolutely at the extreme range of our radius of action, even with flight refuelling. The photographic officer was desperate for someone to get a shot of her, I was keen to get it for him, and to succeed in what had become fierce inter-squadron rivalry. We remained at altitude to minimise fuel consumption going down the channel until, from 35,000 ft, my observer thought he might have her on the radar. To get down to her would put us about 700 miles from the carrier, with very little fuel available for us at low level to identify and get a photo of her. I calculated we could just do it so down we went, and there she was, heading for Beira. With the oblique camera we got a superb shot of her on only one pass and then we had to make a beeline for home, straight up to altitude and fly by the seat of our pants at optimum speed for maximum range. We made it back at our minimum fuel state.

One of the shots on the oblique overlap photo had the tanker bottom left to top right of the frame with us flying 45 degrees across her bow. There in clear white letters on her black hull was her name. The photographic officer was ecstatic.

During our time dedicated to the Beira patrol, from the time we'd sailed from Singapore to the time we got back there we'd spent 72 days continuously at sea. While we were on patrol, with our RFAs coming down from Mombasa on their regular supply runs, we'd had a regular supply of mail and fresh food although, in one letter to Mary, I said I wished we had more fresh fruit. The first mate of the provisions RFA was a friend of mine and I'd introduced him to Mary at some stage. She contacted him when he was in Mombasa storing ship on our behalf, gave him a £5 note and asked him to buy some fresh fruit for her and get it down to me on patrol. Mary had no idea how much fruit £5 could get you in those days. Neither had she any idea of what was involved in actually getting the fruit to me.

As a result, during one of our many jackstay replenishments at sea, I was called up to the flightdeck by a very snotty junior lieutenant in charge of the after jackstay. He pointed to an enormous crate with my name on it, which had just come across from the RFA. He wanted it clear of his jackstay area; it was pretty busy around there. I managed to get four of the squadron sailors for a few minutes and they got it down to my cabin, six decks down, which was quite a feat. We then got it into my cabin where it took up almost all of the not too large deck area. I had to climb over it just to get to my bunk. When I opened the crate up it was packed full of fruit. Bananas, oranges, grapefruit, pineapples, you name it, it was there. On top of that, the crate had been not less than four days in transit, in the tropics, and the fruit had been ripe when it was packed. It was beginning to smell even riper. I started to eat as much as I could but a crate of fruit 5ft long and about 30ins by 30ins holds quite a lot of fruit. I realised most of the fruit would have gone off before I got much further into it and the whole cabin deck would soon know too. I took out what I thought was the least ripe, but I gave the rest to the bridge mess, an officers' mess in the island superstructure, for the use of officers who couldn't get down to the wardroom for their meals while flying was going on. They were grateful. Mary was indignant when I wrote and told her.

Our 72 consecutive days at sea ended when we got back to Singapore. On 9th May the squadron disembarked to what was then RAF Changi and I flew home for some mid-tour leave and to Jo's proposal that we get a divorce. The events of that unhappy leave period are covered fully in the chapter 'Separation and Divorce'. I was very glad to fly back out to Singapore and rejoin the squadron, still at Changi.

One of the better aspects of being disembarked at Changi was that we were accommodated in hotels. The purpose was to allow aircrew a better rest period, out of the ship and in air-conditioned rooms. Since this was May it was pretty warm and humid, and air-conditioning, a hotel swimming pool and even a cabaret by the pool each evening were welcome 'rest and recuperation' assets after weeks at sea in a hot, sweaty carrier with no air-conditioning.

I had returned to the squadron at the end of May and we re-embarked in early June, taking passage across to the Philippines area There we used the US air-to-ground ranges. This included dropping 1,000 lbs inert bombs on a target shipwreck. We enjoyed using real as opposed to practice bombs, albeit inert, until we noticed a few local fishing boats tied up alongside the target ship. When we'd finished the bombing exercise they would then go scavenging for bits of scrap metal, either off the ship or from our bombs. I don't know now whether we were upset because they considered themselves safe beside the target ship, assuming we'd never hit it, or whether they were prepared to risk their lives for the chance of a bit of scrap. We eventually learned from the Yanks that it was the latter.

At about this time I happened into the bar quite early in the evening – there was no night flying that night, and found two of our sub-lieutenant aircrew. Normally, as their senior officer, apart from nodding

Good Evening to them at the bar, we wouldn't have chatted unless I had something routine to say to them. However, the two of them sidled along the bar and offered me a drink, most uncharacteristic. They appeared to want to talk but, being junior, felt embarrassed. After they'd sweated it out for a few awkward minutes I put them out of their agony and asked them what their problem was.

'We want some French letters (condoms), Sir'. Now the navy has always promoted safe sexual activity by encouraging personnel to ask at the sickbay and they would be issued condoms free whenever they wanted. I reminded these two subs about this.

'We know, Sir, but if we asked, the sickbay would know what we wanted them for and we'd feel very embarrassed'. Nothing I could say could persuade them otherwise and eventually I offered to ask one of my medical officer friends to get some for them. They were very relieved, and grateful. I thought this was taking 'looking after the welfare of junior officers' a bit too far but no harm could be done, in fact, I supposed, only good, if it stopped them contracting some nasty sexually transmitted disease. The next day I explained the youngsters' problem to a medical officer chum. He was only too willing to help and said he'd drop some off in my cabin.

Sure enough, the next time I went down to my cabin, lying on my bunk were two unopened boxes of condoms. Each box held 144 French letters. My chum must have known more about my two gay lotharios than I did. They were going to be busy when we got into port. I put the two boxes in an unused drawer in my desk and went off to tell the two pleasure-bent young officers to help themselves whenever. They were delighted, and relieved.

At our next port of call I sneaked a peep into the drawer: both boxes still intact. And at the next port of call, and the next, and the next. The suspense was getting to me. Eventually I collared the two subs, who had appeared to be avoiding me as much as possible, and asked them the reason.

'Well, sir. We realised that, if you'd seen that some of the condoms were missing, you'd know it had been us, and we were too embarrassed to take any!' I gave up.

288 condoms remained in that drawer until the time came for us to disembark for home. We could only take a limited amount of baggage in the aircraft and the bigger stuff would come up to Lossiemouth with the ground party. Packing wasn't my long suit and I tended to empty smaller items straight from the drawers into a large flying clothing

holdall – which is where the two unopened boxes of condoms went. And there they stayed until the holdall found its way, over a year later, to the house which Mary and I were to set up as our first home together in Lossiemouth. This story continues in later chapters.

Having returned to the Singapore area, we were to spend a few more days disembarked again at Changi in early July, before starting passage back west en route home. As we left the straits of Sumatra we were exercising off Butterworth, a New Zealand air force base on the west coast of what was then Malaya. My wingman, Fred Secker., was unable to get his undercarriage down in the carrier circuit and we had to divert to Butterworth with me as his shepherd. I had to land first since Fred would have to make a wheels-up landing and would inevitably block the runway. I didn't have sufficient fuel either to return to the carrier or to hang around waiting for a clear landing run. Over the radio I briefed Fred on what he had to do. He already knew, but he was a youngster and I guessed it would give his confidence a boost if his senior pilot gave him a 'Dutch uncle' chat just running through the procedure with him again. One part of the emergency drill was to jettison the canopy, quite a chunky piece of kit, shortly before touchdown, giving himself time for his eyes to adjust to the sudden rush of airflow, and possibly dust from the floor of the cockpit, before he actually touched down.

Fred carried out a copybook approach and landing. The canopy went at the right moment and he touched down gently, belly first, on the centre-line, managing to keep the aircraft on the line until he'd slowed to the point where the rudder would give no more steerage. He came to rest two feet off the centre-line in an immaculate display of airmanship. As briefed he and his observer then vacated the aircraft as quickly as possible in case of fire.

Fred's handling resulted in minimum damage to the fuselage and enabled the engineers subsequently to jack the aircraft up, manually free the undercarriage and lock it down, and the aircraft returned safely to the ship a few days later.

At about the time the aircraft landed back in the carrier, a deputation of Malayan natives arrived at the air station out of the jungle surrounding Butterworth. Their neighbouring village had found the jettisoned canopy. Could their village have one too?

We must have made a fast passage across the Indian Ocean. I have no flights recorded from mid-July until 8th August when I was flying off Luqa, Malta. A week later we were in the English Channel and *Eagle* disembarked its air group to the various parent air stations. 800

Squadron returned to Lossiemouth via Yeovilton where we refuelled before flying north.

This was to be my last flight from a carrier, and a return to a very difficult homecoming, covered in the chapter on separation and divorce.

The squadron had a couple of weeks much needed leave, returning in September when the first of our Mk 2 Buccaneers started arriving. This was quite an experience after the sluggish old Mk.1's and their underpowered Gyron Junior engines. I hadn't known thrust like the Mk.2's Spey engines since my Scimitar days. The first acceleration down the runway on my initial familiarisation sortie was exhilarating to say the least, and the Mk.2's range was considerably better than it's predecessor.

At the end of September, 1966, Jimmy Moore took over command of the squadron. I'd served under James as the AWI when he was my senior pilot in 738 Squadron, I'd learned everything about a senior pilot's job from him, had a great deal of respect for him and he was one of my role model officers. We'd also sunk quite a few beers and horses' necks together!

By this time I'd been re-appointed: as Commanding Officer of 736 Squadron; my first 800 boss' original recommendation had borne fruit, and it had been followed up by his successor, to be echoed by James Moore, and by Wings and the captain of Lossiemouth.

My last few months in 800 were relatively quiet. I flew a variety of aircraft ranging from the Vampire and Hunter trainers through to both Mk 1 and Mk 2 Buccaneers. At the end of January 1967 I said goodbye to 800 and moved back across the airfield to take over 736.

Despite my comments on the Buccaneer Mk 1's shortcomings, and they were justified, I'd come to love the aircraft, knew all its characteristics, good or bad, and considered it the most stable aircraft I'd taken to the deck. It sat on the approach path, constant at the correct speed, with both engines steady at their optimum setting and you simply arrived in the wires, having been steady 'on the meatball' (the deck landing projector sight) all the way down, day or night. And at night this was a supreme advantage. Much as I was to come to love the Mk 2, its engines had to be throttled back on the approach to land to below their optimum revs making them a little less stable. Even so, I'd take the MK 2 every time. That was really something.

# Chapter 19

## *Bickles and Me*

IT was late1965. *Eagle* was somewhere off Singapore and 800 Squadron had just re-embarked from Changi. My re-embarkation sortie had been like 10 years of Monday mornings compressed into one 35-minute trip.

I'd just spent a week in my room at RAF Changi with what an RAF doctor had diagnosed as Dengue fever. It had to have been something diabolical because the bottle of whisky I had by my bedside had remained untouched. I'd felt so ghastly I couldn't even break the seal, and that had to be seriously serious.

Back in *Eagle* the PMO took one look at me, yelped, and turned me straight in with galloping jaundice. So there I was, laid up in the sickbay, no flying for some weeks and no booze for at least six months. How low can you get?

The no booze thing scared me and I resisted the several alcoholic offerings smuggled into the sickbay by well-intentioned chums, who all departed incredulous, quickly spreading the word that the Senior Pilot must have the jaundice thing really bad, refusing booze!

The no flying restriction was going to be harder to live with. Lying there in my sickbay bunk, feeling sorry for myself about what promised to be a very dull few months ahead, I soon developed an itch to do something: anything.

These cartoons developed during that period in the sickbay.

By the time I'd completed them I'd covered two pages of the squadron's very large line book. The series was entitled "Bickles and Me", Bickles being Mike Bickley, my observer, probably the most long suffering in the navy, who made up the other half of what I liked to think was a pretty successful crew. Mike had all the answers to my idiosyncrasies, dealing with them patiently and with his dry and, of necessity, acerbic wit. He was one of the most professional aviators I ever flew with and the first I'd teamed up with as a crew. I learned a great deal with Mike sitting behind me.

We had a lot of fun, Bickles and me - in my opinion. Subjective, of course.

Bickles and Me

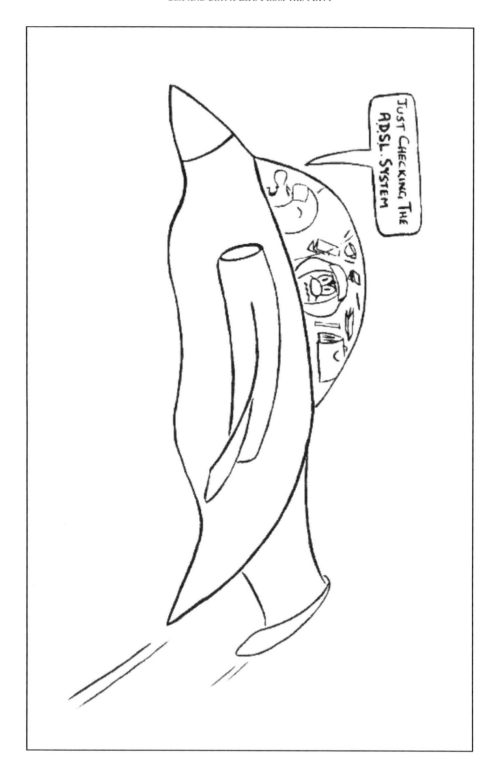

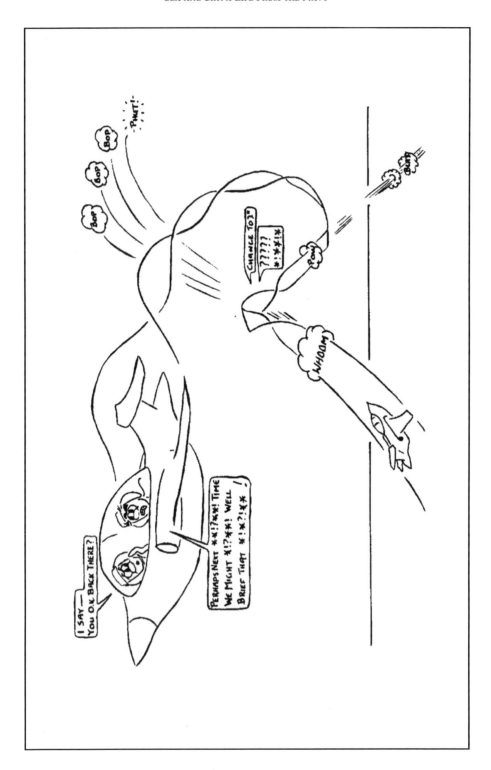

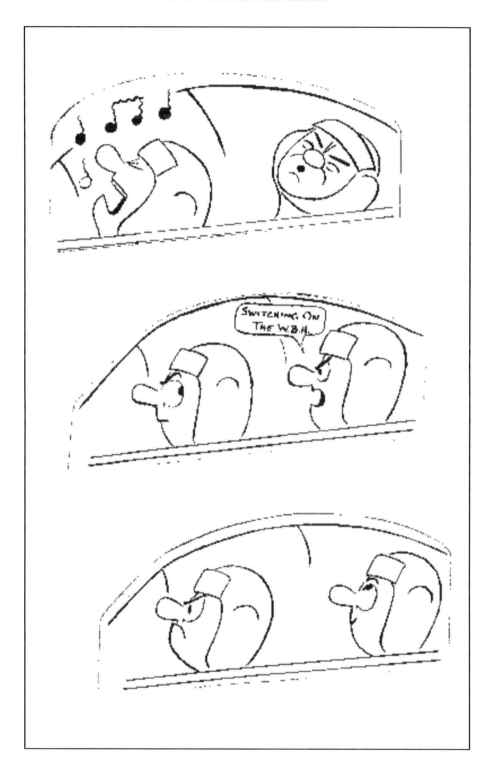

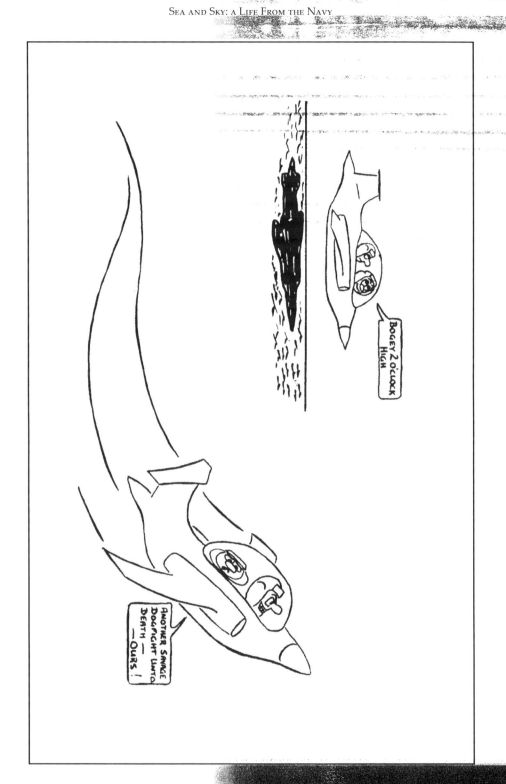

# Chapter 20

## *Separation and Divorce*

ON 9th May 1966, the squadron had disembarked to RAF Changi and I immediately started home for some mid-tour leave. This was a fairly new idea the navy had introduced to try and reduce the separation times families had to endure with such extended periods abroad. A squadron could send one crew home at a time, pilot and observer, as and when it fitted in with the squadron and ship's programme. One crew away did not appreciably add to the load the remaining crews had to bear, in fact it probably improved their lot in that they got in more flying time than they would have done had the squadron remained at full strength. Flying hours were always at a premium.

Singapore's main civil airport in those days was Paya Lebar. I can't remember what sort of aircraft I flew home in but it was a long tiring flight and I felt really grubby and stale when I got to Heathrow; with my long legs I do not do well on extended civil flights! Once I'd collected my baggage I made a bee-line for a men's cloakroom and a freshen up. I was just finishing shaving when the broadcast system asked me to go to the information desk where my wife was waiting for me. I was staggered. Things had not been going too well with me and Jo, as evidenced by the stilted correspondence we'd had with each other in recent months. For her to make this pilgrimage down to London to meet me was a welcome sign that perhaps things might change for the better. I tidied myself up and went out to find the information desk. When I got there I was astonished to find not Jo but Mary. The information desk had jumped to the wrong conclusion!

I had no idea that Mary was coming home, let alone she would meet me at Heathrow, although she must have found out my flight number. She explained that she had come home to start her midwifery training and had finished with Mombasa for good. All news to me. We must have gone into London together because I was due to catch the overnight train from Kings Cross to Aberdeen and thence to Elgin and home.

I arrived home and almost immediately realised something was badly amiss. Jo and I were like strangers, awkward with each other. Pretty soon Jo suggested that "it hadn't been much of a marriage so far and what about a divorce?" I'd scarcely been home a few minutes and my world was coming apart. There didn't seem to be any scope for discussion. Jo's mind appeared made up; she wanted me out, and quickly. I started straight back for the railway station and got the Elgin to Aberdeen train to link up with the Aberdeen to London sleeper.

At some point I must have phoned Mary, told her what had happened and that I had to leave home and was coming south. She said I was welcome to come and stay with her and her mother until I'd got myself sorted out. I had nowhere else to go except my mother's flat in Hove, and still had the rest of my two weeks' leave to run before I could fly back out to Singapore. I decided to go and stay with Mary and her mother in Upminster.

I still remember the train journey down from Elgin. It was a nightmare. Fortunately I was first class and had the compartment to myself and I wept most of the way. I was absolutely overcome with grief and a dreadful feeling of failure. I was desperately worried about the children: how were they going to get on without a father? I knew I hadn't been around for much of their young lives but had been looking forward to seeing a lot more of them once the squadron got home for good. I had my next appointment – I was to be the Commanding Officer of 736 Squadron, the Buccaneer training squadron at Lossiemouth. I was set for a longish spell ashore and able to live at home. Now, it appeared, I might as well have gone back to sea. I'd failed my family miserably and it was all my fault.

There's often one old woman in a squadron and I well knew that one of the aircrew had been writing home to his gossiping wife about what he imagined to be my relationship with Mary (he covered other squadron members too). There was nothing I could do about that, and, on another visit to Mombasa, I had actually slept with Mary although he wasn't to know it but must have assumed that I had – and written his wife to that effect. I wasn't going to deny my shortcomings. These things happen, especially to naval men on repeated long separations. I assumed the gossip had soon reached Jo and that this was why she was so resolute in her wish for a divorce, although she hadn't wanted to discuss any details. She simply wanted me out of the way. On that train journey I was so distressed that it never occurred to me to wonder why.

I spent the rest of my leave at Mary's mother's house, and meeting her friends and relations. It was a rather antiseptic period, except for her mother's house! Her mother's idea of housework and cooking were a long way removed from mine, and "antiseptic" is not an adjective I could apply to either. I was relieved when I had to leave for the airport.

I flew back out to Singapore and rejoined the squadron. Once we were re-embarked I had to tell my boss that I was heading for a divorce.

A few months later we returned to home waters and the squadrons flew off to their various parent air stations, the Buccaneers coming home to Lossiemouth where all the wives and families were waiting to greet us; all except Jo. A friend of mine was there to meet me, and he told me Jo had gone to Aberdeen for the day, to keep out of the way. The door was firmly closed.

I had nowhere to go. Being a married officer, ostensibly living in Llanbryde, I didn't have a cabin in the mess. I only had a small grip with a few clothes that I'd brought in the Buccaneer I flew home in. I had to do two things quickly. I had to get out to Llanbryde to see Jo – was she really still adamant about the divorce? And, if she was, secondly, I had to pick up my things from the cottage and move into the mess. I must have borrowed someone's car to get out to our cottage in Llanbryde. Jo was still out but I managed to climb through a window and sat down, still in my flying gear, to wait for her.

She was horrified to find me sitting there, asked what I was doing and declared emphatically that I couldn't stay. This was the key being turned in the lock. There was no hope of reconciliation; she made that abundantly clear. She couldn't wait to get rid of me, and again it never occurred to me to wonder why. Only much later did I discover, from a senior wren friend, that Jo was desperate that she should not be seen to have done anything that might prejudice the divorce she was so keen on; she was already terribly worried that her relationship with some other chap might be revealed. Unaware of this at the time, I went back to the air station at Lossiemouth.

Back in the mess, still in my flying gear, I had to phone the President of the mess, explain my situation, and get his permission to move into the mess. This he willingly gave me and I got my gear up to my new home – a cabin in the officers' mess! After a shower and a shift into plain clothes I went down to the bar. My junior squadron officers were curious, but kind enough not to ask questions. The boss had let them know the score.

During the next few weeks I had some "coming home" leave. I found the name of a reputable solicitor in London and made an appointment to see him. He agreed to handle the divorce proceedings; Jo was divorcing me and claiming custody of the children and I couldn't dispute either point. I thought I was the miscreant, and as a naval officer subject to separations, could hardly justify any claim to custody. I also agreed that adultery could be the grounds for the divorce and, with Mary's agreement, that I would provide "evidence" in the form of a hotel receipt showing Mary and I had stayed together for a night. By this time Jo had found out what the alimony settlement would amount to. It was the same as the allowance I allotted her every month which, she agreed, she'd be happy with.

During this period several of my friends who'd been at the air station while I was at sea indicated, tactfully, some surprise that it wasn't me divorcing Jo. Only much later I realised that they'd had been trying gently to tell me that they considered it strange that I was allowing Jo to divorce me because they were convinced it was Jo who had been at fault. This never crossed my mind at the time. Apart from the fact that, in those days, men behaved in what we thought was a gentlemanly manner, if there had to be a divorce I assumed this way would be best for the children. They'd not seen a lot of me since they'd been born; half of their short lives I'd been away at sea and there would be more sea time to come. I was the guilty party and I should pay alimony. It would at least guarantee they'd be supported. I paid the alimony for many years beyond the time I could have stopped it.

Long after the divorce became absolute I discovered that, while I had been away at sea, and well before I'd come home on that unhappy mid-tour leave, Jo had been going around with the manager of a local canning company. They had, apparently, been very close but I'm told the relationship with him didn't last.

Jo moved out to Hopeman with the children. While they lived in Hopeman, and about a year after the divorce became absolute, Mary and I were married. We set up home in Lossiemouth, where the children visited occasionally. Eventually they moved down to Stafford and lived with a chap called Moon, the name Jo then assumed although she never married him, presumably to retain alimony payments. I don't know when Jo and Moon had become an 'item'. I did hear that he became an alcoholic and that Jo eventually threw him out. That's about all I do know. I was never inclined to investigate further.

I suppose that attitudes nowadays have changed considerably as far as divorce goes, although I like to think that, with two very young children to consider, any man's attitude would have been similar to mine at the time. I've never been one to discuss my private affairs or lean on anyone's shoulder; however, I am aware that the distress the divorce caused me is not uncommon and I've nothing but sympathy for friends who, I know, have been through the same mill. It took me a long time to get over the sense of failure I felt about the divorce, but this was tempered by my eventual acceptance that Jo had wanted the split – and why she wanted it.

It took much longer to learn to live with the feeling that I'd failed my children.

# Chapter 21

## *Re-marriage*

I proposed to Mary almost exactly a year after Jo and I were divorced and the decree made absolute. Mary's mother had been hoping against hope that her daughter would at last find a husband and, once I'd popped the question, the marriage was arranged in almost indecent haste. My future mother-in-law wasn't going to let me slip through her fingers. I'd proposed in July, 1967, and the wedding took place the following October. I barely had time to get my sword buffed up.

We had to marry in Romford registry office – since then the church has softened its approach to marrying divorcees – and the reception was held at the Upminster Golf Club where mother-in-law was the Ladies Captain and Mary was a member. The event for me was memorable for the hats, great big affairs that made it quite difficult when I was trying to conduct a conversation. I'd gone into my circulating, good naval officer mode trying to have a word with each of the women under these hats, most of whom I'd never met before. Since I'm 6ft 3ins tall and they were all considerably less, the hat became something of a hazard but I managed, and I think mother-in-law was quite pleased with her new son-in-law. I know she was pleased to have a son-in-law

Afterwards Mary and I drove off to Dover, crossed to France, and went on to Rouen. We found a really old fashioned looking hotel, thatched roof and lots of black beams, and Mary decided this was the place. I should have known better. As soon as we got inside the front door we were in reception: one largish desk just inside the door and one even larger, old harridan of a *patronne* clothed in black from head to toe. Mary was undeterred so I asked if there was a double room available.

There was; we followed Madame along passages and up flights of stairs until we seemed to be on at least the fifth floor and right at the end of another passage. The enormous oak door looked as if it had come out of a horror movie set, and sounded like it when Madame pushed it open having first struggled with a huge cast-iron circular handle and latch. But the room was fine and it had an en-suite bathroom so we took it, got rid of Madame and unpacked.

It was quite late by this time and we were hungry. It was difficult locking the bedroom door; the key was enormous and the lock unused to being asked to do what it was for. This worried me a lot. Madame was a villainous-looking old bat and I wasn't keen to leave our bags in an open room. I persisted and finally managed to lock the door. We left the car outside the hotel and set out to find a restaurant. That was no problem and we had a good meal, got back to our hotel, and found our way up and along the labyrinth of passages and stairs. Now fully appreciating just how far we were from the one and only main door, I was determined we were going to be securely locked in. I had just as much trouble locking the door from the inside but, after something of a struggle, I managed it and left the enormous key in the enormous lock. We turned in and eventually went to sleep.

At 2.30 am I woke up. Something was bothering me. I looked around the old room, black beams, low ceiling, stunted old windows through which the moon was casting a long beam: across the room and directly on to the huge door handle. That was what had woken me. The handle was creaking, and slowly turning. Someone was trying to get in, stealthily. For a few seconds my Sir Galahad streak came to the fore. Could I defend my new bride and fight our way down and out to safety? Along all those passages and down all those stairs? No way. Common sense, and my cowardly streak, took over. I jumped out of bed and made a lot of noise stamping around the room, hoping this would deter whoever was outside and make them go away. They did, and I went back to bed, first checking that Mary was alright and hadn't been as frightened as I had. She hadn't. She had snored throughout the whole episode. I didn't sleep for the rest of the night and kept my eyes glued on the door handle.

The first slight disaffection in our very young marriage occurred next morning. Mary thought I was making everything up. I only managed to convince her when I said we had to get out of there fast and make sure we still had a car, and that it hadn't been broken into. It was Mary's car. We got out and the car was OK.

We enjoyed the rest of the honeymoon but took very good care about the accommodations we used. Mary shed her 'go for the olde-worlde charm' attitude and we opted for modern, secure *auberges, chambres d'hotes* and *Logis de France*.

We only had one slight hiccup. We'd heard about an *auberge* run by an English woman, way out in the country and, apparently, very popular. It also offered free wine on an 'all you can drink' basis. This sounded like my kind of place, so off we went for dinner. The first sight we saw as we drove up was a patio with tables laden with several rows of wine bottles: the free wine, red and white. We went in and it seemed quite a nice place except it was full of mainly Brits, which we hadn't wanted. We'd had several most enjoyable evenings in restaurants where we'd been the only Brits.

Someone said the wine was on a help yourself basis, as much as you wanted. We got a couple of glasses and quickly found out why you could have all you wanted, and why there was so much of it on offer. It was the nearest thing to kerosene I'd tasted, all lovingly produced by the English hostess. She could have run a filling station on the stuff. And the food wasn't much better. Or the company. We were learning the hard way, but we were learning, and didn't make that sort of mistake again.

Back in England we loaded Mary's car to the gunwhales and set off for Lossiemouth and our first home, a bungalow named Eilan Mhor in the town.

We already had something of a home down in Wiltshire, an old 'two up, two down' farm labourer's cottage that mother-in-law had bought for her daughter (with Mary's own money) before we were married. It had been modernised to give it a bathroom and kitchen, and the thatch was made good, but it was, otherwise, pretty basic. For two newly weds with, as yet, no children, it made a reasonable holiday cottage. The last farm labourer occupant had walked through the adjoining field to get to his work but had only a footpath for access from the nearest road. We had to buy a small adjoining field to enable us to get a car somewhere near the cottage.

We were subsequently to extend the cottage, for which I took out a mortgage, and to be able to qualify for the mortgage I had to become a part owner. Since the cottage had only cost £900 (it had been condemned and then reprieved!) this was no big deal. Mary and I became joint tenants. I had become a property owner.

The mortgage was an endowment affair, to run for twenty years, and although the payments got a bit steep towards the end of the twenty year period, it paid off handsomely. The bonus I received when the mortgage expired paid for a further much larger extension I was to build later.

The cottage stands in Coate, near Devizes, a village to which Mary's mother and children had moved during WW2 to be near her husband, an army officer stationed at what was then Hopton barracks, now an industrial estate. They lived in another thatched cottage some 150 yards from Wildflower Lodge. Mary's mother had managed to burn it to the ground during the war. Fortunately, nobody was hurt. The only thing left after the fire was a small pile of rubble: what was left of the chimney!

Whether it was her childhood wartime memories or a 'roses round the door' complex that stayed with her for life, Mary's attachment to the cottage was to have a significant, and not always happy, influence on our relationship.

# Chapter 22

## *Buccaneer Training Squadron Commander*

MY first squadron command was primarily Mk 1 Buccaneers and just a couple of Mk 2s. The squadron's flying task was the conversion of experienced pilots and observers to the Buccaneer, and the Buccaneer Operational Flying training of aircrew straight off the *ab initio* flying training pipeline. We were also responsible for training ground crew personnel in all aspects of Buccaneer servicing and operation. In meeting the overall task we had a fairly fluid squadron complement of roughly 360. Flying students or maintenance personnel underwent their training and then left for their front line squadrons. The only permanent personnel were for general administration, training staff for ground crew training and, of course, flying instructors for the aircrew students. My flying instructors were experienced pilots and observers and they were quality. The navy was now a quantum leap beyond the state of instruction I'd experienced when I went through operational flying training just a couple of hangars away in 1955, only 12 years earlier.

Besides maintaining and, hopefully, improving the standard of instruction, with this team I looked forward to developing some ideas I had about new tactics for the Buccaneer. The Buccaneer was relatively new to night operations. It seemed to me that, not unnaturally, we had simply adopted many of the air-to-ground attack techniques used for so long by the all weather fighters. With the Buccaneer's 'under the radar lobe' low level capability and its vastly superior instrumentation we ought to be capable of developing more effective tactics, particularly at night. I was keen to try out my new ideas.

Just over a month after taking command the *Torrey Canyon* ran aground on the Seven Stones rocky shoal near the Scilly Isles. The *Torrey Canyon* was, in those days, a super tanker. She was full of thick, black, glutinous crude oil, which became a nightmare when it washed up on shore, contaminating the shoreline and destroying untold amounts of wildlife. A political decision was taken to set fire to her cargo before it spread too far and, hopefully, before it reached the nearby coasts of Cornwall and Devon. The Navy was the only service capable of the precision bombing necessary to do the job, and Buccaneers were the natural choice, being the Navy's primary air-to-surface attack aircraft.

There were two Buccaneer squadrons available at Lossiemouth: 800, James Moore's front-line outfit with Mk 2 aircraft (the squadron I'd recently left), and 736 with, primarily, Mk 1's and only a couple of Mk 2's. Both squadrons were detailed for the task. James, senior squadron and with all Mk 2's, an operational worked up outfit, was to lead the operation. Then there was 736, with largely a bunch of trainee ground crew, end-of-the queue in modification states and spares, and, except for the experience of my instructors, far from operational. We would follow.

My Mk 1's were a pretty tired old bunch of aircraft. As is always the case, the training squadron only got the fag-end of spares and modification equipment, priority naturally being given to the operational squadrons. We had a lot of work to do to get some of our aircraft into an operational state.

Although Lossiemouth knew its squadrons had been picked to do the job, and that it had to be done pretty quickly, we still awaited the political 'go', and used the waiting time in frantic preparation, not least in trying to get our weapon systems serviceable. That era of Buccaneer used a computerised 'Auto Depressed Sight Line' (ADSL). The computer was archaic and the system difficult to keep serviceable. Thus all 736 pilots were hardly in practice and what aircraft we had to try and get in practice with were scarce, since aircraft bomb release systems also had to be checked over. Aircraft availability was therefore curtailed. We also had our normal flying training task to try and keep running.

My ground crews started work and really got the bit between their teeth. They knew full well how far behind their front-line counterparts they were, and why, but were determined not to be seen as second best even if they were a second-line squadron.

As we got ready, each day the captain, Doug Parker, held a meeting in the Air Traffic Control Tower in Commander Air's office. Commander

Air (traditionally nick-named 'Wings'), Ted Anson, was one of my role model officers. He, the captain, Jimmy Moore and I would review the situation, and discuss progress on serviceability. Needless to say, Jimmy Moore's aircraft were up and running. Mine were struggling but still trying desperately to get operational. I began to realise that 736 were going to be very much 'also rans' when it was all over.

I had to give a lot of thought to the flying aspects of the operation and how the Mk 1's would cope. I was confident (fingers crossed) the aircraft serviceability would meet the requirement, given the effort the maintenance crews were putting in. However I did have my doubts about the ADSL system. What worried me more was the limited endurance of the Mk 1 with its tired old Gyron Junior engines and their poor fuel consumption. The *Torrey Canyon* wreck was at the extent of our operational range (limited by the drag of 4 external 1000lb bombs), given we could land at near-by RNAS Brawdy immediately we'd got rid of the bomb load. Additionally, semi-operational settings such as we were about to encounter usually meant delays of some sort, which would buy up precious fuel. Any sort of delay could mean we'd have to call off our part in the bombing, jettison our bombs in the sea and then divert to Brawdy, in front of much of the world. Embarrassing!

In this morbid state of mind I went along to the next meeting. Doug Parker saw my face and immediately said: 'You look fed up, Dave, what's the matter?' So I told him. Doug immediately said: 'Dave, you'd better go first'. I had had no idea what Doug's reaction would be and almost regretted having opened my mouth. James, my chum, was equally as surprised as I was, and looked pretty fed up. I'd no idea that Doug's decision would 'upstage' 800 and never realised what effect this would have until the operation was over.

So 736 was to lead the operation. A compromise was effected: I would lead and 800's senior pilot would be my wingman.

In the event the operation went pretty smoothly, the wreck of the tanker, and the sea around her, were in flames and the enormous plume of thick black smoke was visible for miles. My initial bombs blew a whole in the side of the tanker. My wingman, Dave Mears, put his first bombs smack in the middle of her. Between us we set fire to the ship and the sea around her to such an extent that thick black smoke started billowing up. Fortunately a fairly stiff breeze blew the smoke reasonably clear downwind from the tanker so that we could still see something to aim for on successive attacks. We then landed at Brawdy to refuel before returning to Lossiemouth.

After landing at Brawdy as I walked in from my aircraft I was met by Brawdy's Wings and a posse of journalists, including TV crews. Wings left me to their mercy and I then experienced my first press interview which, by today's standards, was a relatively tame affair. All I remember really was that I told them we had done what we came to do and were proud to have been asked to do it. When we got back to Lossiemouth that evening we went through much the same routine with more press. I still have several newspaper cuttings with pictures of the smoke plume, and of me and my aircrew relaxing in the crew room back home at 736.

Reconnaissance indicated there was still oil in some of the tanks in the wrecked tanker and over the next two days we flew back to Brawdy, re-armed with four x 1000lbs high explosive bombs, struck the tanker repeatedly and then returned direct to Lossiemouth. On both those days I had a Mk 2 Buccaneer. A Mk 1 would not have been able to get airborne from Brawdy's 2000 yard runway with a full load of bombs. Even so, getting airborne from Brawdy fully laden in a Mk 2 left you wondering. There wasn't much runway left when the wheels lifted off, and I shudder to think what might have happened had the take off had to be aborted at a late stage during the take off run.

When we got back to Losssiemouth for the last time, after it was all over, the impact of what we'd done finally came home to me. Every newspaper in the country seemed to have covered the operation and 736's name, and pictures of her aircrew, and 800's, were everywhere. And, most important, my squadron lads were 10 ft tall. They'd worked their backsides off, their second line outfit had come up trumps, and the whole world knew about it.

I always kept the door of my squadron office open. A few days later I was sitting at my desk when I became aware that a young artificer apprentice, Bradshaw, kept walking past in the passage outside. Each time he passed he glanced in and then hurried by, only to return a few seconds later and repeat the process. After about five passes I thought I'd better put an end to his agony; he was plainly trying to pluck up courage to have a word. The next time he went by I called to him: 'Bradshaw, get in here'. Blushing furiously Bradshaw marched in and stood to attention in front of me, but with one hand behind his back. I asked what his problem was. Turning several shades redder, he produced from behind his back a presentation box and put it in front of me.

'The lads have asked me to give you this, sir'.

*Memories of British Guiana 1952*

*The author about to fly*

*The author and Admiral Sir Michael Le Fanu after a sortie in a Buccaneer Mk 2*

*Seahawks and Sea Venoms of HMS Ark Royal ranged on deck 1957*

*Above: Scimitars armed with Bullpup missiles, 1962*

*Below: A Scimitar, Bullpup missiles on outer pylons, about to launch from HMS Ark Royal, 1962*

*Above: Scimitar about to launch from HMS Ark Royal, jet blast deflector raised.*

*Below: Scimitar approaching to land on in HMS Ark Royal, 1962*

*Buccaneers Mk 1, over the top*

*Above: Buccaneer Mk 1 over the Scottish Highlands*

*Below: Buccaneer Mk 1 in the Aden Protectorate (now Yemen)*

*Above: Buccaneer, much too low on his approach, landing on in HMS Eagle*

*Below: in-flight refuelling pod, hose stowed, drogue basket just visible*

*Above: Buccaneer Mk 2 about to launch from HMS Ark Royal*

*Below: Buccaneer Mk 2 about to take a wire in HMS Ark Royal*

*HMS Lincoln preparing to enter harbour, ship's company in tropical rig*

*HMS Lincoln under way*

*The author, 'Wings', RNAS Yeovilton 1974*

*Night deck landing, pilot's eye view*

I opened it and there was a medal, produced in the squadron workshops, a 'gallantry' cross, with the gaudiest of medal ribbons and, typed in the lid of the box, the following citation from "The Junior rates, 736 Naval Air Squadron"

'Dear Sir,

In connection with your heroic exploits during the offensive action against the helpless, defenceless, stranded tanker *Torrey Canyon*, we have much pleasure in sending you the one and only '*Torrey Canyon* Cross'.

It was a most touching tribute, and my ground crews' way of showing me their gratitude for having achieved such nationwide recognition of their efforts. I had some difficulty in thanking young Bradshaw, my youngest apprentice. He'd drawn the short straw to make the presentation.

I asked him to pass on my thanks to everyone. I still have my *Torrey Canyon* Cross and am very proud of it. I stopped feeling guilty at having unintentionally upstaged James Moore in Wings' office a few days earlier. My second line squadron had acquitted itself with honours.

The squadron continued with its training task, punctuated occasionally with night exercises to try out my ideas for new Buccaneer tactics. These progressed quite well but I had the advantage of being able to use experienced instructors for what were fairly demanding, low level, night operations. My ultimate aim was to be able to train inexperienced aircrew, and everything we did had to be tailored to the requirement to enable young aircrew safely to operate at night. While I couldn't do this in 736, one day I hoped to command a front line squadron and then I would have to work up my young aircrew to the standard I wanted to achieve. Nevertheless, what we achieved in 736 with my instructors laid the groundwork for things to come.

Another 'extra to the normal flying task' was a flypast over the launch of the QE2 on the Clyde. We couldn't afford too many flying hours for this unexpected task but managed a few rehearsals, flying an anchor formation with 13 Buccaneers. We'd been given the job because 736 was the job number allocated to the QE2 when she was building i.e. the 736th ship to be built in that shipyard. We were to fly down to the Clyde area, hopefully not have to wait too long because of the Mk 1 Buccaneer's poor fuel consumption, and overfly the ship as she moved down the slipway on launching. While we were confident we could be overhead the slipway on the proposed dot, we guessed there'd be some delay and we'd arranged to orbit if necessary. We'd also put our tame air station pongo (army officer) up in one of the dockside cranes with a radio and he kept us up to speed with what was going on at the dockside.

Sure enough, come the appointed time there was no sign of the ship moving and off we went into another orbit, rather large because 13 Buccaneers in an anchor formation is a ponderous and unwieldy affair and takes up a lot of sky. On the far side of the orbit and as far away from the slipway as we could be, our tame pongo screamed into the radio: 'She's moving!' I swung the formation into as tight a turn as I dared and we managed, still in perfect formation, to overfly the ship just before she entered the water. By this time my Mk 1s were desperately short of fuel and we turned for home, some of us running straight into the downwind leg rather than do a joining circuit, to save those few precious gallons of kerosene. We all made it safely but, yet again, working with agencies unfamiliar with air problems, we'd been extended uncomfortably.

One incident still mars my memories of 736. We had a Buccaneer conversion student who had had a rough time in his last squadron with the ageing Scimitar. Several of the pilots had had to eject more than once. Fairly quickly it became apparent that this student was no longer up to fast jet flying.

My instructors were not only first class, they were endlessly patient. One in particular, had served with X in that last Scimitar outfit and was, himself, a multiple ejectee. He knew X very well and knew also, just what X had been through, and what his problem was in trying to convert to the Buccaneer.

We kept a careful eye on X and tried desperately to rebuild his confidence but it was no use. Finally we had to recommend X be withdrawn from Buccaneer conversion training.

I wrote a report, based on my instructors' progress notes on X's inability (through no fault of his own) to make the grade. Wings supported the report, which eventually reached the Flag Officer Flying Training for approval.

It was to my great surprise, and even greater consternation, that I was told that X was to remain under training. The navy seemed to be returning to the bad old days I described in Chapter 10.

X finished his Buccaneer conversion under careful supervision and without mishap, although with no improvement. I was so concerned about his future (or lack of it, if my concern proved justified) that I insisted copies of his flying training reports were to be passed to his next commanding officer for retention.

Shortly after that I left 736 and took command of 809 Squadron, covered in the next chapter. A few months later X's new commanding officer told me he intended destroying the reports since he considered X was now competent. Apart from reiterating the concern I'd had as the training squadron commander, there was nothing more I could do.

Only a few days later X was killed. He'd experienced engine failure after take off in a training aircraft and left his ejection too late: exactly the sort of shortcoming that my instructors had found in him, an inability to cope with the demands of fast jet flying.

I went to X's funeral, in the same cemetery I'd had to visit too often at Lossiemouth, and could have wept for the young widow - and her baby child.

Shortly after the funeral I learned, by a roundabout route, that my original request that X be withdrawn from his Buccaneer conversion had been commented on by a captain in the chain above up to Training Command. He'd falsely attributed X's difficulties in the Buccaneer training squadron to 'a personality clash between him and his commanding officer': me. Thus my request had been turned down.

I was horrified. X's case was never discussed with me, and his flying training reports never inspected, thereby ignoring completely all the care and professionalism my instructors had devoted to X. This gutted me completely; and I was helpless to do anything about it. In any case nothing would bring X back. He had died needlessly and in my opinion, which hasn't changed over the years, through the wilful stupidity of a senior officer who hadn't even had the guts, or the common sense or decency, to discuss the matter with me.

# Chapter 23

## *Buccaneer Front Line Squadron Commander*

809 Squadron was an all Mk 2 Buccaneer outfit. The parent carrier was *Ark Royal*, which was undergoing an extensive refit at the time I took over the squadron at Lossiemouth in December 1968. I hoped to be able to stay with the squadron until her refit completed in 1970 and then take the squadron back to the deck and get in some more carrier flying time. This was a pretty optimistic hope but I'm an optimist, and the flight deck to me was like a new train set to a little boy; I was keen to return to embarked flying. I might be lucky but I knew the odds were against me. By that time there were so few fixed wing squadrons left in the Fleet Air Arm that command appointments were like gold dust. I'd be extremely lucky to take the squadron to sea.

I was aware that my predecessor had advised the squadron that it would probably be doing a lot more night flying after I took over: My reputation had preceded me. We started night flying a week after I joined.

In addition to our day flying exercises we flew night strikes, illuminating and then striking targets in the North sea, the English channel, and into the Kattegat against Danish fast patrol boats. For the latter we landed at the Danish air force field at Karup and stayed overnight. The sortie length was over two hours each way and it was an extremely demanding exercise. We took off at dusk and climbed to altitude to in-flight refuel over the North sea in twilight. We then descended in the dark to low level (200 feet) in the Kattegat, searched for and located the target boats, and ran in at 200 feet to illuminate, then attack them under our own illuminants. We recovered to nearby Karup to do a Ground Controlled Approach, land, debrief and stagger off to bed, well pleased with what we'd achieved, but knackered.

To have returned home after that lot would have been too much to expect. Ever since we'd detached from the refuelling tanker at altitude we'd been instrument flying except for the actual visual attack under our illuminants. It was a lot to ask but we'd worked up to it slowly and carefully and it had paid off. My new Buccaneer tactics were developing. So far we'd only used experienced aircrew. Soon we were to involve selected junior aircrew.

I'd long before decided that the only viable close formation at night was a pair of aircraft, rather than the more popular four aircraft unit. A further pair might be part of the same unit but would operate astern of the lead pair and virtually independently except that they would double the striking weapons on target More than two aircraft in a close formation at night was, in my opinion, too demanding for the wingmen for the sort of exercises I wanted to develop. Another decision I'd come to was that our sorties had to be radio silent (latterly known as 'zip lip') until we called Lossiemouth for our Ground Controlled Approach (GCA) for landing, so as not to advertise our approach to an enemy by radio transmissions. The only exception to this rule was, of course, any emergency. This discipline meant that the pre-flight briefing had to be absolutely watertight, and cover every stage of the flight, and every eventuality.

When we introduced junior aircrew we crewed experienced aircrew in one seat with the junior aircrew in the other: an experienced pilot with a junior observer and an experienced observer with a junior pilot. This way we could "break in" the junior aircrew slowly, working up by stages to a full-blown attack sequence. Additionally, once we'd proved to the junior men that they could operate at night we lightened their flying load as much as possible whenever we could. The usual way to do this was for the junior pilot to take the lead automatically, immediately he'd pulled off the target (up to that time the most demanding part of the sortie).

This gave the experienced pilot in the other aircraft the task of joining up on his wing and flying close formation as they came home. In this way the junior man could relax a little, and the experienced pilot could keep an eye on him, in addition to the experienced observer sitting behind him.

It was relatively easy to detect when the junior man was tiring – these were demanding sorties – and it was important to realise this before he got too tired. In some instances it was best to drop away from him and let him forget about having someone on his wing to worry about. He could then return home, not quite on his own – the experienced pilot would be somewhere not too far behind, to monitor from a distance, available for help over the radio should it be necessary. And, of course, there was always the experienced observer with him.

Should it be thought that a back seat man couldn't do anything to help the pilot in front of him fly the aircraft, this simply isn't true. I've been pulled out of some very awkward situations by an astute observer, and regard this as the ultimate in crewmanship.

We never had a problem, which says something about the quality of the junior aircrew, and the quality of supervision of the experienced men. I was always proud of them and I instigated the practice of having a crate of cool beer waiting for the crews when they'd got out of their flying gear and were about to start their debriefing. They'd worked to the best of their professional ability for their individual flying experience, and thoroughly deserved that beer. It was always welcome, and always made for an in-depth, and enjoyable, debrief. And the confidence of the junior men increased noticeably. They were becoming fully operational and were aware of it.

The squadron visited Schleswig, Germany, in June 1969, and we were the guests of the German Naval F104 squadron there. There's a rather peculiar NATO duty free allowance of spirits and tobacco, peculiar in the amount that each man was entitled to take to another NATO country. It was prodigious. I had worked out in advance the squadron entitlement for duty free whisky and tobacco on a per capita basis, and based on the length of our stay. The whisky amounted to over 500 bottles. I can't remember the tobacco total but that too was pretty staggering. I slashed the amount of spirit we'd take by half, with the proviso that we'd come back to Lossiemouth for more, should we need it.

The tobacco and whisky were to be transported, along with the squadron ground equipment and personnel, in RAF Argosy transport aircraft. We needed several aircraft. The aircrew would, of course, fly the Buccaneers. The Buccaneers landed ahead of the Argosies, and I was met by the German Navy liaison officer and, to my horror, a German customs officer. We went out to meet the Argosies and I was alongside the first Argosy, which was keen to unload and get back to the UK, when Customs asked me to sign a declaration that we carried no duty-free goods. I really got to appreciate the qualities of our liaison officer when he lead me and the customs chap round to the blind side of the Argosy to go through the paperwork, while the whisky and tobacco were quickly offloaded into a truck and whisked away. The liaison officer then intimated it was OK for me to sign. To this day I don't know why I was asked to sign this declaration when we were within NATO limits, but the liaison officer obviously foresaw endless complications while it was sorted out and decided to sort it himself. This was my kind of liaison officer!

Before we left Lossiemouth I had made arrangements with a chum of mine, the Commanding Officer of Station Flight, a small flight of communications aircraft for ferry purposes, that if necessary, I could call on him for any support I might need. I had in mind extra whisky! I had to call on him because of, and not for more of, the whisky.

NATO airfields on the European mainland are required to have their living accommodation not less than six kilometres from the operational airfield. The first problem this presented was that our maintenance crews would be down at the airfield when at work, and six kilometres away from their duty free entitlement, which they would get instead of their rum ration (because we were away from their home base). Although they would not be allowed the ration when they were working on aircraft, when they were off duty they could have it. Additionally, we had the problem of how to issue each man his daily ration of the duty free spirit. We had to compromise. We explained the problems to the sailors and got their word that, if we gave them their full entitlement in one issue, they wouldn't abuse it. They didn't. But some of them allowed the Germans to.

Each barrack block on the domestic site at Schleswig had a Bier Keller in the basement, much to the liking of the sailors, who started making firm friends with their hospitable German hosts. In return for the foaming beer tankards they found themselves presented with they decided to return the compliment by offering their whisky. It was very popular, but the recipients weren't used to it and soon became quite ill.

In the men's cloakrooms in Germany it was common to find 'retch' handles for men to hang on to if they couldn't hold their drink and had to void it over the pan. This usually minimises the mess but in the case of the Schleswig German sailors, the handles didn't help much. The cloakrooms became revolting – and my sailors got the blame. Thus, a few days after we'd arrived, I received a deputation of angry German officers accusing my lads of making the mess and what was I going to do about it? I saw no point in arguing with these officers about who might be at fault although naturally I inclined towards giving my sailors the benefit of the doubt.

I had to move fast. First I got my regulating Chief Petty Officer up to the domestic site to investigate the incident and get back to me as soon as possible. He came back to me and explained what had happened. Three of our sailors had been handing round their whisky. None of our chaps had been under the weather, but the Germans hadn't been able to hold their drink and were responsible for the resultant mess.

Next I took the German officers down to my Buccaneer line and climbed into an aircraft. I switched on the long-range radio and got straight on to Lossiemouth. I requested a Sea Prince aircraft to come over and pick up some errant sailors. I then told the Germans what I was going to do to sort the problem. They were impressed at the speed and the manner of my reaction. I had the three unfortunates pack their bags and sent them home in the Sea Prince as soon as it arrived. This was harsh on the sailors but although they hadn't abused their whisky privilege by getting drunk – our main worry – they had abused the privilege we'd allowed them by getting the Germans drunk. I think the German officers felt a little guilty at the effect their unsubstantiated accusation about our sailors had had, but the result was good for us. We had no more complaints, and no more trouble was reported.

There was an important matter to clear up later on our way home. I opted to fly back in the Argosy carrying the lads. I had to reinstate the three I'd sent home in the eyes of their chums. I used the aircraft's internal broadcast to explain that their only offence had been to be too generous to a crowd of Germans who couldn't hold their drink. They'd been unfortunate in their behaviour and unlucky in the result. A complaint had been made and I had had to do something high profile. The lads understood, and we had no problems when we got back.

There's one small rider to this episode. When the Sea Prince arrived back at Lossiemouth the three sailors who'd been brought home offered the pilot hundreds of cigarettes – all the duty-free they'd been issued with but had not had the chance to use. The pilot had been extremely touched at their consideration and their thanks for flying all that way because of their misdemeanour. He had politely declined their gift. He was a pipe smoker.

The rest of our stay at Schleswig was uneventful and enjoyable. Several of our aircrew flew in the German F104s and declared it a worthwhile experience. I managed, politely, to avoid this doubtful pleasure. The 104 was known as 'the widow maker' and I had no wish to endorse this reputation.

Towards the end of our stay we gave a party in the officers' mess for our German hosts and their wives and girlfriends. We still had whisky galore and this was to be the mainstay of the party. I'd detailed one of my officers to be in charge of the booze and, if he thought a re-supply was needed, he was to have one of the stewards bring up a few more bottles. This went very well and, as the evening progressed, the re-supply requirement steadily diminished until, by about 2 am, there was only one German, Gunter and his wife, left in the mess. Gunter was well into his cups but appeared keen to carry on drinking. His wife wasn't so keen. I ordered one more bottle to be brought up and we started getting through it when Gunter, by this time almost out on his feet, put the cork back in the bottle and then put the bottle in his jacket pocket. He then explained German etiquette: as long as a bottle was still available, a guest or guests had to stay until it was empty or they'd be considered discourteous. Gunter had managed to appreciate that he'd had more than enough but he'd decided the best way not to be considered discourteous would be to remove the bottle.

His wife went out to get the car just as Gunter collapsed. She backed the car up to one of the mess windows and we fed Gunter out of the window and through the tailgate. I don't know how she got him out of the car once home; Gunter was a big chap. I thought it best not to ask. He did appear the next day, not too much the worse for wear.

I had many 'Thank Yous' to make before we left Schleswig and I used the whisky to good effect. A bottle of malt whisky went down very well with each of the various recipients.

Soon after we got back to Lossiemouth, I drove down to the squadron hangar one morning only to find my coveted parking spot outside my office had been roped off. I was livid. Parking was always at a premium and one of the few 'perks' a squadron commander had was his own spot. I stumped off to confront my Regulating Chief. He asked me to keep my voice down (outside my own squadron!) and lead me back to the roped off spot, which was gravelled. He put his forefinger to his lips, asking me to remain silent, and then pointed to the middle of the area. It was difficult to discriminate against the gravel background: an oyster-catcher was sitting on its nest – a small hollow in the gravel – and eyeballing me defiantly. I backed off and found somewhere else to park for a few days.

Another oyster-catcher affair had earlier occurred on the other side of the airfield. Each squadron aircraft hard standing had recesses in the concrete to accommodate fire extinguishers but keep them down well clear of aircraft movement. An oyster-catcher had built its nest in one before the extinguishers had been put out that morning. It refused to be budged. The falconer was summoned and duly arrived, a tall burly impressive figure, with his falcon on his gauntlet. The falcon was launched at the oyster-catcher – and the oyster-catcher went bald-headed for the falcon. The falconer retired disgruntled, the falcon in disgrace, and the aircraft kept clear of the oyster- catcher until the young had hatched and fledged.

One Monday morning one of my aircrew requested to see me on a confidential matter. It was urgent. We retired to my office and closed the door. 'I wish to make a complaint against one of your squadron officers, Sir. He made an indecent remark to my wife at the wardroom dance on Saturday'.

Oh dear! Trouble in the aircrew rest room. I said it was a very serious accusation and I'd investigate it immediately. I called the 'accused' in to my office, told him of the allegation and, if it was true, to consider apologising. The 'accused' was an extremely competent aviator, a level headed character and an asset to the squadron; I thought it highly unlikely that the allegation was true. I was also aware that the 'accused' couldn't stand the accuser and could well understand why. The accuser was highly unpopular and, frankly, the squadron would have been better off without him. His wife, although superficially attractive, was well suited to her husband.

A couple of days passed and the 'accused' came back to see me.

'Sir, I've given it a lot of thought and I can't see that what I said to his wife constituted an indecent remark. I'm sorry, I can't apologise'.

'Would it help me get ahead in the matter if you told me what you said. You don't have to tell me, but it could help me make up my mind'.

'I don't mind telling you at all, Sir. I was dancing with his wife and all I said was 'what did you want to marry such a tit for?'

Trying to keep a straight face I replied that the remark was perhaps indiscreet but certainly not indecent. I followed on by telling the now 'unaccused' that my only concern was I didn't want disharmony in the crew room. If he could work towards re-establishing some kind of harmony I'd be happy. I left him to it.

I had requested a reciprocal visit by the Germans which was approved, and we invited them to come over. I had a host team arrange a programme for them and had just got it sewn up when the captain asked me to come and see him; this was just a couple of days before the Germans were due to arrive. The captain wanted to give them a reception. We had already got a welcoming cocktail party lined up for their first evening, after which we'd planned to let them socialise privately with those host officers and their wives who, I knew, were keen to have them to dinner. The captain would have none of it. After the cocktail party the Germans were to be his guests at a reception at his house. I had to accede. The reception would start at 2000.

Our cocktail party in the wardroom went wonderfully, after which the Germans were ferried over to the captain's house, Mary and I remaining behind until the last of our guests had departed. We then went over to the captain's reception only to find a very bootfaced captain and his wife together with a very thirsty crowd of guests all waiting until we'd arrived. The captain was observing what he considered to be an old German custom: nobody gets a drink until the final guest has arrived. Black mark to the Howards. To make matters worse we'd been met at the captain's door by a pensioner steward whose wife, we knew, had been quite ill so, naturally, we stopped to ask after her health. This made us even more late.

We all then got a drink – one drink – while we eyed the buffet table. It quickly became obvious to most of us that there wasn't enough food, and each of us, German guests and us, their hosts, therefore helped themselves, frugally, to very small portions and found a seat. Ironically the host and his wife then made much of exhorting us all to eat up, there was plenty left for seconds

The seating was arranged around the walls of the room but there were no occasional tables for us to put our glasses on while we ate off our laps. The only place for a glass was on the carpet under our chairs, which were squeezed too close together so that you couldn't avoid getting tangled with the person next to you. Needless to say, my glass of red wine spilled over the captain's bilious green carpet, right in front of him. He was aghast, dropped to his knees and started mopping it up, watched by a horrified me and several willing but unbidden stewards. Another black mark – to me.

The evening wore to a rather dreary and embarrassing close, the Germans left and we all said our Thank Yous and followed them. Once in the car I turned to Mary and said: 'We'll never be asked there again!' She asked why and I told her I'd spilled my wine. Mary then said: 'So did I. There was nowhere to put it except on the floor!' So between us we'd racked up a full house of black marks.

The rest of the Germans' visit went as planned, with no further unscheduled interruptions. They finally returned home having had a thoroughly enjoyable time. They were a good bunch and it was noticeable how similar their attitudes and behaviour were to ours, the common denominator being aviation.

There was a rider to that episode in the captain's house. Not too long afterwards I was doing my leaving routine and was passing the Commander's office when he called me in. He asked me what I could have done to upset the captain, so I told him the whole, rather unfortunate tale of the captain's enforced reception, including Mary's and my accidental wine spillage. The Commander laughed and told me that would explain why the captain had added an 'extra' to my 206 (confidential report): 'Bit rough socially'.

Sometime in November 1969 the same captain came bouncing into my office down at the squadron.

'Dave', he said, 'You're coming up on the next promotion selection list (due at the end of the year), so we're taking your squadron away from you'. Good news: this meant I'd been selected for Commander and would put up my third stripe on 1st July the next year. Bad news: I would not be taking the squadron to sea when *Ark Royal* finished her refit. No more carrier flying for me.

This was blind optimism on my part. I should have remembered nobody except the members of the promotion selection board could have known who had been selected, and the selections are never made known until they're published at the end of each half year. However when your own captain tells you, you tend to forget this unbending rule, and I swallowed his tale hook, line and sinker.

He'd told me that I could tell no-one, keep it to myself, which is what I would have expected him to say. However, it's traditional to throw a party when you're selected for promotion and I felt I had to let Mary in on the secret because, if I was going to be relieved of my squadron, New Year's Eve would be the last chance we'd get of giving a party, as well as being the day the promotions were announced. We therefore declared it would be our leaving party and, at the last minute, would make it a promotion celebration as well. Mary kept the secret. And I wasn't selected. Privately we called it the 'Dull Thud' party.

Back off leave in early January after the Christmas leave period, back came the captain to my office.

'I knew you weren't going to be selected and they were going to promote X instead', he announced. I was too low to make any comment.

I left the squadron in February. I'd finished my operational flying career and been reappointed to the Ministry of Defence: a desk job in

London. Mary drove the children, the dog and one very heavily packed car down south. Later I followed in an even more heavily packed second car, with the cat.

# Chapter 24

## *Ministry of Defence (MoD)*

I have to open this chapter by observing that desk work was not my favourite task in the service. I had had no staff training, hadn't had the benefit of what I assumed would have been covered with a Dartmouth training, and paperwork didn't sit easily with me. However, I had adopted one golden rule about it which was to hold me in good stead: I firmly believed that the standard of service writing was important. The routine reports and letters you wrote during your various appointments were often the first, possibly the only, contact you had with higher authority. Therefore the standard of your correspondence would always reflect the standard of the outfit you commanded (in my case to date: two squadrons), as well as you personally.

Whilst I didn't consider myself too adept at penmanship I had at least that yardstick as my guide. I didn't realise how much I had to learn. I was to be fortunate in MOD in serving under bosses who were experienced in service writing and, more important for me, could teach me a great deal. Spiv Leahy was my immediate boss and taught me most about staff writing. Spiv had a memorable teaching style: he would read a wad of your purple prose, take out a black Pentel marker, gently warn you (in Glaswegian) 'perhaps what you meant to say was' and then obliterate great chunks of it. He would then replace the obliterations with a couple of lines. It was surgical. He became another role model for me. However, before I took up the appointment I wasn't exactly looking forward to it other than as a necessary stage in my career which had to be stoically endured. I'd led an all-action life in the service so far, both on the lower deck and as an officer, and although you always knew your front line squadron would mark the end of your operational flying, I considered 'flying' a desk was a very poor substitute.

And so I joined MOD, main building, in the Directorate of Naval Air Warfare (DNAW). As a lieutenant commander you're absolutely bottom of the pile in MOD. DNAW was, at least, on the fourth floor. I don't know who was on the floors below, but I quickly became aware that the floors above housed the more senior and more important mortals, culminating ultimately in the gods (Flag rank officers, senior civil servants and, of course, the Defence Secretary. At my level you shared an office with at least one other officer, and I suppose I was fortunate that it was only one, in a very dingy office looking out on to an enclosed rectangular courtyard with the only view that of offices on the other three sides of the yard.

As an Air Warfare Instructor my job was weapons so I at least had some background knowledge for my duties. My fellow officers kindly set about inducting me into the other important aspects of life in the MOD, not least where I was going to live. I was quickly booked to view several accommodations, usually shared i.e. a tiny private bedroom, shared everything else including my own corner of the fridge. I started a dreary round of viewing these places, all of which seemed to be permeated by the smell of overcooked cabbage.

These were all within easy commuting, or even walking, distance of MOD and relatively low rent, to enable their occupants to make the most of their London allowance. In those days (early 70's) it wasn't generous but, if you were prepared to slum it during your working week and travel to wherever home was Friday evening to Monday morning, you could easily live within it. I wasn't prepared to slum it, or to put up with the smell of overcooked cabbage, so I opted to commute from a bit further out and found more acceptable, albeit more expensive, accommodation. I didn't profit from my London allowance but was much happier – and much more comfortable.

Each office was served by a clerical assistant, usually a lady, who looked after your paperwork, filing and circulation, and usually managed to keep your in-tray piled too high. All drafts went down to a typing pool and I soon realised it was important to pay the pool an occasional visit so that the typists knew the face behind the author of the work they were labouring over. Since lengthy papers you were required to write often went through several stages of massage by your boss before they were deemed acceptable to be passed on to the next level of authority, and since time was often of the essence, getting prompt service from the pool was important. It did no harm to enhance your priority by spending time 'making your number' with these typists. In at least two vitally important, and, as usual, protracted projects I was concerned with, this brief acquaintance proved invaluable.

Because of the complexity of the projects, lengthy papers kept on coming back from the higher levels they'd been forwarded to, requiring amendment in some form. Since civil servants, the other services, and our own flag rank officers were all involved, this, I soon learned, was par for the course, and there was nothing for it but to redraft the paper and try again, guided, of course, by my senior officers within the directorate.

On projects such as these it was not uncommon to find yourself stuck in your office until 8.30 pm or later, and you were not alone, judging by the lights still on in the offices visible from your office window. I suppose if your domestic life really doesn't start until you get home to wherever on a Friday evening, working late doesn't matter too much. It was usually fatigue that finally drove you out of the office, your thought processes too dulled to continue making sense of the work you were struggling over.

During my first year in the MOD Mary and I decided we had to get an extension built on the cottage. Anthony was now two, Katie just a babe in arms and the 'two up, two down' too small. We got the local builder who'd done the modernisation and therefore knew the cottage, and we moved out for the few months that would be needed for the job. Mary and I became joint tenants so that I could take out the 20-year mortgage mentioned in Chapter 21 to cover the cost.

I had joined the MOD in April 1970. On June 30th I was listed for promotion to commander: I'd put up my third stripe on 31st December. This entailed the usual celebration partying and I duly entertained the other directorate officers, who were all too willing to accept my booze as they congratulated me. I think there was also an almost imperceptible rise in my perceived status in the building, (although a commander is only half a stripe better than a lieutenant commander); and even commanders were two a penny.

It was customary for some to get their lunch in one of the nearby pubs in Whitehall. This usually involved sinking a few pints as well as some sort of pie. Pretty soon I discovered that beer at lunchtime did not sit well with an afternoon (and probably half the evening) of paperwork. I'm not a beer man anyway and soon had to give this up. It was cheaper, and more sensible, for me to find a takeaway sandwich and get back to the office and some coffee.

Some of the projects I was concerned with would eventually end up as defence contracts with one of the major defence companies. These companies kept in close touch with all levels of service officers involved in producing the staff papers required along the way to the final contract. Since many of the company representatives were retired service officers I'd served with at some stage this was quite a pleasant association, especially when you were invited out to lunch as a guest of the company. You were always aware of the reason behind this hospitality but it was regarded as a legitimate 'perk'. It also made a welcome change from visiting the company premises for one of the necessary progress meetings. This always required travel and lengthy spells away from your desk.

It was noticeable how the companies differed in their approach. At some, the meeting convened in an elegant conference room and you drank your coffee from a silver coffee service. At others you convened in an inelegant shack and got your coffee from a trolley pushed around by an equally inelegant tea 'lady'.

On one of these hospitality lunches at an up market restaurant, two of us were the guests of a very jovial ex-service mutual chum. We had a splendid lunch and were really hoping to cut and run back to the office. The hospitality was not to end however. Our host absolutely insisted he took us to a 'club', positive it would really be a treat we'd enjoy and not forget. We didn't enjoy it, and we didn't forget it either.

The 'club' turned out to be a strip joint, but we only realised what it was once we were in and seated, in some kind of small theatre. It was an all-male audience and we were three of the very few not in a dirty raincoat! It was the one and only time I, and my fellow desk officer, had ever seen a strip show: to describe it as sleazy was an understatement. Our crestfallen host fortunately realised he'd goofed and got us out of there pretty rapidly. We thanked him, not too profusely, and hurried back to the office, possibly one of the few times we were glad to get back.

After nearly two years in the MOD I'd decided to ask my appointer (the officer responsible for assigning me to my next job) for a staff course at the National Defence College. My time in DNAW had convinced me I needed a lot more experience in staff matters. The appointer asked me to come over to his office to discuss this next job. When I mentioned I wanted to do a staff course he immediately countered with an offer of ship command: a frigate. He strongly urged it would be better for me.

How could I possibly resist, what officer could? This was something I, an ex-boy seaman, had never given a thought. It couldn't happen to me!

I jumped at it.

Soon afterwards I was reappointed as Commanding Officer, *HMS Lincoln*, a Type 61 Cathedral class Air Defence frigate. I was over the moon.

# Chapter 25

## *Ship Command - HMS Lincoln*

IT was with few regrets that I said goodbye to DNAW, took some leave, and then went down to *HMS Dryad*, just north of Portsmouth, to do the Commanding Officers designate course prior to taking command. The course, in June/July 1972, dealt with the operational side of naval warfare, and how to fight my ship in various operational 'hot war' scenarios.

I did some swotting up on my forthcoming command before I went to *HMS Dryad*. As I mentioned at the end of the previous chapter, *Lincoln* was an Aircraft Direction (AD) frigate of some 2,400 tons with a crew of about 240 officers and ratings. Her class, the *Salisbury* class, was distinguished by an enormous rectangular radar aerial atop her mainmast, known generally as the double bedstead (what it looked like), which could 'see' aircraft out to some 200 nautical miles. Thus, in principle, if these ships were stationed well upthreat of the main fleet body they could extend the 'eyes' of the fleet, provide maximum early warning of approaching hostile aircraft, and direct friendly aircraft to intercept them.

The *Salisbury* class all had twin propellors, one 4.5" gun turret forward, an anti-submarine mortar on the quarterdeck, and an unsophisticated sonar capability (since this was not their main role). Each ship was diesel powered, with four engines on each of two propeller shafts. These didn't give much in the way of maximum speed but, since high speed was not essential for their role, were adequate. They did, however, offer flexibility in maintenance since engines could be shut down as required for servicing (given that the operational situation permitted) and they gave reasonable range. *Lincoln* differed from the other three ships in the class in that she was blessed with variable pitch propellors. These are now a standard fit in modern ships but, in those days, were much prized since they enabled much better manoeuvrability in ship handling. They were also 'the best brakes in the fleet'. Perhaps that was why *Lincoln*'s command went to an aviator!

A part of the *Dryad* course I had really been looking forward to was ship handling. The only vessels I'd handled to date had been a variety of ship's boats as a sailor. As an officer, despite having done the requisite six months and been awarded my bridge watch keeping certificate, I'd never actually handled a ship other than making minor alterations of course in mid-Atlantic. However, come the day, the course students were eagerly anticipating the hot word about ship handling. All we got was an instruction to go away and read Chapter 13 of our Seamanship Manuals. Chapter 13 tells you that if you put the wheel over to the left the ship turns to port and, guess what – put it over to the right and the ship turned starboard. I'd have to pick up anything more advanced as I went along. The service had a lot of faith in me.

*Lincoln* was alongside in Hong Kong when I took command in August 1972. I'd flown out to Hong Kong, landed at the old airport at Kai Tak, and stayed for the rest of that day and overnight in accommodation in what used to be *HMS* Tamar, the naval headquarters. I spent most of the day going through a 'Rogues Gallery' of my new ship's company. I'd asked my predecessor for it and he'd kindly arranged for it to be waiting for me. In my squadrons, ever since I'd been a senior lieutenant, I'd always made it a rule to know every man's name. *Lincoln* would be no exception and I got cracking straight away. I was determined I'd know the names of all the officers and as many of the key ratings as I could manage before I first stepped aboard.

*Lincoln* was lying in Victoria basin, a rectangular enclosed basin. It has long since been land-filled and built on but, in those days, was just a short stroll from Tamar. The next morning, in a squeaky clean set of tropical shorts and shirt, I set out to walk over to her and relieve my predecessor, a friend of mine and also one of my ex-AWI students at Whale Island. As I walked around the basin to the foot of the gangway, I eyed my new command. This was a moment I'd never dreamed might happen – boy seaman to command of a ship – and I was elated. I arrived at the agreed time, was duly piped aboard, and welcomed.

Handovers in the service are traditionally short and sharp. There are a few necessary documents to be formally signed for, introductions to be made, and that's about it. The outgoing Commanding Officer leaves as soon as he politely can and the ship is yours.

The limited amount of kit I'd been able to bring in the aircraft I'd flown out in soon arrived from Tamar and I started settling in to accommodation more spacious than anything I'd experienced so far in the service. I had what, to me, was a large day cabin with an inter-connecting door to a steward's pantry immediately aft, and, leading off the day cabin, a small sleeping cabin for'ard, with its own en suite bathroom. Luxury!

Having given me a decent interval to settle in, my First Lieutenant, always known as No.1 in the service, came in for a brief chat before taking me off to introduce me to my new officers. He then gave me a tour of the ship. It soon became apparent that he was not a little doubtful about his new Commanding Officer's ability to hoist in the pearls of seamanship wisdom being offered. It was perhaps a bit too much for an aviator to take in. I took note - and held my peace.

I was particularly interested in the engineering department and later arranged for the Engineering Officer to give me a more comprehensive tour. My interest naturally came from my aviation background: I wanted to know exactly what was happening to make the ship tick, and, in particular, who and what was involved when I gave an engine order from the bridge.

As I toured the engineering department my impression that aviators were considered 'odd', and unlikely to be able to understand seaborne matters, was reinforced. My predecessor was also an aviator and, I knew, was an extremely competent officer, so this prejudice against aviators wasn't just within the ship. It was a 'fishhead/airhead' thing (fishheads = seaborne, airheads = airborne) that, I was to discover, was all too prevalent throughout the service. Previously I'd met this at Whale Island, and in the fairly good-humoured relationship that always existed between fishheads and aviators in the carriers I'd served in. Since we were their *raison d'etre* and they were the means by which we operated there had to be an amicable understanding, no matter how much we pulled each other's legs on the fishhead/airhead line. And pull we did. But now I was in command of a ship with no direct aviation connection other than its Commanding Officer, and there appeared to be some doubt about my ability to understand the ship, or matters afloat on the sea, as opposed to above it.

Nevertheless I enjoyed a traditional 'dining in'. Possibly as an indication of how my new officers felt about aviators, in the ensuing mess rugger, I seemed to find myself at the bottom of each scrum. My shower the following morning revealed another hernia! Aware of the risk, I decided a repair would have to wait. I wasn't going to chance losing my ship.

The following day we put to sea. Victoria basin had only one quite narrow entrance/exit which I managed to clear through safely out into the harbour and then off into the open sea. Since I'd never handled anything larger than a ship's boat I'd arranged with the first lieutenant to have several large cardboard boxes available on the quarterdeck, one to be thrown overboard each time I asked, so that I could practise coming alongside it (until it sank). I was determined to familiarise myself with the ship's handling characteristics: how she responded to wheel and engine orders, try out the variable pitch propellors, then a relatively new facility and, supposedly, those 'best brakes in the fleet'.

I think these practice manoeuvres simply reinforced the ship's company's impression that they had another barking mad aviator in command. Whatever they thought, by the time I'd finished, I was confident I could get *Lincoln* back into Victoria basin safely. The next day I had another session. A chum of mine commanding a minesweeper based in Hong Kong at the time had volunteered to act as another 'cardboard box'. He was also an aviator and knew what I was up to.

It was another useful day of familiarisation and I was delighted with *Lincoln's* handling characteristics. The variable pitch propellors were impressive, and the engine response equally so. With a special sea-dutyman down in the Machinery Control Room (MCR) handling the pitch control and engine revolutions he could move from half ahead to half astern without varying the revolutions. This offered amazing deceleration and, with full wheel on, half astern on the inboard engine and half ahead on the outboard, an amazing rate of turn. Both these attributes were to serve me in good stead in future operations.

I still had a great deal to learn about *Lincoln's* performance, her range, cruising speed, how she handled in bad weather and, above all, how most efficiently to use her engines.

Economical cruising was effected with two engines a side but only gave about 13 knots. Three a side was a far more practicable arrangement. It gave me 17 knots, was better for long range, and also easier in any seaway. Four a side gave a maximum of 24 knots – downhill in a following wind. This was the configuration for entering and leaving harbour, and in any operational situation. Having engines 'off line' also gave the maintainers the opportunity for servicing, provided it was unlikely that the bridge was going to need '4 a side' during the time required for servicing. It was usual for me to allow whatever the engineers wanted in terms of shutting engines down, given that, should I need them back on line, they could be connected fairly quickly. This limitation would only apply should the navigational or operational situation require it. On a long, quiet passage engines could be shut down for longer periods to allow deep maintenance. I was informed when this would be required and we always managed to plan ahead and dovetail maintenance needs into the ship's programme.

My initial 'aviator prejudice' impressions were confirmed quite early on when I did my first 'Captain's rounds'. 'Rounds' is the naval term for an inspection. Rather than stagger through the whole ship on one protracted inspection, my routine covered one department at a time. My first rounds was of the domestic side e.g. mess-decks, bathrooms, heads (toilets) and passages, and I had the distinct feeling that No.1 considered the inspection merely a formality. An aviator couldn't possibly know anything about inspecting a ship.

Going down the first ladder into one of the seamen's messes, on my left there was a 'fan-trunking', the large overhead metal channel through which ventilating air is pumped. As a former matelot I knew that if the sailor who slung his hammock below that trunking was a smoker he would probably have had an ashtray on top of it and out of sight. As I descended the ladder I ran my hand along the top of that trunking and, sure enough, there was an ashtray. It was full. As I set foot on the messdeck I handed the overflowing ashtray to my No.1. This was the first messdeck on my first inspection. I'd made a point. No.1 looked slightly green. And my rounds were never patronised thereafter.

At sea one day I noticed the seaboat's falls were incorrectly rove through their leading blocks, waiting for the boat to return. This was potentially a very dangerous situation and I managed, tactfully, to let No1 know in good time that 'I thought' the falls were wrongly rigged (it was his department and I was keen not to be seen to be interfering). He shot away and rectified matters before the boat was hoisted. He returned to let me know I'd been right. We were getting to understand one another.

My first ship's visit was to the Philippines. This was a brief courtesy visit since, in my predecessor's time, the ship had done magnificent work on flood relief in the northern part of the islands. Our port of call was right at the southernmost tip of the chain, to a place called Zamboanga, where we were to be entertained as a Thank You for that operation. All the officers were invited to a cocktail party hosted by, and at the home of, the head of the local Lions club. This was going fairly well until our host called for silence in order to make a speech. It was quite short and was to thank me for my generous promise of food for the local leper convent.

This was something of a surprise to me since I hadn't even known there was a leper convent locally. I quickly glanced round my officers looking for someone who'd been rash enough to open his mouth. Sure enough one of them looked as if he'd like to disappear through the floor. Fortunately I had a very switched on Supply officer who whispered in my ear that he could produce a creditable pile of canned food not popular with the ship's company. Relieved, I mouthed a few platitudes, agreed to present the food at the convent early the following day (we were due to sail next morning) and left as soon as I could. I got an embarrassed apology from the officer concerned.

The Philippines was about to be put under Martial Law at this time and the Defence Attaché was considering using *Lincoln* to evacuate British ex-pats. To make matters worse a curfew was suddenly imposed between midnight and 7am and there was no way we could let our sailors already ashore know. I got as many officers as I could together and we went round all the bars we could find spreading the word: get back aboard before midnight or stay ashore off the streets until after 7am. We were successful.

Next we called in to the port of Jakarta where the naval attaché there had arranged for me to pay an official protocol call on the governor in Jakarta. This involved an official car and an escort of two very flashily dressed motorcyclist policemen who acted as outriders. The road was absolutely packed with pedestrians, ox or horse drawn carts and a variety of clapped out cars, vans, and lorries. The outriders simply barged their machines into this mass, blowing their whistles the whole time and waving or pushing whatever was in the way off on to the verge. At one stage they were standing on the seats of their machines, no hands, whistles clamped between their teeth, conducting their traffic clearance to allow my car through. My driver, Indonesian military, appeared to be used to this routine and simply drove on completely unconcerned. On our return journey the same thing happened and I was quite relieved to arrive back at *Lincoln* and retire to my cabin.

To my surprise the senior policeman followed me into my cabin and simply stood there. I chatted with him and congratulated him on his motorcycling skills. He seemed to be waiting for something and I was rather nonplussed until I noticed, behind his back, my  Number One signalling from the pantry doorway. He was holding a bottle of whisky and a carton of cigarettes and waving them at the policeman. Then he left them on the side and quietly closed the door. I caught on at last. Telling the policeman I'd like to thank him and his partner for their wonderful escort I went across and picked up the bottle and carton, asking if he'd be so kind as to accept them as a small token of my appreciation. He most certainly would. He grabbed them and left in a hurry.

While we were in Jakarta my navigator was relieved and I met the new navigator shortly after he came aboard. He was brought up to meet me by another officer. They were both dressed in black tie and dinner jackets. The new officer was about to be introduced to the delights ashore. But, unlike his companion, he wore a black jacket which was inappropriate for the climate. We were of a similar build so I lent him my brand new, just received from the Chinese tailor, white jacket, and off they went ashore. The jacket was returned safely and I hope the fact that it was mine hadn't cramped his activities ashore. He more than repaid me; he was an excellent navigator and we were to go through many demanding times to come.

We then had a major stopover for a maintenance period in Singapore and Mary and the children flew out for a few weeks. Kate was still in nappies and Anthony not far out of them. They were on the dockside to meet the ship, as was the senior naval officer – a commodore.

Protocol dictates that the senior naval officer should be first up the gangway, to be ceremonially greeted by myself, the duty officer and a piping party. Thus I was waiting at the top of the gangway, best bib and tucker, ready to salute the commodore as he stepped aboard, but this was too much for Anthony. He'd spotted his daddy immediately and was coming aboard. He toddled away from his mother, over to the foot of the gangway where he arrived at the same time as the commodore, elbowed him in the knee (as far as he could reach up) and pushed in front of him, climbed on to the gangway before an amused senior naval officer and staggered up the rather steep slope to the top where I lifted him down. The commodore came up behind him, took his salute with a big grin and was charming about this slight breach of naval protocol.

After a few happy weeks mostly by the officers' pool at the club, Mary and the children flew home and *Lincoln* continued northwest on our next leg home, heading up the Straits of Malacca and into the Indian Ocean

As we cleared the straits of Sumatra we refuelled from a tanker before setting out across the Indian Ocean for Gan. I then dealt with the next, and really heavy, anti-aviator prejudice incident.

My engineer officer came up to the bridge in something of a state to ask me where the tanker we'd just refuelled from was. I pointed to a smudge of funnel smoke which was the tanker, hull down, heading back into the Sumatran straits.

'Can we recall him, sir?'

On my asking what the problem was the engineer officer told me they'd just switched to a fresh fuel tank and found it full of sea water. *Lincoln* had seawater compensating fuel tanks which filled with seawater as the fuel was used in order to maintain the ship's stability. I asked which tank it was, had a fair idea of its capacity, and calculated we could still get to Gan with an adequate fuel reserve. The engineer wasn't too happy but had to be satisfied with my decision: for a good ten minutes.

He then re-appeared with the Chief Stoker in quite a panic. The next fuel tank they'd tried had also been full of seawater. We had to get the tanker back. I took them out on the bridge wing and pointed to our wake. The only way we could suddenly have lost two tanks worth of fuel was through leaks in the ship's bottom. There wasn't a trace of oil in the wake. Could the fuel have leaked into the bilges? Both of them obviously thought that their aviator captain really was barking mad.

'Sorr' said the chief, a broad Irishman, 'if it wuz in the bilges you'd smell it from up here'.

'Well, anyway, go below and check it please' I told them. They left the bridge a most unhappy pair.

Some 30 minutes later a very red-faced chief reappeared on the bridge. 'Sorr, the fuel is in the bilges'

'How come chief?'

A fuel cock which should have been closed wasn't. The fuel had simply run out into the bilges.

'You've got centrifugal separators. You can run the contents of the bilges through the separators. You won't get all the fuel back but you'll get a lot of it – and we'll get to Gan comfortably. I'm not recalling that tanker!'

Crestfallen, the chief stoker went back down below. The aviator knew much more about his ship then they'd given him credit for, and that, obviously, hadn't been a great deal.

Once at Gan we refuelled and then set sail for a stint on the Beira patrol. This was the rather tired remnant of Harold Wilson's response to Rhodesia's Unilateral Declaration of Independence (UDI) in the mid-60s. I'd first done a spell in *Eagle* in 1966, described in Chapter 18.

We were passing the Seychelles when we were ordered to forget Beira for a while and divert to the Seychelles. We were only too happy and spent a wonderful two weeks there; it's a particularly attractive place and we were treated to their incredible hospitality at all manner of functions. It was a splendid visit after our long passage from Singapore, and something to look back on when we got to the quiet, rather dull period on the Beira patrol, which is where we were sent next. I believe the reason for the diversion to the Seychelles was because our government were about to bring the patrol to a close. Why our stopover in the Seychelles helped this process I don't know, but we didn't complain.

The Beira patrol was uneventful and we spent much of our time at anchor. It was memorable only for the sharks we caught. These were only a few feet long and I knew that if you could get a small shark from the water to the galley and the pan as quickly as possible it was delicious. Shark steak became quite popular. One shark I was glad we never caught was one we christened Beira Bill. He was huge, white and much too wily to take anyone's bait, which was just as well. I didn't fancy hauling him inboard.

From Beira we set sail for Cape Town where we were to spend Christmas. Anticipating a lot of hospitality in Cape Town especially at Christmas, by popular vote we decided to have our own Christmas Day on our way down. The navigator and I discussed whether it might be possible to find an anchorage for the day to reduce the watchkeepers to a minimum. Our track down to Cape Town was through very deep water but there were occasional underwater 'peaks' not too many fathoms down and we decided to try one. We ran across the selected peak a few times until we were reasonably sure we were passing accurately over it each time, then successfully dropped anchor on it and could relax and enjoy the day.

Traditionally on Christmas Day at sea, ships have a Captain's Rounds of the messdecks, not for an inspection as such, but simply to say hello to the sailors. The most difficult thing was to resist the countless offers of beer from the junior and senior rates. I never drank at sea and the ship's company well knew this but it didn't stop them from offering. The other traditional 'must' was a ship's company concert. It's always surprising how much talent there is in a ship's company and how quickly they can put on a show. *Lincoln* was no exception. Needless to say, an amazing amount of mick was taken out of the officers, given and received in good part, and greeted uproariously by the sailors. Then we weighed anchor and continued on to Cape Town.

I was new to South Africa but had heard a lot about the hospitality showered on any visiting naval ship. I wasn't disappointed. The official cocktail party was held in *HMS Devonshire* who was visiting at the same time and with whom I would come home in company. She was a guided missile destroyer, much larger than me and, of course, senior, hence her hosting the cocktail party. Her spacious quarterdeck was absolutely packed with guests who were extremely pleased to see the navy.

Introduced to one chap as the Commanding Officer of *HMS Lincoln*, he immediately handed me a bunch of keys which were those to the annex adjoining his house, which he put at my disposal. He explained that there would be maid service laid on and if, on Christmas Day, I cared to come through the adjoining door to his part of the house I'd be most welcome to spend the day with him and his family. And, throughout our stay in Cape Town, I was free to come and go as and when I pleased.

It was with great regret I had to turn down this generous offer. I had, by this time, collected so many official engagements I felt the only way I could keep up with them was to stay on board close to my wardrobe with whatever rig was required for whatever function, and with the Chinese laundry immediately available. I explained my problem to him. I knew Number One wouldn't be happy staying ashore either so asked if I might let my navigator take my place and he was quite happy. So was the navigator

By Christmas Eve there had been so many invitations received for the ship's company that we had reduced the numbers remaining on board to essential duty men only. Even so, by 2300 on Christmas Eve we still had people coming down to the ship to ask: 'is there any sailor who would like to come and spend Christmas with us?' With regret we simply had to stop responding to all this generosity and hospitality. We had nobody left who could be spared!

After a wonderful visit, and with some regret, we sailed for home in company with *Devonshire*. By this time I was reduced to only five of my eight diesel engines due to major unserviceability, and *Devonshire* was to 'hold my hand' on the long passage back to UK in case I lost any more engines. In the event the passage was uneventful.

We had to make a brief call at Portsmouth before the final leg up the channel to Chatham, our home port. This was my first visit to Portsmouth in *Lincoln* and was another eye-opener in anti-aviator prejudice.

Protocol dictates that every Commanding Officer visiting a port for the first time should call on the senior naval officer ashore. This officer was a full admiral – a pretty big naval banana. His offices were in the dockyard. So off I went wearing my best bib and tucker.

The admiral's first words to me after we'd been introduced were: 'Do you have any trouble handling your ship?' I didn't understand and told him so. He repeated himself: 'Do you find difficulty in ship handling, being an aviator?' Suddenly I switched on: anti-aviator prejudice, and from one of the most senior men in the fleet. Did this chap not know that time, distance, speed and machinery in motion were absolute bread and butter to a pilot? I was shocked at his attitude and simply replied 'No sir.' I was somewhat curt and the meeting didn't last much longer. I came away seething.

I'd more or less quelled this prejudice within *Lincoln* by example. The aircraft carriers I'd served in throughout my flying career had been commanded by senior captains, often non-aviators, who had all embraced aviation readily and with complete professionalism. Yet one of the most senior admirals in the service was, apparently, hidebound in his anti-aviation prejudice. How long must this attitude persist?

We passaged on up the channel and through the Straits of Dover, supposedly the busiest stretch of water in the world. I was reminded of the time I'd flown the First Sea Lord, Admiral Le Fanu, through there low level in a Buccaneer. He was an aviation enthusiast and had roared with delight over the intercom: 'This is the only way to come through here'.

The entrance to Chatham dockyard was through one of a pair of locks well up the River Medway on quite a bend in a fairly fast flowing stream. My Number One briefed me on the problems: the trick was to aim well upstream of the locks until, at the last moment, the ship had moved out of the stream into fairly still water when you could then quickly line up with your chosen lock and move in quite comfortably. This was my first time at Chatham and I made a complete horlicks of it, not aiming upstream sufficiently. I missed the locks, ending up being swept well downstream, had to make a sternboard back down the river and have another, and successful, attempt. To make the episode more embarrassing, the port admiral at Chatham always made a point of coming down to the locks to take the salute from incoming ships. I kept him waiting. I understand I was by no means the first. I took great care not to miss my approach entering Chatham thereafter.

My first lieutenant had come to the end of his tour in *Lincoln* and had been reappointed. Initially we'd taken some time to settle down together but he'd helped me a great deal in my *ab initio* stages and we'd become a sound team. His relief, my new first lieutenant, turned out to be of a similar background to me: an ex boy seaman. He'd obviously been the brainy sort and had gone to *HMS Ganges* for his boy's training. He subsequently entered the communications branch, becoming a communications officer when he was commissioned. Thus we had a great deal in common and were to get on wonderfully well, a relationship which was to stand me in good stead throughout the rest of my tour in *Lincoln*. If he had any anti-aviator sentiments he never once let them show but, in reality, I think we had too much respect for each other's merits – and he had them by the bucket load - to allow prejudice to cloud our judgment.

After some leave, much needed repairs in the engine-room, and other routine maintenance, the ship then started exercising in UK waters, visiting the other naval bases: Portsmouth, Portland, Devonport and Rosyth and generally preparing for our sea inspection at Portland in May.

On our next visit to Portsmouth I had been allocated a berth immediately astern of *Ark Royal* lying at South Railway jetty. Llandaff, the same class of frigate as *Lincoln*, was immediately astern of my intended berth and there wasn't a lot of room to spare either ahead or astern of my slot. I slid in passing close up Llandaff's port side and tucked myself in astern of *Ark*. Within minutes my Number One came up to the bridge grinning from ear to ear and brandishing a signal we'd just received from the port admiral, a rear admiral, whose offices overlooked our berth. It said: 'That was the best alongside I've ever seen'. I was chuffed, as was the whole ship's company who got to know about it pretty quickly.

I hope the port admiral's congratulatory signal eventually found its way on to the desk of the bigoted admiral I'd called on previously but I doubt it would have made the slightest bit of difference to such a dyed-in-the-wool anti-aviator type.

I managed one more congratulatory signal from the port admiral. We had been exercising our gunnery system and had had some obscure and quite serious fault develop which required a spare part in a hurry. We had to go into Portsmouth to pick it up and the Solent was socked in with thick fog. We closed up the blind pilotage team in the operations room and started a completely blind approach up the buoyed channel into harbour. This was a first for me and quite eerie until I got used to it. Monitored by the navigator on his bridge radar, the operations room below kept me informed on the bridge about all traffic coming down the channel, its range and how close down our port side it would pass. Since there wasn't much room in the channel it was always going to be pretty close even though we were ourselves pretty close to the channel marker buoys passing down our starboard side. One by one each reported contact appeared eerily out of the fog practically as it reached our bow, and passed safely clear down the port side.

As we closed the actual mouth of the harbour we broke out in clear sunshine, and going through the entrance we got another signal: 'Bravo Zulu' from the port admiral. This is standard naval speak for 'Well done'. We came up harbour, went alongside, collected our much-needed spare part and sailed again. By the time we got back to the harbour mouth the fog had cleared.

We were in and out of Portland fairly often. When we were out we exercised in the adjacent sea areas which meant sustained periods on the bridge amongst quite busy shipping. In just such circumstances I had my frigate squadron leader, a senior captain, on board one day when I was called down to the operations room to talk to the Portland Operations officer, a friend of mine. He asked me if I'd mind changing my assigned berth when we got back in that evening. I assured him it was no problem, noted the new berth and returned to the bridge.

I forgot to let my navigator know the berth switch. I was so busy that even when he briefed me before coming into harbour (to the original berth) I didn't twig. Thus we went into the old berth in fine style, half astern both, stopped absolutely on the spot, dead alongside, so neatly that the sailors didn't bother with heaving lines – they simply passed the berthing wires down on to the jetty. I had been trying to impress my squadron leader and thought I'd done pretty well, until I noticed him stumping along the jetty. He'd been first ashore and seemed a little put out. Then I noticed the Operations Officer jumping up and down and waving his arms at me from down on the harbour wall. I shouted to him 'Something wrong?'

'Dave, you're in the wrong berth'.

And so, eventually, to the dreaded Portland sea inspection. The procedure for the inspection was that the inspection team, several officers and senior ratings, came to sea with us for a week and watched the ship's company go through a variety of exercises designed to extend us and to highlight any weaknesses in our procedures. We were then to be debriefed thoroughly on what had gone wrong and what was needed to be done to put things right. Then we were to go back to sea to practise until we'd got everything right, re-embark the inspection team and go through the inspection proper.

For my part, the final debriefing of the first stage was to take place in my day cabin where I was to entertain the various heads of department to lunch (at my expense, best steak and wine) while they told me just what rubbish they thought my ship was and what I needed to get done to improve things to an inspection standard. The lunch meeting was going fairly well until there was a knock on the door. I didn't call to the person knocking to come in (as I normally would). I didn't want to advertise the fact that the senior inspection officers were apparently having a whale of a time at my lunch table.

I got up to open the door myself. It was my Yeoman of Signals with a priority signal for me. *Lincoln* was to proceed forthwith for an Icelandic patrol, taking time only to store ship before getting underway.

This was a 'pierhead jump'. It meant MOVE and quickly. I had always acknowledged that a full sea inspection would have been good for the ship, albeit painful at times, but in the circumstances it was with not one iota of regret I had to explain to my guests that the party – and the inspection – was over. The ship was to leave as soon as possible for Icelandic waters and would they please finish up their lunch and disembark. We had a lot of work to get through, and quickly, before we sailed.

They left!

# Chapter 26

## *Cod War 2*

ITALICISED sections of this chapter are taken from the book 'The Royal Navy in the Cod Wars' (Captain Andrew Welch, Royal Navy (Rtd) ), copyright for which is noted at Page iv.

***

I arrived in Icelandic waters in mid-July 1973. Initially I was ordered to join a more senior ship in the northwest fishing area but very soon was detached to go down to the southeast area to relieve another frigate. En route, somewhere off the northern coastline of Iceland, I had my first encounter with the senior Icelandic gunboat, *Aegir*. He had obviously been notified there was a 'new kid on the block', and come to try me out. He closed in on my starboard side to within about 30 ft. I simply stood on, holding a steady course and adhering to the Rule of the Road at this stage. The sea between us became quite choppy and *Aegir* took a large wave inboard along the port side of her upper deck which unshipped her ship's nameplate from a screen and washed it overboard. One up to *Lincoln* and I hadn't moved a muscle! *Aegir* moved away and left me alone.

On 17th July as I came down the eastern seaboard of Iceland towards the southeast fishing area I refuelled from a tanker and listened in to the VHF frequency the trawlermen used. We had it on open broadcast on the bridge. It was obvious that the trawler skippers were a very unhappy bunch, and that there appeared to be little cooperation between them and the frigate I was to relieve.

This was to be my first experience of defending the trawlers and, if necessary, getting between them and whichever gunboat might be threatening their warps, his object being to cut them – an expensive disaster for the unfortunate trawler concerned; both the nets and the catch were irretrievably lost. The defensive manoeuvre of positioning your ship to keep between the trawler and the gunboat was known as 'riding off'. It wasn't in any rule book and there had been no instruction on the best way to go about it. You just picked it up as you went along and as the circumstances at the time dictated. I was on another steep learning curve.

On the VHF net we learned that *Aegir* was the gunboat loose among the trawlers. He'd cut down inside the 12-mile limit, forbidden waters for us, and arrived in the area well ahead of me. I guessed he'd be trying to regain the face he'd lost after his nameplate had been washed overboard when he 'tried me out' on the way down to the southeast fishing area.

Refuelling complete, I took over from the other frigate 2 cables (400 yards) on *Aegir*'s port beam, heading towards the trawler group.

I'd earlier decided that a little psychological warfare might not be amiss. *Aegir* had his warp cutter streamed astern of him, at a short stay until he let it out for a cutting run. I had a length of anchor chain streamed over my stern with the end just below the waterline. It worked. As soon as *Aegir* had seen me he'd abandoned his approach to the trawlers and dropped astern to have a look at my anchor chain. I gently altered course away from the trawlers, he followed me, and decided to play 'chicken' again. He slowly got closer and closer. He had a raked bow which eventually ended up overhanging my transom. This close, from his bridge he was blind to my transom and had no way of judging his distance. In trying to scare me he overplayed his hand and nudged my stern, opening up some plates at deck edge level, well above the waterline. This had two dramatic effects: it cleared the two special sea dutymen from the tiller flat below the quarterdeck (I apologised to them later), and *Aegir* backed off rapidly. Once again he'd lost face and he made off fast back towards the trawler group, now some distance away, presumably to try and exact some revenge and regain face with his onboard media.

I overhauled him about halfway back to the trawlers as a report came in over the VHF net that one trawler had his nets snagged on the seabed. He was stuck fast, unable to move, and a sitting duck for *Aegir* who'd also heard the report. He started a run for the helpless trawler, and my induction into riding off began.

> *I moved into a close mark on his port beam, holding him off from being able to make a direct run at his intended trawler victim. At about 17 knots I passed the trawler at approximately 30 feet on my port side with the wheel hard-a-port, half astern on the port engine, full ahead on the starboard. Lincoln spun around that trawler keeping the gunboat outboard throughout and safely clear. Aegir then backed off.*

I now gave thanks for my variable pitch propellers. They, and the team in the Machinery Control Room, had done me proud.

This incident had several repercussions:

1. *The trawlers went from being a surly uncooperative bunch to suddenly showing a lot of respect for Lincoln. The first sign came over the trawler net immediately: 'Chr…ist, I didn't know an effing frigate could effing turn like that'.*
2. *I was subsequently offered shedloads of fresh fish; on one occasion we were unable to hoist the sea boat until we'd unloaded most of the fish, which had been above thwart level! The donating trawler had had no baskets to spare and had simply emptied several of them down into the seaboat.*
3. *When I returned on patrol in September Aegir was very wary of Lincoln during our first 5-hour brush on 19 September, 4 hours in thick fog. I don't attribute his caution to my railway lines!*

*I had a specially embarked photographer who filmed the whole of this incident. The film was dispatched to the Ministry of Defence and was never seen again. I was later informed that it had been 'lost'.*

That was my only close encounter with the gunboat on that patrol. Although *Aegir* stayed around he was never again a serious threat to the trawlers under my immediate protection. On 27th July I was relieved and returned home to Chatham. I would be back on another Ice patrol in September.

Chatham dockyard appeared delighted to have an 'operational' repair. The dockyard 'mateys', as we had always called the dockyard workers, set about patching up my transom quickly, and very soon I was completely shipshape again.

We spent the next few weeks in or close to Chatham prior to our next Ice patrol and I gave a lot of thought to how best to protect myself should a gunboat decide to have another go at me. My major concern was my stern section: my rudder, my variable pitch propellers, which I now regarded as invaluable, my engine room, and my MCR (Machinery Control Room). Diesel engines may not have been the fastest propulsion unit but their response was great. Under the expert hands of my best team in the MCR, my propellers and engine response were a primary asset and enabled me to match *Aegir* for manoeuvrability. I also had a speed advantage over him. The main difference between us was that he could afford to be offensive, even dangerous, in order to garner press publicity and influence world opinion. I was purely defensive at all times, simply doing the job I was sent up to do: protect our trawlers as they went about their legal business on the high seas. So how to protect my stern?

*Chatham dockyard seemed to be strewn with old railway lines and it occurred to me that, were we to meet again, a pair sticking out through my after fairleads would at least keep Aegir away from my stern. Apart from his strengthened stem, I assessed that the rest of his ship's plating would be vulnerable if he were rash enough to risk impacting what was purely a defensive measure. I was also particularly anxious to protect my rudder and my variable pitch propellers. The latter had been invaluable during July's riding off affair.*

*When I was detailed for my next patrol, I had a pair of railway lines smuggled on board, cleaned up, wrapped in canvas, painted ship's side grey and stowed as unobtrusively as it's possible to stow a package that large in a relatively small frigate. En route to Iceland we refuelled in Loch Striven, and rigged the railway lines, buttressed against the anti-submarine mortar on the quarterdeck and fanned out through the after fairleads: the 'porcupine look', as it came to be known.*

On 16th September I was once again back in the southeast fishing area. This time I had a liaison skipper, a retired trawler skipper, Bill, to facilitate communication between *Lincoln* and the trawler fleet.

*On the afternoon of 19 September, I had arranged a rendezvous with Ranger Briseis to transfer mail for the trawler fleet in the southeast DFA.*

*We were to meet up north of the Whaleback bulge. The whole area was in thick fog. As we approached the rendezvous we got a report from the Olna's Wessex helicopter of a fast moving contact heading northeast towards us. We had trawlers fishing fairly close, east of us, and I decided to lie up 'in the grain' and behave like a trawler while I waited for Ranger Briseis. The fog delayed Briseis getting to the rendezvous, which happened to be in the only small clear patch in the fog.*

*When the contact was still some way off, I got a request to come down to the ops room: a Wasp pilot wanted to talk to me personally. The pilot was an old chum of mine, Dick Ward, and he told me he could see, just above the layer of fog, the yardarm and topmast of what he took to be a gunboat but he couldn't see her hull and wondered if I could identify her from his sparse description. It was Aegir.*

*Back on the bridge it became touch and go whether Aegir got to me before Ranger Briseis. I couldn't let Briseis know that Aegir was coming up fast. It would have given the game away. I had to watch Briseis lower her inflatable, which started crossing the clear patch towards me. Exactly halfway across, Aegir broke out of the fog. I've never seen a hastier retreat but, to my relief, the inflatable reversed course and got back to mother safely. The gunboat realised she'd been duped and made off for the nearby trawlers.*

*For the next 5 hours, 4 of them in thick fog, Aegir and Lincoln manoeuvred in close company – Aegir attempting to get at the trawlers and Lincoln thwarting her every move. Twice Aegir came within a few feet of Lincoln, intent, so it seemed, on causing a collision. He did very nearly hit me. Only my starboard 30 prevented him from raking down my starboard side after he'd deliberately turned into me from close range on my starboard beam. Aegir had a press party and a Swedish TV team on board and this may well have been the reason for close-quarters manoeuvres in fog. However, the immediate effect of the media's presence was that UK shore authorities became aware of the railway track defences. FOSNI approved of this initiative and arranged for other ships to embark railway track.*

MoD, however, prohibited their use, concerned that it could be construed as an offensive measure, and one likely to cause casualties.

I had been on my own in the southeast fishing area up to this point and, in view of *Aegir's* reckless behaviour, thought it prudent to ask for assistance. This was readily provided by my operational commander and that afternoon I was joined by *HMS Whitby* commanded by another aviator chum of mine, Jim Flindell, and by two of the defence tugs who were assisting in defending the trawlers: *Welshman* and *Englishman*.

*On 22nd September, Lincoln and Aegir clashed once more - and once more the press were present. Who can say which is cause and which effect, but in this much more media-savvy age, we expect a certain degree of 'acting up' for the cameras. Even at the time there was a strong belief that Aegir was seeking to construct an incident that could be portrayed advantageously, both to garner international support and to heighten the domestic pressure on the Icelandic government.*

*HMS Lincoln was in charge of the south-eastern DFA and was patrolling the southern end of the area, with HMS Whitby to the north.*

*The weather was good, as was the visibility, and about 50 trawlers were enjoying rich fishing with Englishman and Welshman in close company.*

*Aegir was first detected on radar by Olna's Wessex and then, at 0830, identified coming out of Nordfjord by a Wasp helicopter.*

We'd assumed our usual 'Action Stations' and damage control state, with a dubious bonus – since our weapons were not manned (guns remained covered) the hands normally manning them were available as extra damage control teams.

*She stopped and appeared to be waiting for Lincoln to join her, then at 0915 headed north towards some trawlers, with Lincoln marking. As they neared the first trawlers, Lincoln took up a defensive position and, for 45 minutes, kept Aegir at bay. When clear of the trawlers, Aegir continued on Lincoln's port beam until, from about 30 ft, accelerated ahead and, either intentionally or because of a lack of understanding of the pressure and suction effects, despite emergency engine and helm orders in Lincoln, just caught one of her guardrails on Lincoln's port anchor. Aegir then retired, presumably to brief the media, feed them and prepare for the afternoon session.*

I now had another dimension to factor into my riding off philosophy. Up to this point I'd become increasingly aware that *Aegir* was a sound seaman, prepared to take risks in pursuit of his aim, but never to risk his ship. Now it was apparent he would do just that to give his onboard press and TV the scoop they wanted.

I had to be prepared for a deliberate ramming, and by an opponent who had a strengthened stem.

*At 1445 the performance resumed, with Whitby now also in company. Aegir made for the nearest trawler and Lincoln marked from the up-threat bow. Aegir came up on Lincoln's starboard beam, slowed down, and Lincoln sounded 'Uniform'(the International Code for 'you are coming into danger'). At about 50 ft, Aegir turned to port and hit a nearly stationary Lincoln hard amidships at 1504. An hour later, after another session of close marking and riding-off, a similar situation developed with Aegir on Lincoln's port beam at about 100 ft. Both ships had just altered to port at 12 knots, when, Aegir having steadied up first, she suddenly turned starboard and hit Lincoln amidships. Harassment attempts and riding off by both frigates continued for another two hours.*

*As so often during both the Second and Third Cod Wars, both sides could argue that they had right of way, but in reality the Rule of the Road was irrelevant because no professional seaman would have got himself into such close quarters in the first place, unless he had very good reason to. Plainly both could have avoided collisions had they given up on their aim – in Aegir's case to harass trawlers and gain good publicity and in Lincoln's to protect the trawlers from warp cutting.*

*The TV crews were busy throughout; there was a second crew overhead in a Coastguard Fokker Friendship from 1445-1630, surely a further indication that this was a deliberate attempt to garner publicity, in which it succeeded. The airborne film, grainy and disjointed as it was, was shown on Icelandic television where it demonstrated, to those who were already wishful believers, 'proof of the British frigates' policy of ramming gunboats'.*

I reflected that my learning curve in ship handling had become pretty steep during this episode. We went into these close quarters situations (as all 'riding off' encounters must be) as fully prepared as we could be – Special Sea Dutymen (our best team) closed up, at the highest Damage Control State of preparedness, with the additional bonus of having extra manpower available because our weapons were not manned.

Now we were in a different ball game. Not only was I riding off to protect my trawlers, I had my ship and ship's company to protect. My hull integrity was of paramount importance.

My most vulnerable points were all well aft. If *Lincoln* had - God forbid – to be rammed, where and how to take the blow?

It had to be somewhere forward. I decided on the flag deck area: my maximum freeboard (deck height above the water line). Anywhere aft of the break of the fo'cs'le would mean *Aegir*'s bow could, and twice did, overhang my ship's side. If he came inboard the damage could be catastrophic. My flag deck was the same height as *Aegir*'s bow and that strengthened stem. If I had to, I'd try and take him there, avoiding direct head on impact from that strengthened stem.

How to take the blow? First, in what little time I might have, I had to get on to as nearly the same heading as the gunboat; it had to be a ship's side to ship's side impact. At the same time I had to adjust my speed so as to be as close to that of the gunboat as possible, to prevent her raking along my side and spreading the damage.

In both of the collisions that afternoon I managed to turn a deliberate ramming attempt into an unavoidable but serious collision. *Lincoln* was a little bent but otherwise intact.

Thankfully there were no more ramming incidents, and no trawler lost their warps during the entire day's operations.

During these 'riding off' episodes my Liaison Skipper, Bill, had been invaluable. He knew all the trawlers and their skippers personally.

Whereas during my earlier patrol without him, communication between *Lincoln* and any trawler during 'riding off' confrontations had been by my Principle Warfare officer on the VHF radio net e.g.: 'Trawler fine on *Lincoln*'s starboard bow please move away to starboard'. Bill was now on the radio and would simply say: 'Eh up Charlie, f--- off to starboard'. The trawlers response was immediate.

We 'lost' Bill one day after we'd been given yet more fresh fish by another generous trawler. No1 had searched high and low for him and was getting worried – a man overboard in these waters couldn't have survived very long, and Bill was not a young man either. I had a feeling I might find him and went below to the main galley. There he was tucked away in a corner, happily filleting cod. He'd borrowed one of the chefs' knives, honed it to razor sharp, and was filleting cod for them. It was a delight to watch. He put his knife down behind the gills, sliced right down to the tail in one stroke and lifted the fillet. He then turned the fish over and repeated the process. Thus in two deft strokes he'd reduced a very large cod to its skeleton, attached to the head, and two perfect fillets. Nothing at all was wasted. I could have spent a good while watching his artistry but had to get back to the bridge.

On 24th September my patrol finished and I was to come home but for a Force 10 storm which blew up. In view of my collisions MoD was concerned about my hull integrity and I was advised to heave to and sit out the storm, rather than take passage through what promised to be very heavy weather.

Once the weather abated I then set course for home on an uneventful passage except for an encounter with a Soviet satellite tracking ship which made a bee-line for me, presumably having heard about the collisions and keen to get a few photos. I ordered four engines a side and outran her before she could get anywhere near me.

Coming home we did everything we could to improve the ship's appearance which was looking a trifle tired after a pretty tough period at sea. I had a chat with the shipwright to see whether he could do anything to cover up at least one of our dents, our plan being to use large sheets of plywood and then paint them ship's side grey. My only problem was which side? The shipwright had only enough plywood to cover one side's dent. I had to make a guess: port or starboard. I opted for the port side since this had been the side I'd presented to the port admiral each time we'd gone into Chatham. Chippy made a pretty good job and after it was painted I was certain we would make a good showing as the admiral took the salute when we locked in.

The other, most important part of our appearance was the two railway lines still projecting from the after fairleads and which, thanks to the press, had gained some notoriety. The first lieutenant had told me there was a strong feeling amongst the ship's company that we should keep them shipped but smarten them up and he had many volunteers (including my supply officer!) willing to crawl out along them with a pot of paint and 'tiddely' them up. The ship's company had also produced a huge white banner to hang between the ends of the railway lines just before we locked in. On it they'd painted, in large red letters, 'Lincoln Junction'. I agreed we could enter the lock with it in place.

As we approached the Chatham locks we were ordered to use the starboard lock. This meant I'd guessed the wrong side and a very large, rusty dent would be presented to the Admiral as he took our salute! In the event all eyes were on the railway lines and the banner. The Admiral was almost doubled up with laughter and thoroughly approved.

This was quite a homecoming! My ship's company were, to a man, feeling 10 ft tall. They were extremely proud of their ship and what they'd achieved up in Iceland, yet again, and I doubt they ever bought their own beer when they went ashore! – a status they well deserved. They'd done me proud.

As we'd passaged home I'd received quite a long signal from the Ministry of Defence advising me that there would inevitably be a press conference as soon as we'd arrived back. *Lincoln* had received a lot of TV, radio and newspaper publicity on this patrol, because of our railway lines, the two major collisions and the nearest of near misses with *Aegir*. MoD also provided a list of likely questions I'd get from the press and suggested the sort of answers I might care to give. There was no pressure on me to stick to what they advised but it seemed prudent to use the help offered and I was grateful for it.

Sure enough, almost as soon as we'd berthed, the press swarmed on board and were shown up to my day cabin together with the deputy leader of my frigate squadron, a captain, and the officer who drafted my confidential reports for the squadron captain to approve and sign.

I soon realised the MoD were on the ball with their anticipated questions and I duly gave the suggested answers they'd provided me. To the best of my memory there were no low fast balls. I quickly became aware that some of the members of the press were getting fed up with what, they thought, were stonewalling replies to their many questions. They were after something sensational – and I was not about to give it to them! Finally the Daily Express reporter expressed his disgust by chucking his pencil across my desk and looking daggers at me: he'd come for a scoop and wasn't going to get one. This more or less brought the meeting to a close and they started to file out of my cabin.

As they went the captain in attendance leaned over and said quietly in my ear: 'I suppose you think you're going to get the OBE for that Howard'.

Apart from welcoming this captain aboard for the press conference I'd never met or spoken to him before. His obvious antipathy, even hostility, towards me was quite a shock, and totally unwarranted. Suddenly it struck me: this was anti-aviator-prejudice again – and this was the officer who wrote my confidential reports! I was horrified – and helpless. I could only respond with the truth: that I'd never given such a thing a thought, I was just doing the job I was sent to do. I then saw him off the ship.

I discussed this incident with my first lieutenant later and he explained some of the antipathy I'd experienced. In addition to the reputation *Lincoln* had gained on Ice patrols, apparently every time we entered or left harbour, if he was in Chatham, the deputy leader would be on his upper deck, telescope to his eye, checking that every detail of our appearance was top notch. It was part of Number One's job to ensure that it was and he never let me down. We were never picked up once for our appearance and that must have rankled with a fishhead. I obviously had a senior officer antipathetic to me and to *Lincoln*. Judging by his remark about an OBE – very anti!

Another incident worried me rather more. Shortly after the press conference I was visited by a constructor lieutenant – one of the technical specialisations concerned with ship design, construction, and hull and equipment integrity. I welcomed him aboard and he explained that it was his department that had advised that I heave to and ride out the Force 10 storm just before I left Icelandic waters for home. He then asked me to come down to the starboard waist with him to the seaboat's davits. He was carrying a paint scraper with him – a large piece of naval kit which was basically a two-inch wide flat metal bar with a right angle bend for about two inches at one end. Each end was sharpened into a scraper edge. Immediately abreast the after boat's davit he applied the scraper to the freshly painted deck (Number One's tiddelying up before entering harbour!).

The constructor lieutenant dragged the scraper through the paintwork down to bare metal, exactly straddling a crack in the deck plating. 'That's why we asked you to heave to and ride out the storm Sir. It's a weakness in this class and they always show it in that position'. Quite shaken, I expressed my surprise, and thanked him for demonstrating so graphically why MoD had been concerned about *Lincoln*.

# Chapter 27

## *Hull*

CHATHAM dockyard mateys once again set to work on *Lincoln*, now having more serious damage to make good: a major dent on either side below my flag deck. They wasted no time even though one collision had displaced major communications equipment internally. Within roughly a week we were repaired. I had asked the chefs to make a large 'thank you' cake to present to the workers on completion and this was presented to them on the bridge together with a glass of champagne and a short speech from me.

It had occurred to me that a crowd of dockyard mateys might not know what to do with the enormous amount of cake remaining after they'd all had a generous piece. I suggested to them that they might like to present it to a local children's home. This was well received and our thank you was much appreciated.

During that week the fleet operations officer called me. Due to our enforced stay for repairs in Chatham we'd missed a scheduled visit abroad. Where would we like to go for up to a four day visit instead? Four days was all that could be spared before our next assignment. I asked him if he had any suggestions and he immediately came up with Hull. 'You could meet up with those trawlermen you've been protecting'. This suggestion was a great idea and I immediately agreed. And so we went to Hull – not too far up the east coast from Chatham.

As is the tradition, on the first night in Hull we gave a cocktail party in the wardroom. This was, of course, with the agreement of the First Lieutenant who was the president of the wardroom mess; the captain only goes down to the wardroom by invitation. As always, Number One was only too willing. The cocktail party was a golden opportunity for the officers to mix with and get to know the locals and was invariably well received by those locals. The wardroom could hold about fifty guests and, with the ship's officers, made for a cosy, if a little crowded, gathering. It was left to the civic authorities to make up the guest list.

The party was going with quite a swing. *Lincoln's* reputation on Ice Patrol was well known locally and the ship was a popular visitor. The fleet operations officer had got it absolutely right. About halfway through the party Number One introduced me to a very pleasant chap, the manager of a local night club. He very kindly invited me and all my officers to be guests at his club after the cocktail party. He explained that the club had several bars, restaurants and a large dance floor. We would be offered dinner and could drink whatever we wanted whenever we wanted – all on the house. From Number One's expression I could see that the manager had been working on him at some length beforehand, and that Number One was willing me to say Yes. I thanked the manager for his generous invitation and said we'd all be delighted to come. The manager and Number One were beaming as they moved away to circulate. A few minutes later Number One was back with the manager: would I mind if we all came in uniform? I most certainly would mind and with great regret had to refuse: we just didn't go ashore in uniform any more, not least because of the security aspect; we could attract a whole lot of trouble. The manager was visibly disappointed but again moved away with Number One, only to return after another short interval: could I possibly reconsider please? Number One was obviously hopeful and the manager made it easier by offering to ensure that taxis would take us from the ship straight to the club and bring us straight back to the ship afterwards. Reluctantly I relented and the manager went away elated.

I had a quiet word with Number One: the club would be the only port of call for us that evening; please make sure that every officer understood, and also that I was uneasy about things, play it cool. I had no doubts about any of my officers but I was worried that some of the locals might start trouble if they spotted our uniforms.

We were already 'scrubbed up' and in our best uniforms so going ashore after the cocktail party was no problem: straight into the taxis and then straight into the club, where we were looked after like kings and all had a wonderful time.

My worries had been groundless. What I'd overlooked was our reputation in a fishing port. The manager knew what was going to happen: a great many of the predominantly young people in the club that night wanted to see us, even stopped us in the street as we crossed the pavement to the club entrance. 'Were we from the visiting ship which had been up in Iceland with their trawlers?' They were really interested and asked a lot of questions. Hull was a fishing community, these youngsters were part of that community and keen to get to know us. I left that club with a great deal of respect for the young people of Hull, and for that club manager. He knew his clientele but had really had to twist my arm to agree to us wearing uniform ashore, and in a night club to boot!

Soon after that evening all the officers received an invitation to visit the fish market. We were amazed at the speed of the transactions as well as the fancy footwork of the auctioneer as he moved from the top of one pile of boxes full of fish to the next. Even more impressive were the filleting ladies. Their speed and dexterity were a joy to watch and there appeared to be not a vestige of wastage on the skeletons remaining after only two skilful passes with knives so sharp you could have shaved with them. My liaison skipper up in Icelandic waters, Bill, must have had lessons from them.

In return for this visit we asked the trawler skippers aboard for a drink. They had asked if they could come at 10.30 am which seemed to us rather early to start drinking but we'd heard the trawlermen could put it away so agreed. We waited for them to arrive but no one turned up - until midday, the whole group of them, and all three sheets to the wind. They piled down into the wardroom and quickly got stuck into the whisky, and chatted and drank, and chatted and drank, and chatted and drank, with no apparent effect considering the state they'd arrived on board in.

By about 1.45 pm Number One and I had been exchanging anxious glances for some time. There was no sign of our guests leaving, none of the officers had had a chance to eat, I certainly had had more whisky than I was used to, and I had an official dinner to go to that evening. I needed food and rest: and I was in danger of being drunk under my own wardroom table. I was aware that Number One felt the same way. And there appeared to be no relief. The trawlermen were hard at it and looked set for the afternoon.

The wardroom armchairs were covered in the standard, rather shiny red leather and some of our guests were using them, including the senior trawler skipper. He got us out of our troubles by simply sliding off his chair on to the deck, prostrate, and blind drunk. There had been no warning. One moment he had been chatting away and drinking. The next he was out like a light and horizontal on the deck. For the rest of the trawlermen this was, apparently, the usual way they ended a party.

Two of the trawlermen stood up. 'Great party, skipper' they said to me, and then picked up the prostrate senior skipper, slung him between them, an arm round each of their necks, staggered out of the mess and up on to the upper deck to the gangway. The rest of the skippers followed suit, thanking me as we saw them over the gangway in the wake of their two senior mates still dragging their unconscious chum between them. Presumably they all went off to the nearest pub. The amount of liquor they'd consumed on board had been prodigious. Heavens only knows how much they'd had before they arrived, or had after they left.

On our final evening before leaving Hull I had to attend an official function and was clearing up a bit of paperwork in my day cabin prior to getting showered and changed to go ashore. There was a knock on my cabin door and, with noticeable pleasure, the duty officer ushered in a very attractive young lady: 'Miss X sir'.

I offered Miss X a seat and a drink; fixed the drink and asked her what I could do for her. She explained that the manager of the night club had sent her. No further explanation, and I was too thick to understand. I told her I was about to get ready to go ashore to an official function so we chatted for a few minutes, had a second drink and then I apologised but said I'd have to bid her Goodbye. I escorted her along to the gangway, saw her safely over the brow and into a taxi before going back to my cabin to finish my drink and then jump into the shower. Very soon there was another knock on the door. It was the duty officer again, rather anxious.

'Where's Miss X sir?' I explained I'd just seen her off the ship; I had a function to attend. The duty officer was crestfallen. 'Do you realise, sir, the club manager sent her along as a Thank You for letting us go to the club in uniform the other night?' The penny at last dropped. The duty officer must have thought his captain was pretty green.

'Do you know where she lives sir?' During our brief chat she'd mentioned the area of Hull she lived in. I said that was all I knew, except for her name of course. 'Would you mind, sir, if I got in touch with her? I'd like a date, and if you don't mind I could get someone else to stand my duty for me – assuming I can get in touch with her'.

I wasn't sure about the propriety of this situation but this was one of my best officers – look after your assets! I had a shore telephone on my desk together with a local directory. I looked up the girl's surname and, sure enough, found her listed in the area she'd mentioned. I reckoned she'd just have arrived home from leaving me in a taxi, so called the number. She answered immediately. I explained who I was and she was quite surprised to hear me again. I said I had a duty officer beside me who'd like a word with her. 'Would she mind?' She didn't mind.

Having set my duty officer up, in my cabin, on my telephone, I retired to my sleeping cabin to let him arrange his assignation in private. My duty officer then thanked me profusely.

I never saw him again until the following morning. He'd obviously had a very enjoyable night. He thanked me again – profusely!

# Chapter 28

## *Denmark*

THE ship was scheduled to visit a small Danish fishing port, Kolding. To get to Kolding involved transiting the Kiel canal. The canal runs from Brunsbuttelkuge on the Elbe estuary up to Kiel and into the southern part of the Kattegat, and you require a pilot for the transit. To get into the canal you lock into massive locks capable of dealing with much larger vessels than *Lincoln*. There was no cross-stream flow (as at Chatham) to contend with either. After Chatham, locking in there was no problem. Before we started up the canal we embarked the pilot, a pleasant young German officer.

A canal can present a problem if you get too close to the side. The ship's movement creates an area of low pressure along the ship's side and this can suck you in towards the bank. The pilot instructed me to keep well out towards the middle, which was fine until you met traffic coming the opposite way down the canal. It meant passing what looked like impossibly close to the opposing vessel and it took much urging by the pilot ('keep up tovards ze middle plees') to get *Lincoln* sufficiently close to the middle to satisfy him. Only after we'd safely passed several ships as large as, or larger than *Lincoln* did I begin to have confidence that, notwithstanding the low pressure suction area along the ships' sides, the areas of high pressure at the bow and stern of each vessel would keep the two ships apart. Thus the proper way to transit a canal is to keep well up to the middle i.e. slightly starboard of the centreline and well away from the canal side; and try and relax. I found the last bit quite difficult; in fact after the first few encounters with oncoming vessels I was composing my court martial defence!

Before we'd entered the canal we'd sailed through the Dover straits, possibly the busiest narrows in the world, and up into the southern part of the North Sea, again pretty crowded; I was on the bridge for all of this passage. The canal transit had also required my presence on the bridge the whole time. Thus I'd been on the bridge for quite an extended period when we finally got into the Kattegat. Again it was quite busy but I managed to get some rest before we picked up another pilot for the passage up a narrow channel to Kolding. This was uneventful except that we slithered through mud at one stage. There was an almost imperceptible deceleration as we passed through, and the navigator and I exchanged 'how come' glances. The pilot had assured us that our draft would comfortably transit the channel. He hadn't said we might meet a little mud!

Kolding harbour is tiny, and there was just enough room to turn *Lincoln* in comfort. Once facing back out the way we'd come in we berthed and prepared to meet the civic dignitaries on the jetty waiting to greet us. It was 9 am! My golden rule was never to drink at sea, and my grog locker remained closed, always from the day before sailing, until we were finally berthed at our destination, when my steward opened it. And even though it was only 9 am it was, apparently, de rigueur for the welcoming Danes to be offered a sociable drink. When asked, the dignitaries requested whisky. I, of course, was expected to join them, and did so with some reluctance! Not only was it a bit early for me; I was pretty tired.

Kolding was more than kind to *Lincoln*. The ship gave the usual cocktail party on the first evening and thereafter it was difficult to keep up with all the hospitality offered. It was even more difficult to avoid being caught out by the Danish propensity for toasts – always in neat aquavit, and always downed in one! That was swilled down with Carlsberg lager and then another toast followed. When I queried this custom I was informed that the first and the last toast were always taken in one gulp and when I asked the obvious question, how do you know which toast will be the last? I realised my leg was being gently pulled. However, the Danes all appeared to drink every toast in one gulp and I decided against trying to keep up with them, prudently keeping my responses to sips. Aquavit is powerful stuff for me.

After a pretty aquavit-impregnated and very enjoyable few days *Lincoln* said her farewells to the many new friends we'd all made, and sailed for the UK. Again we used the Kiel Canal with a pilot but, with the experience of the first passage through, I was almost, but not quite, blasé about 'keeping up tovards ze middle'. I never quite got used to how close we passed ships coming up the other side of the channel. We locked out at Brunsbuttelkuge into the Elbe estuary and thence the North Sea and back into Chatham.

Several months later the Fleet Operations Officer told me that *Lincoln* had been voted by the Danes as the ship they'd most like to visit again. Would we like to go back there? Would we! Yes please. So off we went, back up the Kiel canal, no worries this time about 'keeping up to ze middle', and back into Kolding harbour and to our old friends. Again my grog locker was opened at 9 am to host the local dignitaries waiting on the dockside to greet us.

By this time *Lincoln* had two Ice patrols under her belt and I was just a trifle anxious about our reception by the Danes because of their association with Iceland. At the ship's cocktail party on the first night I was chatting to the wife of a fairly VIP Dane, the Swedish consul in Kolding. This lady was British and had been in Denmark all her married life. She spoke fluent Danish of course and I mentioned that I was going to have to make a speech at a reception to be held in our honour in a few days' time. I had thought, with the speech, I ought to try and smooth any anti-British feelings there might be and wished I spoke some Danish.

The lady didn't think there was the slightest problem with the Iceland question but, if it would make me feel any easier, kindly offered to vet and translate an English draft into Danish and teach me how to pronounce it phonetically; there wasn't time to get into grammar. Subsequently I produced a suitable draft and, over several lagers, and many rehearsals, eventually managed a passable effort: in pidgin Danish.

On the second morning of this visit I was confronted with a perplexing defaulter. When I asked what excuse the defaulter had to offer all I got was: 'I don't wish to say anyfing, Sir'.

Junior Seaman Jones: a Captain's defaulter, two and a half hours adrift off leave, was a repeated offender before me for punishment. Jones had love bites everywhere above the neckline; he was purple from the neckline to his jaw, or from his collar to his hairline viewed from the back. Some half a dozen officers and senior ratings in the room were bursting to find out how the youngest and most junior man in the ship had managed to score so heavily on his first night ashore in Kolding. And he didn't wish to say anything!

The First Lieutenant had pre-briefed me on the case, what was uncovered at the preliminary investigations (the accused had consistently said nothing but had pleaded guilty), and the standard punishment. Only offences sufficiently serious were ever passed to the captain (this was a repeated offence); the First Lieutenant dealt with the less serious. With a guilty plea I merely had to award punishment.

We had then adjourned to the 'court', the sonar control room, a small compartment not in use at the time, where a prosecuting and defending officer, the offender's divisional officer, any witnesses, and the Master-at-Arms (really a clerk of the court) were in attendance. I stood at my high, podium-style desk, and the defaulter was marched before me by the Master-at-Arms who ordered 'Off cap' and read out the charge.

Jones wasn't a rogue; just a very inexperienced youngster, not too bright, and prone to trouble. I had no doubt he would develop soundly given time and the right treatment. He was perfectly entitled not to say anything, and he'd patently been told by his messmates that he didn't have to; just plead guilty and say nothing. There was no question about his guilt; his father was the ship's Chief Gunnery Instructor and had happened to be duty when Jones came aboard adrift. Father was waiting for him, gave him a sound clip around the ear and put him on defaulters' report.

I was as curious as the rest of the officers present about the lovebites. Although Jones hadn't 'wished to say anyfing, sir' I felt I had to prise it out of him somehow. I assumed my 'seriously angry' expression, tweaked the peak of my cap down and glowered from under it. Then I picked up the podium and deliberately slammed it back down on the iron deck with a resounding crash.

'Jones' I barked, 'You're bleeding from ear to ear and you don't wish to say anything. Something must have happened?'

Success! Too young to recognise pure bluff when he saw it, Jones assumed he'd made his captain angry and his resistance crumbled.

'It was the girls, Sir'. As soon as the assembled staff heard the plural the curiosity grew, almost tangibly. Ears were twitching.

More barking. 'Girls, Jones. Girls. More than one?'

'Yessir', as if it were a perfectly normal, even a regular occurrence for Jones.

'How many, Jones?' I barked.

'Only two, Sir' Jones gasped, thinking it might be prudent to demonstrate that he had exercised some restraint.

It was still an orgy! The youngest man in the crew had got himself into an orgy. Jones was suddenly the object of not a little admiration from the staff. How could this notoriously rather foolish young sailor have scored like a tall dog on his first, and shortly to be his only, night ashore in Denmark?

'Two, Jones. Two?' Flabbergasted, I was almost lost for words; I had to say something! 'Both together or one at a time?'

'One at a time, Sir'. Jones obviously thought admitting two together would have been pushing his luck, and felt he ought to play his restraint card again.

'And they gave you all those?' I waved a hand at the lovebites.

'Yessir'

Every man bar Jones quietly wondered what he looked like below the neckline. I daren't ask.

It was now imperative that I put an end to the proceedings. It was becoming difficult to restrain the laughter that was, at the moment, confined to broad grins on everyone's face, except, of course, Jones, now quaking in his boots (what was he going to tell his messmates?), and me, still trying to maintain my 'seriously angry' look.

Jones' punishment was predetermined before we started and, although he was too inexperienced to know it, his messmates would have known, hence their telling him to say nothing. The ship's company knew I always stuck to the Green Guide, a Fleet recommendation for what punishment to award for what offence. I didn't have to think about it, just get Jones out of there quickly before somebody exploded into laughter, possibly me.

'Fourteen days stoppage of leave and pay' I decreed.

'On cap. About turn. Quick march' ordered the Master-at-Arms hurriedly. Jones went.

It was some time before we were sufficiently composed to deal with the next defaulter; and the Danish vampires from the bacon factory on the dockside opposite *Lincoln* would have to find fresh prey that night.

My speech in pidgin Danish was very well received at a reception a few days later, held in the equivalent of their town hall. The reception could only adequately be described as a banquet. Open sandwiches seemed to be a speciality, loaded with smoked salmon, and gravadlax. It hardly needs telling but aquavit and Danish lager flowed freely, with the usual Danish 'down in one' toasts, and many of them. This time I was careful with the 'when will be the last toast' question and was in no danger of getting caught out, managing to sip when all the Danes appeared to be gulping

The bacon factory vampires didn't appear again and I certainly never noticed any more of my ratings 'bleeding from ear to ear'. One young Danish chap, Mrs Swedish Consul's nephew, went to the assistance of some of my sailors ashore who'd been set upon by a gang of the local youngsters, probably because the sailors were too popular with their local girls. The unfortunate gallant young Dane received a dreadful black eye for his troubles, from one of his own countrymen! However, that young man did illustrate the depth of the goodwill towards *Lincoln* generally.

The visit was another success and we finally sailed having strengthened even further the bonds of friendship we'd formed on our first visit. We again transitted the Kiel Canal, exited from Brunsbuttelkuge, into the Elbe estuary, the North Sea and back to Chatham.

During the passage home No.1 notified me that there was a deal of pornographic literature now on board, there being any amount of it freely available in Denmark. The ship's company had bought it just as freely. We were aware that Customs were hot on confiscating anything of this nature, and worried that they might institute some kind of proceedings against offenders caught with such material in their possession. I discussed the matter with Number One and we agreed that I should use the ship's broadcast and have a 'dutch uncle' chat with the crew. I told them of my concerns and ended by saying: 'I've never cared to talk about women, read about them, or look at pictures of them, naked and posing provocatively. I'm a player, not a spectator'.

Not one of the ship's company was picked up with porno literature. There may have been a trail of it in our wake after my chat; I'll never know. I was just relieved they got the message!

# Chapter 29

## *Flagship Lincoln*

AMONG the several duties *Lincoln* was detailed for in the next few months one was to be the flagship for the Flag Officer Scotland and Northern Ireland (FOSNI). He wanted to tour his command which covered a pretty large area and needed a ship to take him. *Lincoln* had the privilege. This FOSNI, a Rear Admiral, had been my operational commander when I was up on Ice patrols, he well knew *Lincoln*, and we'd met in Rosyth, his base headquarters, at a reception he gave and to which he kindly invited me.

I immediately took to this admiral and I like to think he took to me. I'd been a bit of a maverick on Ice Patrol and he'd had to administer the very gentle slap across the wrist over not informing anyone about my railway lines. But he'd approved of my initiative and, indeed, had requested railway lines for the rest of current and future patrol ships. I guessed that, although he could never tell me, he also approved of *Lincoln*'s conduct with *Aegir*. I would also conjecture that the admiral had protected me from not a little flak from MoD. I was just grateful to him for his operational control, direction and restraint when I was in the thick of things with *Aegir*. He was the sort of guardian angel that inexperienced ship commanders like me needed when the chips were down. He also would have been well aware that there were no rules written about riding off gunboats and, accordingly, ship commanders had to play every confrontation 'by ear', dependent entirely on the circumstances they found themselves faced with at the time, the ship-handling response of their command, their ability to use that response to maximum advantage, and the team they lead. I could be flattering myself but I think the admiral had a bit of a soft spot for *Lincoln*. Possibly that was the reason she was chosen to be his flagship for the tour of his parish

The only problem when you have an admiral embarked is that courtesy demands that the Commanding Officer vacates his cabin for the senior officer. I then moved into Number One's cabin, the only other cabin equipped with intercom with the bridge and which a Commanding Officer has to have available. Eventually, after several officers had 'rolled over', somebody took the bunk in the sickbay. In the event the admiral only used my accommodation during the day. Evenings he went ashore, met up with his wife and they spent the night with friends or in an hotel.

We started the admiral's tour of his command in Oban and then covered four other stops, three in the islands and one more on the mainland west coast. At all these places we gave a cocktail party to which all the local dignitaries were invited, made their number with the admiral and appeared to enjoy themselves greatly.

I had a golden rule at cocktail parties. *Lincoln*'s wardroom could only accommodate about fifty guests and I tried, usually successfully, to get to know every guest's name before they left. I was only thrown once. In the Kyle of Loch Alsh we had six couples named Macrae! One couple were spinster sisters – that was easy. The other five were husbands and wives and I had some difficulty with them, but no one seemed to mind – except me. I felt a bit of a failure at not being able to bid all of them Goodbye by name.

The tour went well and we only had one mishap. In Skye, anchored off Portree, the admiral and I went in by boat, best uniforms, to make a protocol/courtesy call on the provost. It was low water and the landing stage at the foot of the steps up to the top of the jetty was covered in thick dark green seaweed. First out of the boat, the admiral unfortunately slipped on the greasy surface and went flat on his back. I spent the first few minutes picking strands of wet seaweed from him; luckily he hadn't hurt himself.

We soon found the provost's house and knocked on a huge, centuries old, oak door. But the provost appeared from around the side of the house, in full highland regalia, and let us in. He sat us down, fixed us up with the traditional malt whisky, and apologised for his wife who was out but would soon be back. A large collie type dog then appeared. Its coat was dreadfully matted especially around its rear end, and it smelled appallingly. The provost, a colonel, apologised for the animal ('got something wrong with his back end') and barked at it a few times to get under the piano. The dog just looked blank. Then the provost's wife arrived and also barked at the dog – only once. The dog shot under the piano. The smell remained!

We chatted for several minutes and then got up to leave. After we'd said our thank yous Mrs Provost took us out into the hall. This was square, fairly large and lined on every wall with cages of stuffed birds, from floor to about three feet from the very high ceiling.

'Let's see' croaked Mrs Provost, in a throaty Hermione Gingold voice, 'who can spot Ozzie'. I caught the admiral's eye; we were both non-plussed. When she'd assessed we didn't know who or what 'Ozzie' was Mrs Provost pointed up to a corner. We had some difficulty, discriminating among all those birds, that Ozzie was a live owl. He had a horribly mangled wing. She explained 'We found him and he had this broken wing. We set it ourselves' she said with some pride and sense of achievement 'but he's never managed to fly at all'. I was rather glad Ozzie had never attempted to. Had he done so his maladjusted aerodynamics were such that he would have done what, in aviation terms, was known as a 'graveyard spiral'. The admiral and I muttered due platitudes about Ozzie and returned to our waiting boat, this time safely negotiating the seaweed.

We disembarked the admiral at the end of his tour and *Lincoln* then joined up with several other ships to participate in a maritime exercise to be conducted off the Scottish coast and around the islands.

We exercised in and around the Inner and Outer Hebrides for a few days, sometimes in fair weather and, for a couple of days, in a blizzard. Replenishment from an oil tanker was scheduled and my slot for refuelling was in the middle watch (midnight to 4 am). Being the Junior Joe in the group I had expected this. The senior captains always got the more comfortable daytime slots. I hadn't expected to be refuelling in a blizzard though and really felt for my sailors, having to work darned hard when the snowflakes were coming at them horizontally in the dark. They managed as usual, and had a hot snack available when they finally went below.

I had a supply officer who had been a lower-decker himself and really knew what made sailors tick. He knew that good food, and piping hot food when appropriate, would keep them going for as long and as hard as was required, and, when they'd finished, a hot snack would enable them to sleep. Well-rested, well fed sailors are happy sailors and I was lucky to have a supply officer who never forgot this maxim. The food in *Lincoln* was superb.

As the junior Joe, *Lincoln* was ordered to 'disappear' for four days, and reappear on the east coast to rendezvous with another one of the group and form a SAG (Search Attack Group). I had to avoid detection at all costs and would be hunted by surface and air units.

I shut down every method of transmitting, radar, sonar, ship-shore telephone, radio telephone, no signals, nothing was to go out at all. We were to remain absolutely silent for the entire four days.

Sod's law then surfaced. The navigating officer and a stoker both had wives who were about to give birth. Could they use the ship-shore telephone to confirm all was well? No, they couldn't; but I felt I couldn't let them down. I knew a loch at the head of which was a phone box. I'd used it as a low-level navigation marker from the air many times. We'd go into the loch, lower the ship's boat and they could go ashore and use the phone box. This would also serve as a suitable beginning to *Lincoln*'s four days' disappearance.

Although the ship's company had, by this time, seen enough of me to know that what had frequently seemed to be a barking mad aviator's actions usually turned out to be sound, incredulity from the navigator and the stoker were strongly in evidence. The captain had really gone bananas on this one! However, since I remained adamant: there would be no transmissions whatsoever, they had no option but to accept my word, hope for the best and jump in the boat. They went off, highly sceptical.

While we waited for their return *Lincoln* circled deep inside the loch, and we saw several search aircraft overflying the seaward end of the loch looking for us. We weren't spotted or, with no giveaway transmissions, detected, while we were so vulnerable waiting for the boat to return. The navigator and the stoker were beaming. They'd easily found the phone box, got through to their respective wives who were both doing well, and were delighted to get the calls from their anxious husbands. The latter were very grateful to their barking mad aviator skipper.

We left the loch and passaged up the west coast of Scotland, maintaining our electronic silence. This required the officers of the watch on the bridge to use visual bearings to fix the ship's position regularly, rather then radar which was, of course, shut down. After some initial anxiety all the watchkeepers got used to, and quite enjoyed, this 'old fashioned' style of navigating.

I was worried about crossing the Orkney/Shetland gap when we'd be quite exposed to any searching ships or aircraft. Therefore we planned to transit the gap by night, at slow, trawler-like speed, and burning trawler navigation lights, hoping to avoid detection. We succeeded, and rounding the northwest of the Shetlands, my navigator and I started looking for another spot to hide.

We opted for Blue Mull Sound, a deep water narrow cut which lead down south east through the island group. If we could lie up inside the sound somewhere for a couple of days all we had to do to end our four day 'disappearance' would be to slip out from the sound at the south east end and make our rendezvous. Entering the sound I had deemed it prudent to switch on the echo sounder for our passage across the bar at the entrance – our only transmission throughout the entire four days and, since it only read the depth under our keel, hardly likely to be detected. We had ample water over the bar and once we were through the entrance and into deep water again, the sounder was switched back off.

Some half way down the sound we found an anchorage close up under the east side and settled down to wait. To aid our concealment it started snowing!

We were reported. An old crofter had spotted us, thought we were a Russian ship up to no good, hiding there in the sound, and reported us to the local RAF radar station. They alerted RAF Buccaneers who came looking for us – unsuccessfully. That night we saw them passing the seaward end of the sound but they never came inland and we remained undetected from the 'enemy' forces.

Early the following morning we weighed, slipped down the sound and out into the open sea to make our rendezvous. We'd 'disappeared' for four days.

# Chapter 30

## *Dartmouth*

*LINCOLN* was detailed as guard ship for the Dartmouth regatta. Dartmouth is an awkward place to get into; there's a formidable rip through the bottleneck entrance to the river and you have to time it just right. The aim is to enter late on the ebb tide and moor, in mid-stream heading up river, before the flood gets underway. Arrive late and it could present a problem when the sudden, rapid flood racing through the bottleneck could get under your stern whilst trying to moor in a narrow river cluttered with small craft.

We found a yacht lying in our berth and unwilling to shift. I stopped close alongside him and we moored safely. His yard had just touched the side of my flag deck. He immediately screamed blue murder, but took care to leave harbour in a hurry before the harbourmaster could board him and inspect the extensive damage he claimed to have suffered. I understand he was inspected in Portsmouth some days later and was awarded some compensation. I was told this is a practice that more unscrupulous people afloat will attempt – and often get away with.

My guardship social duties weren't too time consuming. Mary had driven down to Dartmouth for the few days we were there, and we managed to see something of the local countryside, which was fairly new to both of us. One evening we were having dinner in a restaurant in the town. It was only a small place and pretty full. The waitress asked us if we'd mind if someone shared our table.

It was a pleasant young man, on his own, rather full of himself and inclined to chat. Before he'd placed his order he extolled to us the attractions of Dartmouth and explained that he had to keep coming back 'year after year' because he liked it so much. It quickly struck both Mary and me that, with his evident youth, he couldn't have been 'coming back' for too many years; he simply wasn't old enough. He had to be a midshipman at the naval college. He then asked me if I was in the guard ship.

'Yes'.

He started digging himself a hole.

'Was I the engineer officer?'

'No' – pause for effect, but don't let this young ass dig himself too deep.

'I'm the Commanding Officer!'

The poor chap didn't stay for his meal. Well, he had been laying it on a bit thick!

After a few days I had to shift berth and move up to a small jetty further up the harbour on the West side. There would be insufficient room safely to turn *Lincoln* on a normal approach, so that we were facing to seaward, either before we tied up or when we left. The river shallowed abruptly just beyond the new berth.

I discussed my intentions with my navigator. I wanted the ship starboard side to on the jetty, facing downriver to seaward. On the last of the ebb we would approach with the jetty fine on the port bow, let go the port anchor and then turn the ship, on her engines, anti-clockwise, keep the anchor cable 'growing' (laid out) fine on the port bow, and lay up alongside starboard side to. Facing to seaward, the anchor would give us a back-up safety measure to ensure our propellors got nowhere near the mud should there be any tendency to drift astern in the flood when we cast off for our departure.

The navigator worked out our approach and his final position or 'fix' for letting go the anchor.

Late during the approach I was hard put to contain my anxiety, and not to interfere. Directed by the navigator we seemed to be getting uncomfortably close to the jetty. This was what I'd asked of him – and I was getting it, in spades! But I'd given no thought to how this unusual method of coming alongside would actually look – daunting.

On deck the seamen were preparing heaving lines and hawsers for coming alongside and would be well aware this was an unconventional approach. But they'd seen a lot of unconventional, nevertheless sound and successful, seamanship from their skipper and were now philosophical about him – he was an aviator, pilot's wings on his sleeve. Said it all, didn't it?

My Number One kept me well informed about morale and I was aware my ship's company were as proud of me as I was of them. They were a great team and had always come out with flying colours in the many awkward and unusual situations we'd been through. And they were my sternest critics – armchair experts on their skipper's ship handling ability. Their reputation was at stake. This was so not just in this ship but any and every small ship in the fleet. How their ship performed in close quarters situations, particularly coming alongside, reflected on them personally. Any ship's performance was always watched by other ships in the vicinity and, good or poor, word spread fast. On this occasion there were no other ships present but the ship's company would still be as critical as ever

So what was their 'old man' doing this time? O.K. He was a barking mad aviator – they're all barking mad – yet he'd proved he could handle the ship. But this was something different.

On the jetty, besides the civilian berthing party, were a couple in plain clothes. Unheralded, an old chum, also a naval aviator, had arrived with his wife on a surprise visit. He knew the river well, that it shallowed off immediately beyond the berth, way above the ship's draft, into mud – 'putty' in naval speak, and that this presented a problem getting a ship alongside. He was intrigued to see how his old friend managed it, and recognised immediately that this would be no normal approach.

We were heading upriver into the last of the ebb tide, cautiously creeping the final few yards to the point, just short of the berth, for letting go the anchor.

As a boy sailor I had been taught this manoeuvre as one of several methods of coming alongside. Why boy seaman needed to learn such finer points of seamanship I'd never understood, but what a boy learns at that age sticks and that knowledge had stuck. All I needed was a good navigator – and I had one! We'd been through a lot together and trusted one another completely. I'd never tried the manoeuvre but both of us were entirely confident that when the navigator got the ship to the position he'd calculated I could finish the job..

In the event, as we approached along the navigator's requested compass bearing, with the jetty, as ordered, fine on the port bow, it seemed to be getting horribly close. I was willing my navigator to ask for the 'let go' long before we got to the anchor drop point. With difficulty I kept my thoughts – and my tongue - to myself.

As ever the navigator maintained his customary cool. Although I had experienced this, and been thankful for it many times, particularly during Cod War 2 gunboat confrontations, now I found it almost exasperating, but held my peace.

After what seemed an eternity we reached the navigator's cross-reference compass bearing, he reported 'let go, sir', and I snapped out the executive command. We were now in slack water. By restrained use of the engines, slow astern on the port, slow ahead on the starboard, stopping engines when necessary, I managed to keep the anchor cable 'growing' slightly ahead, and we slowly swung round anti-clockwise through 160 degrees to lay up alongside the jetty, starboard side to, without 'cracking an egg'.

The ships' company was visibly impressed. None of them had seen it done before, not even the navigator. But to them I was still barking mad. I was an aviator, even though I'd started naval life as a sailor. The pilot's wings on my sleeve were almost stigmata!

Our departure from the berth went as planned. On a flood tide we eased off the jetty and weighed anchor. The anchor cable was thick with mud, hosed off as it came up through the hawse pipe. The anchor itself seemed to have half the riverbed attached. Once it cleared the water it too was hosed clean, and we went back to sea.

# Chapter 31

## *Gibraltar*

IN early 1974 *Lincoln* was detailed as guard ship again, this time in Gibraltar. I was keen to meet the Flag Officer, Gibraltar, a rear admiral. As a Lieutenant Commander, he'd been my first lieutenant in the *Armada* when I was a leading seaman. I'd admired him then but I'd been warned that he was pretty feisty in Gibraltar. He was a bit of an insomniac, walking his dog around the harbour in the small hours of the morning - and woe betide any ship in which he didn't find the quartermaster and bosun's mate where they should have been: somewhere near the head of the gangway and alert. I'd also been warned that his wife, an Australian lady, didn't suffer fools gladly and could be extremely abrupt.

Another 'must' in Gib. was to call at the naval hospital and ask them to arrange an appointment for me in the UK after we'd arrived back home. I had to get my introductory mess rugger lump seen to (Chapter 25 refers).

The admiral kindly invited *Lincoln*'s officers to a reception and he and his wife were absolutely charming to us all. I chatted to the admiral about our time together in *Armada* and I think he was surprised and not a little gratified to find one of his ex-leading seamen in command of the guard ship. His wife also was interested to know the admiral and I had served together, and she was good company.

I planned to invite the admiral and his wife to lunch in *Lincoln*. Before I issued the invitation I did quite a bit of homework researching whether or not the sort of food and wine I wanted for my guests was available ashore. It was.

I sent out the invitations for a couple of weeks ahead and quickly got a response – WMP - with much pleasure. I then had my supply officer arrange for the purchase (from my own pocket) of the food and wine, and had a chat with my leading steward who'd be serving the meal. He was delighted and was looking forward to the occasion. The meal would be based on lobster as the main course, with a suitable starter and dessert, followed by cheese. I'd managed to track down my favourite white wine to go with the lobster, and a suitable red for the cheese course.

*Lincoln* had quite a bit of time alongside in Gibraltar and this was a golden opportunity to give my Seaman officers some ship handling experience. It was something I'd wanted to do ever since I'd taken command. I'd had no ship handling training whatsoever: there'd been none on my Commanding Officers' designate course. I wasn't happy with this state of affairs and now could at least offer my officers some experience. They were all keen!

Perhaps the most important part of ship handling is coming alongside; there's the harbour wall, often ships ahead and astern of your berth and all watching! And, of course, your ship's company, always your sternest critics, for whom their Commanding Officer's ship handling performance was a matter of pride, or, regrettably in some cases, not. We would be practising coming alongside.

I was allocated a suitable stretch of the harbour wall to set up this practice session on, with a pair of stout catamarans, presumably to protect the wall. I mustered all the seaman officers on the bridge, we had a brief discussion on the ship's handling characteristics, I answered any questions they had and I briefed them on what I wanted them each to do: leave the wall and clear into mid-stream, do a circuit to bring them round for an approach to coming alongside, and then bring the ship alongside. I hoped to give each officer at least two circuits, the second to make good anything that might have gone wrong on the first. The weather was fine and we were inside the harbour mole in calm water, so there were no extraneous factors for them to have to take into account like wind or current.

The session went remarkably well. Some of the officers were a trifle nervous but I'd briefed them that, if everything was becoming a can of worms, I'd have no hesitation in taking over and sorting it out until I could hand control back to them. I never had to take over although we did have one rather hard bump on the catamarans. This was my fault; that particular officer was nervous and a bit hesitant and I'd not wanted to shatter his confidence by intervening. I accepted we were going to bump, but safely, and then explained how he could have prevented it. This was the first time these officers had ever handled a ship, least of all coming alongside. They learned a great deal in only the short time I could offer them, and I was proud of what they'd achieved. They were delighted to have been given such an opportunity.

I ventured up to the naval hospital to see a Medical Officer (M.O.) and ask him to arrange an appointment at a naval hospital in the UK when we got home. I should have known better. The M.O. immediately demanded to see my lump. I had to drop my shorts and Y-fronts to show him and he nearly had a fit. He was only a surgeon lieutenant commander but he gave me, a commander, the biggest bollocking I'd ever had in my life, finishing up with: 'If you weren't *Lincoln*'s Commanding Officer I wouldn't let you out of here until that lump had been fixed'. With my tropical shorts round my ankles and my Y-fronts round my knees, being bollocked by a junior officer holding all the cards, I assessed if I were to ask him to stand to attention while he bollocked me, it might lack the degree of authority I felt I ought to assert! Additionally, by religion I'm a sincerely devout coward and have long stuck to my personal maxim: never upset the person about to wield the knife or the needle on me. It seemed more than appropriate at that time.

He hadn't finished. 'When do you sail?' It was nine days hence.

'If you can get here by 0830 tomorrow morning I'll operate and have you back in the ship the day before you sail. If you can't make that you'll have to stay behind. I can't allow you to leave Gibraltar with that hernia'.

Checkmate!

I had to move fast. I asked for an emergency meeting with the Admiral and explained my predicament. I had to request his permission to turn the ship over to Number One , telling him I had no doubts about his ability to take command. I also had to explain that Number One would be hosting the lunch I had planned for the admiral and his wife. The admiral didn't mind. His only comment about the whole business was: 'You know, of course, Commander, that when you get a lump fixed on one side you invariably get a lump on the other side'. I needed that advice like hole in the head but thought it prudent not to respond, other than to thank him.

I then had to get back to the ship and talk to Number One. I explained what the doctor had insisted I do, and asked him if he'd mind taking command, not only while I was away in hospital, but during my convalescent period afterwards. I told him that I'd informed the admiral

I'd be happy for him to take over and he'd given his blessing. Number One was over the moon. Opportunities like this were like gold dust.

Next I asked him if he'd host the lunch I had planned for the admiral and his wife. I explained that the food and wine was organised, told him the meal I had planned, and was he happy? He was delighted.

Finally, I asked him to come ashore for a meal that evening. I had no doubts about his ship handling capability. All I wanted to discuss with him was what to do if you got into any difficulty; in other words how to make a silk purse out of any sow's ear you may have contrived in coming alongside. We had a great evening and Number One was grateful for the few tips I'd passed on. I didn't think he'd have the slightest problem but would have been remiss if I hadn't explained a few tricks of the trade. By the end of the evening I was content. So was Number One. In fact he must have felt like Father Christmas had just called.

I went off to hospital and Number One went to sea each day, handling the ship immaculately. He had to host a visiting army staff course at sea for one day, in company with another frigate, and managed to beat the other ship in most of the evolutions they laid on for the army.

When I woke up after the operation I was pretty sore, thick headed from the anaesthetic, and lying on my right side (the repair was on the left). The first thing I saw was a single, beautiful yellow rose in a vase on my bedside cabinet. I reached for the card with it. It was from Sheila, the admiral's wife. It was a much-appreciated kindness and, when I returned aboard, I sent her a card thanking her.

When I was up and about around the ward after the operation, with a bit of a squint from a hospital window I could just see *Lincoln* coming back alongside each day. It was copybook stuff and I was proud of the way Number One handled her.

I had a pleasant surprise one morning. Unheralded, the admiral came to visit me in hospital. He asked if there was somewhere more private where we could talk, rather than the open ward but the only place we could have used was the ward sister's office. Reluctant to ask her to vacate, we went into the sluice room for a chat. The admiral was quite happy. Not so the ward sister who was terribly upset that I'd received such a distinguished guest in the sluice room of all places.

The M.O. was as good as his word and, the day before *Lincoln* was due to sail, there was a naval car waiting to take me back to the ship. Unfortunately, before a hernia operation you have to be shaved all around the groin area. One week later the stubble had started to appear. It was distressingly prickly!

I was wearing tropical rig, white shirt, shorts and stockings and had had a very uncomfortable time getting dressed. Walking was a difficult business and I didn't want anyone to see me hobbling along in the agony I'd experienced simply leaving the ward and getting down to and into the car. I planned to sneak aboard quietly.

As the car drew up alongside the foot of the gangway I was horrified to see that Number One had 'cleared lower deck' (all hands topsides) to welcome me back aboard. I think the most courageous and most painful thing I've ever done in my life was to walk, normally, up the gangway, fifty yards along the iron deck in the waist, through a screen door and up to my cabin. Along the route I'd had to maintain a cheerful grin, as I said hello to all the officers and ratings waiting there to greet me, despite the red-hot fire in my shorts.

Once in my cabin I collapsed into an armchair which is where Number One found me, almost gasping in agony, when he came along to see me. He was alarmed to see me in pain and asked if I was OK. I told him my problem, and that I deserved a medal for what I'd just done. From the grin on his face I assessed there wasn't a lot of sympathy around that day. He came back later to report on the events of the week I'd been away. He'd obviously had an absolute ball.

# Chapter 32

## *Finale*

SHORTLY after I returned aboard from the hospital we finally sailed from Gibraltar for home. Number One retained command during our passage up the Atlantic, across the Bay of Biscay into the South Western approaches and up the channel. I convalesced, sitting lazily in my captain's chair on the bridge, and behaving entirely like a passenger. I let Number One realise I had no intention of interfering in any way and was quite content to sit back and watch. I knew the ship was in safe hands.

On the way home we were asked if we'd visit Penzance for their Spring festival. We duly anchored in the bay off Penzance and had to make quite a lengthy boat trip inshore. Nobody seemed to know anything about our visit. It was probably best summed up by one of our sailors who'd gone into a local pub.

'Hallo, Jack, what are you doing here?'

'We've come for your Spring festival'.

'What Spring festival? News to us!'

Wires crossed somewhere!

When we left Penzance I resumed command and we set sail for Chatham, up the channel, through the maritime Piccadilly Circus they call the Straits of Dover, up into the River Medway and finally home to Chatham – for the last time.

I had no relief to turn the ship over to. *Lincoln* was going into Reserve and later a lieutenant commander would take her over until her future was determined. I don't remember all my round of farewells but I did call on my frigate squadron leader, a very likeable captain who'd come to sea with me a couple of times. He recommended me for another sea command.

More memorable was my farewell call on Commander-in-Chief Fleet. He seemed pleased with *Lincoln*'s performance under my command but surprised me by asking how we issued the beer ration in *Lincoln*. I was puzzled and told him so. I also told him each rating drew his beer ration from the canteen daily.

'Did you have any alcohol problems in *Lincoln*?'

'No sir. None at all'.

The C-in-C was surprised. Apparently there were a few alcohol problems in the Fleet.

One up to *Lincoln*! I like to think it reflected favourably on my ship's company. They were a happy bunch, one hell of a team, and we'd achieved one hell of a lot.

Come the day of my departure I said Goodbye to my officers. Number One had again cleared lower deck for me and I paused halfway down the gangway to give them all a wave and say Goodbye. Then I was away; and couldn't look back. Mercifully, naval farewells are surgically short.

I drove off to some gardening leave before taking up my next appointment – Commander (Air) at the Royal Naval Air Station, Yeovilton.

When I was an operational aviator I had always considered that, if ever I was lucky enough to achieve command of a squadron, it would be the pinnacle of my career. In that position I'd enjoyed enormous satisfaction and fulfilment. But I'd never given a thought to a future beyond that stage. It had simply never occurred to me that I might one day get a ship command.

Thus I could have had no idea of the sense of achievement and fulfilment that a ship command might bring, the pride in a ship's company operating efficiently as a complete team, the knowledge that that team could be relied on anywhere, any time, in any circumstance, and the knowledge that the ship's company, every man jack of them, was intensely proud of what they'd achieved.

Nor could I have anticipated the problems that would have to be dealt with along the way, more memorably three deaths among the crew, two of them buried at sea, the ice patrols and the tangles with the gunboat, the collisions, winning the hearts and minds of the trawlers, dealing with the shedloads of fish they presented us with, trying to keep up with their drinking in Hull, and so many more.

The ship's company took everything that was thrown at them in its stride, and came away with another achievement under its belt, something more to enhance their pride in *Lincoln*.

The ship had a "war cry", frequently demonstrated in company ashore after sufficient stimulation with alcohol:

*Ship's*
*Chanter      Company*
"Give us an L":........"L",
"give us an I":...... "I",
"give us an N": ......"N",
"give us a  C":........"C",
"give us an O".:......"O",
"give us an  L". ......."L",
"give us an N":......."N",
"Who are we?"......."LINCOLN"
"Who are we?"......."LINCOLN"
"Who are we?"........"WE ARE THE DRINKIN', STINKIN', LINCOLN".

Bellowed with justifiable pride by a ship's company who often all felt ten feet tall when they got back into harbour, I was no exception. Our war cry was famous in the fleet.

# Chapter 33

## *Commander Air*

I joined the Royal Naval Air Station, Yeovilton, as the new Commander Air on the day of the annual Air Day in 1974. Initially I was to sit in the Air Traffic Control tower alongside my predecessor and watch an Air Day procedure, a useful introduction to my new job. I would take over formally when the hangar doors closed after the show.

Traditionally known as Wings, and as Head of the Air Department, Commander Air was the officer responsible for the whole conduct of the air show from the initial planning, the date, contacting and booking the various display aircraft or teams, compiling the programme, arranging accommodation for the aircrews, their aircraft and ground crews, rehearsals, display timing and, finally, the show itself. There also had to be a poor weather alternative display should the cloud base on the actual day preclude vertical manoeuvres. It was a colossal task and, assuming it went well, a colossal achievement. I was grateful to have the chance to see it all in action before I actually took over.

It was a brilliant show and I realised I had a lot to live up to in my time at Yeovilton. I could expect to be responsible for two Air Days.

One incident marred that otherwise perfect day. An RAF Harrier pilot did a superb display, taxied back into dispersal, and forgot to put his lower ejection seat safety pin in before he stood up on the seat to vacate the aircraft. Sadly he stood on the lower ejection seat handle and activated the ejection seat. In front of a horrified crowd he was thrown a couple of hundred feet into the air before he was killed when he hit the concrete hard standing.

In the tower we never actually saw the incident. The dispersal was just out of our field of view. However, there is a sickening 'crump' when an ejection seat fires on the ground and both I and my predecessor knew what had happened before the unfortunate pilot hit the ground. It was a sad end to a superb Air Day but there was nothing that could have been done. It is the pilot's responsibility to ensure his ejection seat safety pins are in place before he vacates his aircraft; and, unfortunately, activation of the seat occurs in only a fraction of second, as it's meant to.

I was sorry for my predecessor: it was the final few minutes of his tenure and a ghastly note to have to leave on. The Air Day is always followed by a cocktail party, usually in a giant marquee in front of the wardroom, attended by hundreds of guests. It was a somewhat subdued affair, not least for me: I was now in the chair. Commiserations all round.

Initially Mary and I moved into married quarters just outside the wardroom at Yeovilton – Skid Row as it was known – and we kept the cottage going as a weekend retreat. Keeping two homes going proved to be an expensive business – the married quarters rent for a commander at that time was over £1,000 a month, and then there were the normal overheads, electricity, water, telephone, for both places. I also had a mortgage on the cottage. It was too much for us and we decided that it made more sense not to bear the additional expense of the married quarter. We moved back into the cottage and I became a weekend commuter.

We soon agreed that we'd put the cottage on the market and find somewhere to buy down in the Yeovilton area. We started looking and found several very attractive possibilities within a few miles of the airfield. However, we could only buy if we managed to sell the cottage in Wiltshire. I lived in hopes. But months went by and there was no word from the estate agent about any offer so I arranged an on-site meeting with them. When I told them I was rather disappointed at the apparent lack of offers the agent was surprised.

'But, sir, your wife asked us to take the property off the market six months ago'.

Mary and I owned the cottage jointly but she'd not said a word to me. I was the one paying quite a substantial mortgage but it seemed to me that Mary not only wanted to remain at the cottage and wasn't really interested in moving down to Somerset, but that she considered the cottage hers and hers alone. We'd spent a lot of time looking at possible properties we might buy given the cottage would realise most of the purchase price, but Mary had known, almost from the start, that it was never going to happen. She gave no explanation. Feeling rather sick about the whole business I resigned myself to a continual life of weekend commuting. There was no question of daily commuting. Apart from the 50 miles each way, the airfield was usually night flying three nights a week and I was required to be available until completion, although not actually on the airfield.

In 1974 Yeovilton's primary task was the training of Commando helicopter air and ground crews and the parenting and support of the front line Commando helicopter squadrons. The air station's additional tasks were fixed wing flying for the Fleet Requirements and Aircraft Direction Unit (FRADU). Fleet requirements meant mostly providing target aircraft to the Fleet for gunnery practice, and training for seaborne Direction officers. The latter also received training at the air station. FRADU were equipped with Hunters and a few Canberras for the tasks and these aircraft were to provide me with regular flying practice as well as letting me see how my Air Department coped from a pilot's point of view.

The Commando helicopter in those days was the Wessex 5. It was a completely new world to me and I set about doing a Wessex 5 conversion with the training squadron. I had already done a basic helicopter course at RNAS Culdrose so it wasn't all completely new to me – a fixed wing man all his flying career. Even so I found the Wessex 5 an interesting challenge. The principles of helo flying are so different to fixed wing and it required both hands on all the time. Thanks to a great deal of patience and professional instruction the training squadron eventually got me flying solo and I became a qualified Wessex 5 pilot.

I had no intention of pursuing this pastime. It would have denied the training squadron flying hours that were better spent on the squadron task – training pilots destined for operational squadrons. What my limited Wessex 5 flying did for me was to teach me a great deal about Wessex 5 operations and as much as I could learn in a training environment about Commando helicopter scenarios. Even now I shudder at landing in a simulated jungle clearing, with the rotor blade tips apparently only a very few feet from the trees. That is for the birds – literally! The whole experience left me with a lasting respect for helo pilots, and 'Junglies' – Commando helo pilots – in particular..

During my early days as Wings, Prince Charles, at that time a young lieutenant, was doing his Wessex 5 operational flying training in the training squadron. He not only coped with the demanding requirements of flying instruction, but, in the evenings when other young officers under training were able to relax in the wardroom, he had his despatch boxes to deal with. Additionally, Prince Charles was then the most eligible bachelor living and every mum with even a remotely eligible daughter seemed to ply him with dinner invitations. He was a busy young man.

On the rare occasions when Prince Charles had a free evening he would sometimes ask the president of the mess (the Executive Commander) if he might have a drink in the bar and then dine in the wardroom. If any of the officers wished to join him in the anteroom before dinner he'd be delighted to meet them – and their wives if they so wished. My lasting impressions of this pleasurable experience were that I envied him his tailor, and that he was a charming, courteous young officer (he even called me Sir!).

Yeovilton was a fun place to work. I had a splendid team in the tower and each working day got to see many of them at the Meteorology briefing at 0800, which I made a point of attending. Part of the team was my civilian staff officer – Ginger – who'd been doing the job for years, knew all the pitfalls and smoothed my working day immeasurably. I had no hesitation in going off to fly, or to do Rounds, and leaving the office for a couple of hours. The office – and the air station – would still be running smoothly when I returned!

Throughout my flying career I've been lucky. I never lost an aircrew, and only three aircraft - one in each of my squadron commands and the last at Yeovilton when a Hunter's engine failed immediately after take off and the pilot ejected safely. The aircraft landed in a field. I was on the radio in my personal mini and on the scene before the crash crews, to see the aircraft lying pancaked on its belly, its ejection gun prominently and forlornly extended from the cockpit. I'd already been informed on the radio that the pilot was safe so by that stage I was only interested in whether or not there had been any damage to property. Fortunately, apart from a deep furrow in the field, there was none.

Both the Air Days during my time at Yeovilton were successful and uneventful. The tower team and the Air Engineering Department put in a tremendous amount of time in meticulous planning and it paid off handsomely. We put on a pretty good show and the crowds of thousands went away well satisfied each year. The Supply Department also put in a great deal of hard work ensuring that the traditional wardroom lunch before the flying display and the cocktail party after the show were first class. Yeovilton Air Day is an annual social 'must'.

There was an enthusiastic gliding club on the air station and a small hangar was allocated to it. Much of the aircraft maintenance was done by civilian club members in that hangar, which was on my Rounds route. The first time I did Rounds there I was horrified to find a deal of flammable material lying around – paint, dope, and rags on or close to the gliders. The hangar was an accident waiting to happen. I ordered a rescrub – another inspection - after matters were rectified. This greatly offended the club. Wings was the honorary president of the club and my insistence on applying the same rules to the gliding club as the rest of the air station was infra dig in their eyes. Even so, it was my Air Department and they were part of it. They complied.

I was encouraged to glide and even allocated an attractive young gliding instructress as temptation. She managed to get me up to solo but my heart wasn't in it. I had a strong impression that I was being buttered up to take the heat off that very scruffy hangar and their bad safety/cleanliness habits. Furthermore pleasurable flying for me meant having at least one powerful jet engine strapped to my backside and not relying on thermals for lift. I didn't glide much!

I managed quite a bit of Hunter flying. The aircraft were T8s – twin seat trainers – on which I had already gained a lot of experience at Lossiemouth. I even managed to fly several of the ground crew who'd expressed an interest and thus saw the airborne side of all their labours on the ground.

The RN Historic flight was based at Yeovilton and I qualified on the Swordfish. This lovely old World War 2 bi-plane was a delight to fly and I would take it all over the country to flying displays at weekends through the summer

The Swordfish is a three seater. The middle cockpit was invariably occupied by Ben, a burly, bearded Petty Officer Air Fitter who knew the aircraft inside out and did all the servicing during our trips away from base. Ben was also invaluable for navigation – never my long suit – and could guide me around the country using railway lines, motorways, power stations and, once, a Swan lager silo, as navigation markers. We made a good team. The rear cockpit was usually for an additional maintenance rating.

Because the Swordfish cruised at a mere 90 knots sorties were generally quite lengthy and the aircraft was equipped with a urinal system consisting of a funnel in each cockpit connected by piping to a reservoir behind the rear cockpit seat. If we had to stay away overnight the only stowage for baggage was in place of the reservoir which was stripped out, the individual cockpit funnels then being sealed off. This was usually not too inconvenient except for one visit, to an airfield which I will not name. We had landed there after a long trip, to refuel, fly our display and then depart for Yeovilton – some two and a half hours away.

As we climbed away, over the intercom I heard an anguished scream from the rear cockpit number: 'Where's the effing p-tube?' Ben explained over the intercom. that the system had been stripped out to make way for the baggage.

From the rear cockpit: 'Oh that's effing marvellous innit! The loos were so disgusting at that airfield I couldn't use them. Thought I'd wait till we'd finished the air display and then use the p-tube. Now it's two and a half hours till we land. What am I going to do?'

I was having convulsions in the front. 'Tell you what Chief' I said coming to his rescue, 'I'm going to kick on full rudder and we'll skid sideways while you pee over the lee side. OK? Tell me when you're done'.

I just kept my fingers crossed that no aircraft enthusiast had their binoculars on us; the Swordfish attracted a lot of attention. Luckily I had no complaints waiting when we landed.

Other aircraft I flew at Yeovilton were the Tiger Moth, as a re-familiarisation with propeller driven machines before I flew the Swordfish, and the Chipmunk which we used to tow gliders airborne (this became my major contribution to the gliding activity).

I served almost exactly two years as Wings, enjoyed every minute of it and was eventually dined out at a memorable and pretty hilarious mess dinner in the wardroom.

I had been wracking my brains for something special to do for my farewell after-dinner speech. I happened into the Deputy Air Engineer Officer's office and explained my predicament. Without batting an eyelid he went over to a flying clothing locker in his office and pulled out a six feet tall pair of wings. 'Will these help sir?' They'd been the product of a staff inspection improvisation exercise the department had been set and were quite the real McCoy – feathers and all.

Next I went along to see the Commander – the president of the mess – to ask him if he had any tips on speaking in the mess. He told me it was always candlelight and really too dark to read any notes you might want to use, especially as you would almost certainly be shouted up on to the table for your speech and be well above the candles. I went back to the DAEO and explained my problem. Once again with not a flicker of expression, he went across to the same locker and pulled out a large illuminated halo with a small battery and switch which you kept in your trouser pocket. 'Will this do sir?' Darned right it would!

The actual dinner was also a Ladies Night and Mary was beside me. This was her first Ladies' Night with the navy and I doubt she ever forgot it. When the president called on me to speak there were the usual shouts of 'Up,up,up' but I didn't get up on the table. I had the stewards waiting in the wings with a very tall step ladder which they duly brought out. This more than satisfied the cries for me to get up on the table.

I then recounted the tale of my search for inspiration for my speech, my visit to the DAEO and his deadpan handing over of a solution. The stewards then reappeared with the pair of wings and handed them up to me. I put them on and the mess almost had hysterics, the DAEO with them.

I next went on to tell of the Commander's warning about difficulty in reading your notes, my return to the deadpan DAEO, and his producing the halo which I'd earlier attached to the back of the wings. At that point I switched it on. Then the mess did have hysterics. It was some time before I could continue.

The rest of the speech went down very well helped along by an entire side of one long table manned by the whole air traffic control tower team who had armed themselves with numbered boards, 1 to 5, and would all hold up a score each time I cracked a joke.

As I climbed down from the ladder I received quite an ovation which was followed by a presentation picture – a large original Tugg Wilson cartoon featuring me. It's one of my most prized mementoes. Tugg was a brilliant and famous cartoonist and an old chum of mine. He never lost a chance of pulling my leg. The cartoon was no exception!

I already had my next appointment which was to SACLANT – Supreme Allied Commander Atlantic – based in Norfolk, Virginia, USA. I had a few months leave in which to arrange with an agent to look after and let the cottage while we were away in the States, and to pack everything we'd have to take, some as accompanied baggage and the bulk as sea freight. We'd be over there for two years.

# Chapter 34

## *The States*

IN March 1977, the family flew out from Brize Norton in a VC10 – not the most comfortable of aircraft but then apparently the only RAF means available for ferrying service families around. We landed at Dulles, Washington, and then took an internal flight down to Norfolk, Virginia, where we were met by the officer I was due to relieve.

Most families arriving out there for the first time moved into an hotel and then spent their first few days looking for a house. Often, but not always, a family would move into the house of their predecessors and also take over at least one of their cars – you simply couldn't get about without wheels. Although we had one or two reservations about the house, this is what we opted for. We weren't keen to have to spend too long in an hotel with the children. We wanted to get them settled into their new schools as soon as possible, which meant choosing a locality and house quickly.

The 'ranch style' house backed on to water – a creek at the bottom of a garden about 60 yards – the creek opening into Broad Bay, one of the many inland waterways in Virginia Beach which we were to come to love and spend a great deal of time on.

Both Anthony and Katie, eight and six respectively, managed to fall into the creek within minutes of our moving in and staggered back up the garden covered in thick mud. The first impression our neighbours got of us was of me hosing down the children in the garden – the temperature was reasonable and this appeared to me to be the only practical way to clean them up without muddying the route to the bathroom and the bathroom itself. So the new Brits immediately acquired a reputation for eccentricity!

It quickly became apparent to me that we had to get ourselves a boat, and soon. There was so much to explore. We had already been given a boat tour of the local waterways and had immediately fallen in love. It was usual for naval officers to choose small cabin cruisers but I realised that their draft limitations meant there'd be an awful lot of shallow water we'd be unable to explore unless we found a boat drawing only a few inches. The boat I chose was an aluminium hulled Starcraft, sixteen feet long and with a 25 HP outboard engine. Being so light the 25 HP motor would produce some 25 – 30 knots depending how many passengers we carried. If I tilted the outboard until the water cooling inlet was just below the waterline I could run it in water only six inches deep. The family were subsequently to spend a great deal of leisure time in this craft and I did a lot of fishing, including picking oysters and clams by the score.

In the Supreme Allied Commander Atlantic (SACLANT)'s headquarters in Norfolk I started my new job, meeting all the senior officers I needed to call on and generally settling in. My immediate boss was an RAF Group Captain, a charming chap and one I was to car pool with since we lived in the same vicinity in Virginia Beach: Alanton.

I soon discovered that the Brits were known as the 'wordsmiths' in the HQs. When I called on the US navy vice admiral he asked me if I knew anything about anti-submarine warfare. Still wet behind the ears in my new job I said 'Some, sir' and was immediately co-opted into the HQ's new anti-submarine warfare group. Furthermore, I was detailed to write the standing orders for the group. I'd only been in the HQs a few hours!

I'm not a desk man. I'd had two years in the MOD and had learned a lot about staff/service writing – mainly because I had a very patient boss – but had come away all too glad to get out from behind a desk and resume a more active life. SACLANT was not an enjoyable work experience. At that time there were thirteen maritime NATO nations (there are more at the time of writing) and getting a collective decision out of them was usually an agonising long drawn out process. Thus it was improbable that you'd see any return for your labours in your time in the HQs, generally two years, although I was, unusually, to serve four years.

A Brit friend who was more than half way through his two-year tour warned me that, in his opinion, a job in SACLANT was a super job 'outside working hours'. He wasn't wrong. However, I was lucky. Not too long into my first two years I was detailed to organise a biennial maritime conference – Sealink – which took place in Annapolis at the US navy's college there. This affair was attended by four and five star officers and also by the Secretary General of NATO, at that time Dr Joseph Luns. My job was to arrange the two day programme – a series of addresses by the VIP attendees, organise accommodation for them and their staffs, arrange a welcoming cocktail party, fix transport wherever and whenever required, and be the general factotum.

It got me out of the office, and up to Annapolis regularly and I was grateful to someone (my boss?) for volunteering me for the job. I did the job for two consecutive conferences and both functions were a splendid success. The experience gave me an insight into the American way of life. I had to distribute some 400 personnel, ranging from the Secretary General to an Able Seaman, through the variety of hotels in and around Annapolis – deal with the college officials for all sorts of requirements, venues, food, drink, leisure activities. My lasting impression was that, if you'd done your homework and could state your requirement positively and clearly, you got what you wanted. I'm aware that being a Brit also helped and as soon as I heard the standard 'Gee I just love your English accent' I knew I was well on my way to getting maximum cooperation and help. I had no hesitation in laying it on thick!

On the domestic side one of my early ventures was to build a proper dock at the foot of the garden so that I had a sound berth for our boat and the family could get into and out of it easily rather than scrambling up or down the creek bank. This involved sinking half telegraph pole sized piles deep into the mud and then building a boarded platform between them. My wife always described my building projects as affairs you could sail across the Atlantic in or on, and I'd guarantee the dock is still there and in good nick. We certainly used it extensively.

By this time we had acquired a dog. Americans seem not to regard dogs as one of the family but as a status/security symbol, to be kept out in the 'yard' (garden), and to suffer indifferent treatment. This dog strayed into our garden one day and the children immediately adopted it, although Mary and I were a little concerned – the dog wouldn't let us near her for several days, she was so wary of adults. She was a big handsome animal and must have had an unhappy time previously. Eventually I allowed the children to give her some food and slowly she settled down and became less wary of us. We found the owner – who didn't want her back, so the children named her Sheba, and she became one of the finest dogs we were ever to own. But how she hated Americans! We sent her home and into quarantine three months before we finally left, which meant we only had three months to wait before we could get her out and bring her home in England. She lived to be sixteen.

Sheba loved the boat as much as we did and she'd stand with her fore-paws up on the fore-deck like a figurehead, with her ears streaming in the airflow as we shot along at speed. She soon became known as the sea dog.

Exploring the waterways of Virginia Beach was one of our favourite pastimes. There were countless narrow cuts and creeks as well as open inland bays and everywhere along the banks and shores we'd see herons or egrets like sentinels, waiting for a fish to make a fatal move and become another meal.

One of the beaches was what we called 'Brit beach' and many of the Brits who lived on or close to the water would congregate there, running their boats aground in the shallows and wading ashore. A feature of this west facing beach was that you could see bad weather approaching and many times I had to bundle the family into the boat and head fast for home about two miles away. As we scampered up the garden the thunder would break and the rain start pelting down.

All these waterways were tidal, the open ocean being only some three miles from our dock.

Another favourite, purely family pastime was catching crabs, the blue Virginia crabs that abounded in the local waters. We found the quiet spots where we'd discovered they were always plentiful and, armed with 'past their sell by date' chicken legs bought from a nearby food store, and a large igloo to keep our catch in, we'd space ourselves round the boat and dangle the chicken pieces on lengths of line over the side, just touching the sandy bottom. Very soon someone would feel a tug on their line. Gently and steadily hauling in until they could see the crab, below the waterline and still hanging on to the chicken, I would be ready to scoop their crab up with a homemade wire net on a pole, bring the crab inboard and drop it into the igloo. It had to be a wire mesh net – untangling a crab from a string net can be a painful and protracted business. Mary, Anthony and Katie became adept at crabbing and, because they were guaranteed continual action, never bored of it.

When we'd caught a substantial number, small as well as large, we'd up anchor and come home for a crab feast. The bigger crabs we dropped into a large pot of boiling water for a few minutes. When they were cold, using nutcrackers to open them up, we "picked" them, savouring the sweet meat. If the smaller ones were soft shelled we deep-fried and ate them whole. If not they went back into the creek to fight another day. Deep fried soft-shelled crab is quite a delicacy.

I discovered oyster beds in creeks too shallow for other boats and would come home with a big igloo crammed with the large Lynnhaven oysters, too large to swallow in one – you had to chew them. In those days these creeks weren't polluted and you could safely eat the catch. I believe there has been so much development since our time there, each house having a septic tank, that it is now out of the question.

Another delicacy I found was a clam bank. The bank was under only three feet of water and almost at the mouth of the cut out to the open sea, well flushed by the tides. I would anchor the boat, hop over the side and tread for the clams in the sand. Mary's clam chowder became famous.

The fish I caught weren't that appetising. The water temperature was too warm but I solved this problem by building a smoker and smoking them over a charcoal fire. They then became quite tasty and we would offer them at cocktail parties rather like smoked salmon. They were very popular.

During this early part of our tour Trevor and Jenni, respectively nineteen and seventeen, flew out to stay with us. We had a happy time showing them the country, and the waterways we'd so come to love and which they enjoyed too. They had always got on well with Mary who was delighted that they'd managed to get out to see us; likewise Anthony. I regret I can't say the same for Katie. One evening when Jenni and Trevor had kindly offered to babysit for us, once we were out of the house Katie simply screamed her head off in one prolonged tantrum. Jenni and Trevor came away firmly convinced that Katie was thoroughly spoiled. She was, although I didn't realise quite how much at the time.

Anthony had not settled well at any of the several schools we'd tried. Every Brit child was assessed with the IQ of a genius, which is what Anthony appeared to live up to – for the first few weeks, when he got rave reports. Thereafter he appeared to coast, as if it was all too easy, and we had to change schools, to no avail. We were getting desperate. His eleven plus was looming soon after we were due home and he was not going to make it. We had to send him home to boarding school where he settled down and did well. The headmaster had to be good – Anthony disclosed to us that one of the most valuable lessons he'd learned there was how to pour a glass of wine without letting a drop run down the outside of the bottle! Apparently the boys acted as hosts whenever the school held a parents function, and were responsible for distributing the wine. More appeared to be drunk in the kitchen than was offered to the guests!

I missed Anthony greatly when he was away at school, especially on our boat excursions. I had tried teaching Mary how to bring the boat alongside anyone falling out of the boat in case the anyone should be me, or I was out of action for some other reason. She couldn't get the hang of it so I switched to Anthony, eight going on nine years old. He picked up all the safety and handling considerations, quickly becoming expert at getting back to the person in the water as soon as possible (psychological), approaching upwind of them (so as to drift down on to them once he'd cut the engine), and cutting the engine before reaching them (to avoid injuring them with the propeller). We practised many times using a dummy and he was a natural.

I'd let him handle the boat in open water before but now had no hesitation in letting him handle it coming alongside and leaving the dock, and was proud of what I fondly regarded as his being a 'chip off the old block'.

We took a few days leave and did the Disneyland trip to Florida. We had to take the children out of school for a few days which gave us the advantage of visiting Disneyland when it was relatively uncrowded – we rarely had to queue for a feature, which meant we could go once round everything, let the children decide their favourite features, and then go back to whatever they liked best. Small, Small World proved to be their absolute favourite – and ours too.

We also visited a waterways wildlife complex in Florida where the major feature was the indigenous alligator. They seemed to be everywhere, and not too friendly. When we got back to our berth – stern to – I noticed one of these beasts, just nostrils and eyes visible, swim across the lagoon and tuck itself under the stern gangway we'd just walked across. I thought I'd better report it so found one of the staff. 'Oh yea, that's old Fred. He comes across every evening, ever hopeful. Nobody's fallen in yet'.

In the second year of our supposedly two year tour, despite the assurances of a civilian doctor that a lump in Mary's breast was nothing to worry about, a second opinion at the US naval hospital in Norfolk diagnosed a serious cancer. It meant an immediate mastectomy and the hospital phoned me at work. Our world collapsed. My boss simply said: 'Go on leave and come back only when you can'. I went straight to the hospital.

Much later I had to leave Mary at the hospital and drive the 20 plus miles home to break the news to the children when they came home from school. I was forced to pull over at one stage. I couldn't see through my tears.

Mary's operation was successful but she was committed to chemotherapy for two weeks each month, the other two weeks being recovery time from the extremely debilitating effects of the treatment.

Mary's cancer was oestrogen based and, were she to become pregnant again, she could contract more cancer. One of us should be sterilised immediately. We had been asked to meet another consultant who had to advise us on the implications for each of us. He was thorough, and concluded by telling us that it was the hospital's policy to recommend that the partner who was ill should be the preferred choice but that that choice could only be ours. Mary and I discussed the matter thoroughly and, backed by her nursing and midwifery experience, decided to accept the consultant's advice. She went back into hospital for the operation.

Mary showed an incredible degree of courage and determination throughout this devastating period. She vowed to me at her hospital bedside that she was going to see her children grow to adulthood, knowing, with her nurse's background, that her chances were pretty slim. She withstood the dreadful effects of the chemotherapy, managed to retain her hair, and, with her prosthesis, participated fully in all the many social activities, be they full dress dinners or beach parties. She was determined to be as normal as possible. She succeeded. And she was to win herself an eighteen-year remission.

Meanwhile my next appointment was scheduled: I was to be the naval attaché in Copenhagen. A friend of mine was nominated to relieve me at SACLANT. Mary was still being treated by the USN oncologist, a doctor whom Mary had come to like, and to trust implicitly. After not much thought it seemed to both of us that Mary's best chance of a successful recovery would be to stay with him and not have to transfer to another doctor on the other side of the Atlantic. I applied to be allowed to stay on at SACLANT and was granted a further two years.

Mary's mother flew out to be with her daughter at this time. She had accepted that the mastectomy was a necessity. The sterilisation was too much for her. She was a staid, old-fashioned woman who found it difficult to talk about such matters. Her recourse was to wait until we'd gone out for some shopping and then get blind drunk on my gin store. When we returned she was almost legless, but determined to challenge me: why hadn't I had a vasectomy instead? Her elder son had had one and told her it was the greatest compliment he could pay his wife. I forebore telling her that her elder son was a basket case (which he was), and explained in detail how Mary and I had come to the decision we'd reached after we'd listened to the consultant.

I was never forgiven, and this was a bone of contention for the rest of her life. She even managed to convince Mary that I was in the wrong and that it was me alone who was responsible for her sterilisation. It then became a serious bone of contention between Mary and me, although I believe Mary finally came to realise her mother was horribly wrong. Their accusations did untold harm to our relationship.

The harm that interfering old woman caused still rankles, as does the fact that her inability to discuss women's problems had prevented her from letting Mary know that she'd had breast cancer herself as a young woman. Mary would never have continued to accept that civilian doctor's assurances about the lump in her breast had she known.

One of my hazards during this period had been the HQ's Wives club – with an overbearing of US navy wives. With one accord they sprang to the aid of the poor helpless husband with two young children to look after while Mary was in hospital. And their help was to come in the form of food – the man couldn't possibly cook, could he? – and that food was MACARONI CHEESE! - by the barrow load. It was well known that every US wife always responded in this sort of emergency with macaroni cheese. I had anticipated the problem and discussed it with my boss' wife, quietly available at any time if I needed help. She volunteered to act as a macaroni cheese filter and let it be known that all offerings for me should be directed through her and she would pass them on. I don't know where she passed them – I can't stand macaroni cheese – but not one dish of the stuff ever reached me and I'm eternally grateful to her.

Mary put her cancer behind her and got on with life. We bought a small caravan and did a lot of touring, through Virginia, West Virginia, the Carolinas, and up into New England through New York state and into New Hampshire and Vermont. We visited Niagara Falls, crossed into Canada and got as far as Toronto. We flew to Denver, rented a car and went up into the Colorado mountains, staying in a log cabin from where Anthony and I would get up early and go and catch trout for breakfast. Everywhere was eye-catchingly beautiful, and the further away from the east coast we got the friendlier the people got – the preponderance of military in our local area in Virginia Beach seemingly not as warm and open as the people further inland.

One of the HQs duties that I enjoyed greatly was being a regular member of a NATO touring team. A team consisted of four commander level officers from four different nationalities and a team leader, a USN rear admiral. We would have an itinerary of usually about four visits spread around the country and we'd fly anywhere from the deep south up to Chicago and New York, and the east coast to the west. Our hosts were usually a Veteran Retired Officers association and we were always accommodated in luxurious hotels.

Our aim was to spread the word about NATO to our audiences who, quite often, had never even heard of the alliance. After a short introduction by the team leader we took it in turns to give our part of the briefing, usually prefixing it with a few minutes of chat to give the audience time to get used to four different nationalities' ways of speaking. Typically the audience would have to get used to English as spoken by a Norwegian, a German, a Dane and a Brit. In this manner I saw a lot of the states that I never would have managed otherwise, and meeting people all over the country was a lot of fun. I never knew so many Americans had so many British ancestors. One young man even confided to me that his grandfather came from 'over there'. When I enquired where he proudly told me: 'Newfoundland'!

In New York I had two memorable experiences in short order. My hotel didn't do breakfast and I had to walk out, in uniform, into town for it. As I left the hotel elevator two chaps walked by and I heard one say: 'British Airways'. Ouch!

Minutes later I'd found a breakfast bar run by two charming Greeks. They couldn't understand a word I said and I not a word of theirs. This must have happened quite often because, hanging from the overhead, there were dozens of signs each with a breakfast item printed on it in English. By pointing to everything I wanted I accumulated a splendid meal. I was happy and so were the Greeks.

Back at home Mary would probably be preparing for another party. With thirteen different nations in the HQs the social round was a busy one, ranging from cocktail parties, through boat parties and beach parties to full-blown dinner parties. We had discovered the only way we could return hospitality was to hold dinner parties for up to eighteen people at a time. Mary's cooking became a popular feature and she regularly laid on a feast of goodies. If it was a dinner it would be a four course affair. If it were a cocktail party we'd always have a cold buffet table groaning with delicacies such as cold crab, smoked blue fish, beef, ham and stacks of homemade bread. We could never stand the 'polystyrene foam' stuff sold in the shops so we made our own, usually, for a party, in French sticks. When the last guest had left the only thing remaining on the table, apart from empty dishes, would be crumbs!

Our final two years were much, much happier than the first two. Although she had to check in with her oncologist regularly Mary had been given the all clear and she enjoyed life to the full. We made the most of the boat not only in the local waterways but towing it far and wide to explore other areas. Mary discovered Williamsburg, Charlottesville and many other popular tourist attractions, and introduced me to them. We enjoyed Christmas American style which is invariably very pretty if somewhat over the top by our standards, and frequently entertained and were entertained by the many American friends we'd come to know. And so our four years drew to a close.

We crated up and despatched all the contents of our home, moved into that hotel again for our final few days, and finally flew home on my fiftieth birthday – bad planning on my part! Our cottage was waiting for us and none the worse for the four years it had been rented out. We'd been lucky with our choice of house agent.

# Chapter 35

## *The Final Leg*

MY appointing officer had asked me where I'd like to serve for my last appointment. There was a job available in Wilton, just a few miles from home, with a joint services unit based in the Army Headquarters. It seemed to be a good idea at the time so I opted for it. That was a mistake! It was one of the dreariest jobs going and I regretted it greatly. However, I'd made my bed and had to lie on it. I don't take kindly to desk work and this job was all desk work – and hardly challenging. At least I got home every evening.

We worked 'army' hours, 9 – 5 with a generous lunch break. I've never been much use after drinking at lunch time so used to give the bar a miss and get out into Wilton, or sometimes Salisbury, as often as possible. Occasionally we did have a lunch time session in one of the local pubs to say Goodbye to an officer who was leaving. Keeping awake at my desk afterwards was a problem.

The one advantage this job had to offer was, when in my final few months, I started my Resettlement courses, I could be spared with no problem, and was reasonably close to wherever the courses were held, London and Portsmouth mainly. I can't say any of the courses I attended taught me anything that has stayed with me, with one brief exception. A retired army major started his lecture to an audience of anything from 3-star officers down to Chief Petty Officers by emphasising: 'The one thing every one of you has to learn – and quickly – is that the only thing that matters in civvie street is this' and he pulled out a banknote and held it up. He was right!

Through the Officers Association I went for a few interviews for possible jobs. This was another mistake. What was on offer was based on rank and a Commander, rather as in the MOD, was very small fry. What I was offered – and the environment that went with it – was depressingly dreary. I decided that I'd be better off finding myself a job.

And so, on 22 May 1984, the day before my 53rd birthday, I left the service and ventured out into civilian life after 37 years since my first day at *St Vincent* as a boy seaman.

My last appointment apart, I'd been fortunate with every other job both as a sailor and as an officer. I'd been a 'small ships' sailor, a light cruiser the largest, then destroyers and a minesweeper. As an officer and a pilot I'd served in *Bulwark* (Seahawks), *Eagle* (Seahawks first time and later Buccaneers), and *Ark Royal* (Seahawks and Scimitars). As the arrestor hook/catapult carriers phased out I was one of the last aviators lucky enough to have commanded two fixed wing squadrons – one a training squadron, the other front line. I'd enjoyed a full and exciting flying career without mishap and had been accepted on to the General List for a permanent commission quite early in that career. I'd been given command of a frigate and, for most of that command, had been a private ship (operating on my own), and I was Head of the Air department (Wings) at RNAS Yeovilton.

All of these jobs, all of the ships, had been rewarding. The earlier ships, particularly as a young sailor and later a junior officer, had taught me lessons in life, as well as seamanship, airmanship, self respect, self -discipline and self confidence in any situation. I'd left home and accepted that the Navy would take the place of a mother and father. This the service had done – in spades. And I'd come from the bottom of the pile.

I'd collected a few unforgettable memories along the way: action in the disastrous Suez affair in 1956, the honour of being in front of the gun carriage at Winston Churchill's state funeral, bombing the shipwrecked oil tanker, the *Torrey Canyon*, and two Iceland patrols in Cod War 2, both involving serious confrontation with the senior Icelandic gunboat *Aegir*. Many more indelible memories are recorded throughout these chapters.

I was a lucky man; as a sailor my divisional officers had had faith in me and pushed me forward. As an officer I owed a great deal of that luck to four officers. Never having had any Dartmouth training, and aware of many gaps in my background training, I recognised in each of these officers, as they occurred through my career, qualities that would teach me a lot, which I admired, and, if I could, I should develop. They were milestones for me. I have referred to them as my role model officers and I am eternally grateful to them. They became my firm friends.

# Chapter 36

## *Life Without the Navy*

ANTHONY had just finished at Canford and Kate was about to start there. The fees were pretty steep but the service had contributed half – until I retired. Now without the help of that half I had to find some money quickly. I had my gratuity, which wasn't going to see me very far, and I commuted half my pension, which realised the capital I'd need to pay for Kate's school fees for the two years she'd be there in the sixth form.

Since Mary would only qualify for a half pension when I died I also invested some capital hoping to make up the other half so that she'd at least have the equivalent of a full pension.

On both these two major financial considerations I got it completely wrong. Kate's school fees were a total waste of money which I've bitterly regretted, as I have the sums I wasted on her later.

On the second consideration – Mary's pension – that was an unforeseeable disaster. I couldn't have known that I would become a widower instead of the other way around. The money I'd used to 'buy in' for the widow's pension is irrecoverable. Somewhere in the small print all those years ago it said that the scheme would only apply to widows who'd been married to officers at the time they bought in. I only discovered much later that were I to re-marry and pre-decease my new wife, she would only qualify for a pittance. Thus I've paid for a widow's pension but lost that investment for good.

In hindsight I would have been better off not commuting half my pension and not sending Kate to Canford. Hindsight rarely reflects true life and can throw up a lot of regrets, even though what I did at the time I did with the best of intentions.

One further mistake: I had assumed the navy would take care of any medical problems I might have after retirement. How wrong could I get? When my GP approached the navy he was told it would be something like a two years' wait for an appointment and a further eighteen months before that appointment materialised

I had to find a job and start earning. While I looked about for something I started a small saw-milling business with a mobile sawmill which I used to haul to wherever a client's timber might be and cut it up into whatever dimension timber was required. This proved to be an interesting outdoor activity. I had to learn from scratch but managed to grasp the essentials fairly quickly and became reasonably proficient. I'd discovered a wonderful old saw doctor, Arthur, well past retirement and out to grass with a major sawmill – sweeping up and making tea! He was a mine of information and only too glad to chat to someone who was keen to listen and to learn. I learned. And I was earning.

On the lookout for other employment, now keen on remaining outdoors, and having worked on several estates sawmilling, I went for an interview for an estate manager's job down in Hampshire. A house on the estate went with the job. It was an attractive job on an attractive estate but the move was singularly unattractive to Mary and she wouldn't hear of it. The job was out of the question.

It became apparent that Mary had no intention of moving. And she'd be most unhappy were I to move to where the job was and weekend commute. I was therefore anchored to our cottage home. I bought a bigger and better sawmill and went into mobile sawmilling full time.

I liked the idea of being my own boss, and the work appealed to me not only for its outdoor nature. I got to work in some very attractive places, mainly estates, and because the work was flexible I could work when I wanted and, to an extent, where I wanted. If I didn't like a possible job (or the client) I could turn it down.

Being self-employed also offered me the chance of working until I wanted to retire rather than being turfed out at 65. I was, by now, fitter than I'd been for years so had every prospect of continuing well past that age.

I'd bought my new mill on the strength of a big job on yet another estate. That job paid for the mill. I wasn't earning big money, but I was earning steadily and the major part of my equipment was paid for.

Another mistake I made, and one which, I understand, several newly retired officers make, was to build another extension to the cottage This at a time when what we really needed was a small, three bedroomed cottage – which is exactly what we had. Mary wanted a bigger house. She had the idea that, if all our children (two of our own and two by my earlier marriage to Jo) were to marry and have children, wouldn't it be nice if we could accommodate them all at the same time?! I had always wanted to build a house so went along with the idea of adding a much larger extension to what we had.

I'd been paying what was now quite a substantial monthly sum on an endowment mortgage I'd taken out in 1971 for our first extension. I'd also been receiving regular bonus notices informing me of the latest bonus sums, which were getting quite large. I asked the building society if they'd advance me a loan on the strength of the guaranteed bonus and they couldn't get the money across the counter fast enough. So the bonus on the mortgage for the first extension paid for the second.

Once I'd obtained planning permission I set about buying the building materials. I planned to build up to the eaves but get professional trades to put the roof on, thatch it, and then plumb, wire and plaster it.

It was going to take some time to build because I was trying to earn a living at the same time. The build was further delayed when I had a bad fall, smashed my pelvis and six ribs and punctured a lung. Rushed to hospital, ambulance siren blaring, I was glued back together. The process entailed a few operations. I then had to convalesce, part of the time in a wheelchair, before I could get going again.

During this period Jenni got married in Stafford and Mary had to drive me up for the wedding. During my time in hospital I'd lost 35 lbs in weight and was, and looked as if I was, skeletal. In the wedding photos I managed to conceal my crutch behind Jenni's quite full, and very attractive, wedding dress but my morning suit, ordered before the accident, hung off me like a limp rag, much too large. I'm afraid I ruined a lot of the photos – what bride wants an ill-dressed skeleton of a father, looking like death warmed up, beside her at such an important time?! Nevertheless, I was extremely proud I managed to take part in her wedding.

The land on which the new extension was to stand was a 'made up' site. When we'd first moved in the garden had been a jungle and we'd had to clear the brambles, nettles and weeds and then level it. Thus where I had to build had a mixture of topsoil and the green sand sub-soil down to six feet. Since the topsoil would produce further growth I had to get below it before I could put down foundations. I'd recently acquired a JCB digger, mainly for moving logs about. It dug out the entire foundation area so that it looked more like a swimming pool in the making then a house.

I'd borrowed some do-it-yourself building books from the library and set about pegging out the marker lines for the foundation trenches. It all looked very professional and when the building inspector arrived he declared it was 'text book stuff'. I never told him that was exactly what it was! Later, when I was half way up the walls, on one of his visits I was checking with my spirit level I'd still got the wall vertical.

'Mr Howard, a few centimetres either way wouldn't matter'.

I was horrified. I told him a few millimetres either way was unacceptable to me. He declared it looked as if I knew what I was doing and he was going to leave me to it. I was rather sorry; he'd been enormously helpful all the way so far. He continued to be so, but over the phone mostly.

After the build, roof joists, thatching and the first fix plumbing and electrical work, the plasterers set to work on what, to me, seemed acres of walls. Then, with Anthony's help, I put up stud partitions, laid all the floors and fixed skirting boards. The rest was completed without mishap and Anthony and I started the monumental task of decorating.

Mary and I were eventually able to move into the new extension in 1993.

At about this time my sister Paula and one of her daughters, Nicki, came over from New Zealand to visit and we were discussing old times, particularly the period when my stepfather had been alive. I knew Paula had loathed him as much as I had. I then found out why, over 40 years on.

We had been discussing the flat in Hove, in Ventnor Villas, when Paula and her little daughters used to come and visit my mother. Nicky said: 'Of course, you know that was the 'hands in knickers' time for Pip and me'. I had no idea what she was talking about until she explained that whenever they were alone with the stepfather he interfered with them, putting his hands in their knickers. Afterwards he told them that they must never, never tell anyone about it. They were little girls of about four and six. Then Paula explained that he'd also tried to have a go at her when she was in her teens. I was absolutely aghast. I'd had no knowledge of my stepfather's behaviour. Suddenly what it was about him that I'd detested so much, but couldn't put my finger on, became all too clear.

He was a paedophile. I'd left home to get away from a paedophile. Worse still, my mother must have known about it. Paula told me she'd been sent away to boarding school to get her away from him.

In 1996 Mary and I took a trip to India. Having once done the journey from Calcutta to Bombay, by train, Mary had always wanted to go back. We started off in Madras and journeyed around using internal flights. In Kerala we went up into the hills in the east of the province but had to cut our stay short when Mary slipped in a tiled hotel bathroom one night and broke her wrist. There was no doctor available, and the telephone was out of action. We had to wait until morning and then get a taxi the long journey back to Cochin. There she went into a tiny hospital where the staff was absolutely charming, and much too deferential, and her wrist was set and plastered. When I asked how much I owed the hospital the equally charming Indian doctor asked me how much I had on me. Stupidly I told him. Surprisingly, the bill came to exactly that amount! One of the first things we had to do when we left the hospital was to cash some travellers cheques.

Soon Mary started to get seriously ill. Fortunately our visit was just about at an end and I was relieved when we finally got aboard the aircraft for the flight home. Mary was having difficulty eating. Back in the UK her GP could find nothing wrong with her, but her appetite just got less and less. We took a trip down to Bordeaux to stay with Mary's aunt, the widow of her late much loved uncle, hoping that Mary would pick up. She didn't, and could do nothing but rest, either in bed or on the settee, eating virtually nothing. After five days, on a Friday, I drove like a madman all the way up to Cherbourg and we got on a ferry home. Mary was now in a bad way and I took her to see our GP the following morning. His only observation was: 'Now, now Mrs Howard. You mustn't think every time you feel unwell, you've got cancer again'.

We didn't know it at the time, but this was the beginning of the end for Mary. Only a few days later, in the middle of the night I was so alarmed I called the duty doctor – fortunately not our GP. He took one look at Mary, called an ambulance, and she was rushed to Salisbury Hospital. She had a tumour as big as a rugby ball in her lower abdomen, and had to undergo an immediate emergency colostomy. I brought her home a few days later to recuperate and try and gain sufficient strength for an operation on the tumour, and, of course, chemo-therapy.

The surgeon was so concerned for her he told her if she was in any doubt I was to bring her back straight away. It wasn't long before I had to take her back. She was immediately re-admitted, and then began the sad process of events that gave rise to the succeeding chapters. Mary's eighteen years' remission had run out, but the vow she made when first diagnosed with cancer in the States, she'd managed to keep. She'd seen her children grow up and even acquired two grandsons.

Chapters 36, 37 and 38 were written soon after Mary died. Chapter 39 I wrote many months later. I found writing them therapeutic, and the process helped me greatly along a road I considered, with my background and resilience, I could negotiate with relative ease. I was so wrong – again.

# Chapter 37

## *Bad News Teapot*

SOMEHOW I had shut down to reality, simply couldn't accept what was almost screaming out at me, as I passed most of those next few days after Mary's operation at, or close to, her bedside.

Mary's friend Tricia had volunteered to feed and walk my dogs so I had no other domestic commitments. I was free to wait – by Mary's bedside on the ward, when she woke, or in the hospital corridor until she was wheeled back from theatre. I needed her to know I was still there, waiting for her, and refusing to give up hope.

Then one morning the ward sister got up from her central desk and hurried across to me at Mary's bedside. She asked me quietly if I'd 'come and have a word in private' with the doctor. She scarcely looked at me, and she never looked at Mary at all. Her abruptness was unlike her, and ominous.

I wasn't surprised that she hurried. The staff worked so hard on this ward they sometimes never had time for a coffee break, although they always found time from somewhere to comfort visitors in distress – get them a cup of tea, keep checking that they were O.K.

I was surprised that sister never looked at my wife; that presaged badly for Mary – a Nightingale – one of that talented band of St Thomas' trained nurses who, justifiably, regarded themselves as the *crème de la crème* of nursing, past and present. Although the ward sister wasn't a Nightingale, Mary recognised her professionalism, admired her for it and they had become firm friends. So there was no doubt in Mary's mind about the unusual absence of eye contact.

Mary suspected that her days were numbered – her cancer had returned yet again, this time far worse than before – a massive abdominal tumour that must have been developing for years. With her nursing experience she would have guessed that this 'private word' would be formal notification that her suspicions were well founded.

I followed the ward sister down the ward, telling myself as I went that I could no longer refuse to accept what had been staring at me for months. I was about to come face to face with stark reality. I could no longer not acknowledge to myself that Mary was dying.

I suppose I must be one of those people who simply refuse to countenance the worst until there is absolutely no chance left. Mary had always known I would never give up hope, until there was no hope. All through the last few months, as her quality of life had been progressively degraded, I had simply not allowed the worst to enter my mind. Perhaps I had been blindly stupid, but, even now in hindsight, I know there was no way I could have discussed with Mary the possibility that she might die, until I was certain. And she knew this. Only later did I hear from our daughter that Mary had earlier told her she had no wish to continue in the dreadful state of debility she'd been reduced to. She'd endured and beaten the mastectomy eighteen years ago in the States. Now a colostomy - plus the prospect of more chemotherapy before an operation for the tumour . But she would never have said as much to me until I acknowledged to her that the end was inevitable.

This doesn't mean that Mary gave up, even for a moment, or lost one iota of the phenomenal courage she always showed, and would continue to show, right to the end. She was just being far more realistic than me. Her only comment on the point was to visiting girl friends the following day – she hadn't expected it to be quite so soon.

Sister showed me into a private room where the doctor was waiting. We shook hands and he waved me to a chair beside him. Sister pulled up a chair directly in front of me. This surprised me initially, until I realised it had been pre-arranged that she should be present, that she would need to look after me in what was likely to be intense distress.

The doctor was young and, I knew, capable, and he looked extremely upset. He and Mary had also become firm friends, even though she'd been through a very painful operation under him and his consultant surgeon. She enjoyed his humour and trusted him implicitly. I, too, liked this young doctor who had so conscientiously given untold care and attention to my wife.

He ran through all that had happened to Mary since she'd first been admitted to hospital several weeks before. I wasn't helping him. I'd been unable to hold back my tears almost since he started talking. It must have been a few minutes, but to me it seemed only seconds, before he reached the crisis point: Mary's tumour was just too large and aggressive. She had only a few days left to live.

By this time I was crying uncontrollably. The tissues I had brought with me were a useless, soggy mess and sister fed me more. In comforting me she held my forearms, leaving my hands free to dab continuously at my eyes. Between my sobs I managed to stammer out a request that Mary might die painlessly.

After reassuring me that this would certainly be the case, the doctor left us. He was considerably more upset than when we'd started, but at least he'd managed to control his feelings. I wondered how many times this young doctor had had to deal with middle-aged men in my situation. Women are expected to give vent to their feelings with tears; in their boyhood men are usually exhorted never to cry – 'be brave, it was cissy to cry'. As a result there are too many tears to shed in manhood, an unusual experience that I was never allowed to learn to handle, and that I now find difficult to cope with, or to control.

Sister stayed with me, waiting for my heaving sobs to subside, talking gently to me – I don't know what about – calming me, but, above all, staying with me. Are women naturals in these circumstances? It struck me that she was very, very good at her job. Do they do courses in compassion? Is this why she was a ward sister?

Slowly my sobbing eased, albeit I couldn't stop my tears. Sister asked me if there was anything she could do for me. I was conscious that she had already done so much for me, given so much of her precious time. I knew she'd be completing her paper-work well beyond the end of her shift. I said I could murder a cup of tea. There was a ward tea trolley just outside in the passage, and I thought it would only take her a few seconds. She went out to get it.

I then realised I had to pull myself together, and quickly. When I left that room the first thing I'd have to do would be to go back to the ward and tell Mary – even though I knew she more than half expected it. But she would want, and the doctor and the ward sister would want, me to be the one to tell her.

How do you tell your wife she's going to die – and soon. Suddenly 'until death do us part' was right there, was about to become reality, but I'd never even given it serious thought. After all the gentle things, the tender things, the happy words, the angry words, the jokes that made her eyes light up, the laughter. How do you say: 'I'm sorry, you're going to die, and very soon'? How do you, as gently as possible, tell your wife the worst news you could ever have to break to her?

Sister came back, and only when she reappeared did I appreciate she'd been gone rather longer then it took to get a cup of tea from the tea trolley. She carried a tray, and on it, the most magnificent, ornate teapot I'd ever seen – gilt and enamel, with fluted sides, and a long, curved, elegant spout. It was large enough to pour at least six cups without a refill! With it were a cup and saucer to match. This was obviously part of sister's 'comfort for anguished visitors' procedure, brought out only in special circumstances.

It was good therapy. It took my mind off my distress a little, and I started to calm down. As my cup of tea was poured I admired the Victoriana style – possibly genuine – teapot.

I dubbed it the 'bad news teapot'.

The ward staff gave Mary and me time to recover after I'd gone back to Mary's bedside. Somehow I'd managed to tell her what she already knew. Now it was out in the open between us. Even then I hadn't really hoisted it in. I was punchdrunk.

Reality started to bite the following day. Several of Mary's girlfriends were visiting. I'd left them to it and was hovering at the ward entrance. A senior nursing sister came up and introduced herself. In the gentlest manner she explained that there was now a bed available for Mary in the nearby hospice.

Every member of the hospital staff concerned had somehow managed, in the gentlest and most considerate way, to bring me to this point: this would be a one-way trip for Mary.

At last I fully acknowledged the bad news.

# Chapter 38

## *The Urn*

AS I wandered around my desolate home, out to the garage, back to the cottage, upstairs, downstairs, kitchen, living rooms no longer alive, kitchen, kitchen, kitchen, I wept steadily. In the kitchen I had just cut up, into as small pieces as I could, the polythene urn that had held my wife's ashes. I was going to burn the pieces, even though I knew it was only symbolic, that it couldn't affect her in any way, that she had really gone, irrevocably, finally, never to return to that cottage, her garden, her children or to me.

The urn, very ordinary looking, dark brown, surprisingly large, had been quite tough to cut up, but there it now was, shredded, so that I could incinerate it, all those pieces, just as my wife's body had been incinerated on the date given on the label.

It might only have been symbolic but I could not bring myself simply to throw the pieces of the urn into the dustbin, as refuse, to contribute, mixed with every other kind of household detritus, to some unknown landfill site.

I was going to burn them on the garden bonfire – with all those cuttings, even weeds, from the garden my wife had worked so hard to make her own individual shrine. She had loved her garden, and there was no more appropriate way to dispose of the urn.

We had scattered the ashes that afternoon up on the Marlborough Downs, toward the eastern end. It was quite a few weeks since the funeral – it sounded a long time to wait – but the day had been the first that was clear and breezy and that I and our two children and grandsons could all be together. My wife had never decreed how or when her ashes were to be scattered, only where. I had chosen the how and the when, and the conditions had to be perfect, as they had been on today.

As so we'd all gone – my son and daughter who, aged nine and eight respectively when my wife had first been diagnosed with cancer, had vowed she would see grow up, with the two grandsons she adored, and with the two dogs she had loved so dearly and which had so loved her, and me - we'd all climbed Walker's Hill. My son had taken the urn from me, ostensibly to make it easier for his father to climb. More probably he had wanted to hold, for the last time, some positive, physical reminder of his mother. They had been close.

Towards the top we had stopped on a crest, where it looked out down Pewsey Vale to the east, across Salisbury Plain to the south, and west back to where our cottage lay, too far to see. Behind us had been Milk Hill and its nipple, and, further back the White Horse.

Gorgeous little Jake rising three, had managed to walk up, holding on to his mother's hand. Oz, the other, equally gorgeous, younger grandson who had looked so much like his grandmother, had ridden happily on his uncle's shoulders.

As we had come up to the crest, what had been a slight breeze at the foot of the climb had become almost a gale out of the southwest. The visibility had been as good as when my wife, years back, had first brought me up there to marvel at the panorama spread around and below us. I knew I'd chosen the right day, the right conditions, to say this final Goodbye.

And so we, first father, then son, and then my daughter, slowly allowed those grey ashes, all that remained of our wife and mother, gently to trickle from the urn and to blow down the wind: to disperse across, over, the Downs she had loved so much, and which she had looked out on from our bedroom. Had she some premonition that the furthermost point she could see from that bedroom window would be her final resting place; or rather, the point from which her earthly remains would disperse, across the Wiltshire she had loved?

None of her ashes had immediately fallen on the grass. As she had wanted, she had simply drifted down the wind – and gone.

And only the urn had remained: and her bereft family – all weeping openly, and praying silently – on the windblown, empty hill, as we had watched down the wind, the way she had gone. Even her two little grandsons had been silent. The last physical attachment had been severed.

We'd stumbled back down the hill, grandchildren now, fortunately, keeping us in the real world: Jake with grassy hillocks and slopes to run up and fall down; Oz back again on his uncle's shoulders, urging him to do the same, shouting and laughing, unaffected, happy, boisterous little boys – life has to go on.

Driving home in the car father, son and daughter were all quietly grieving, but recovered slowly with the therapy of two little boys chattering to anyone who cared to listen, Jake quite intelligible, Oz half words, half scribble, but an active participant, communicating with us and his brother. The boys had unwittingly eased our painful distress, unconsciously drawing us back into the real world, their world, and away from the world of the grandmother they had known and loved, but had now almost forgotten.

My son had gone back to work. My daughter had returned home with my grandsons. The gaping void in the cottage was that night cavernous, and almost tangible.

And now I'd cut up the urn. Tomorrow I would cremate it.

# Chapter 39

## *Cathartic Therapy*

I had always wanted to write about events when Mary was so ill, those last few desperate weeks until she died, and her funeral. I knew I couldn't start writing too soon – I was too close to the tragedy. I also knew I could never be objective – what man could who has sat and watched his wife slowly die – but there had to come a time when I wouldn't be totally subjective, when I was able to talk rationally about events that had occurred. It would be another milestone behind me, another indicator that I was starting to get my grief under control. I don't know whether you ever do get it fully under control.

I also had an instinctive feeling that such writing would be good therapy for me, would somehow help ease that grief.

The hospice staff – forever my heroines – warned me that grief could suddenly leap out and bite at the most unexpected moments, with no warning at all. How right they were. How many times, blinded by tears, had I stumbled out of church, utterly riven – by a line, or even a word in a hymn, the organ music? Or simply by the reminder that this was where Mary's funeral took place – where I and my children knelt, and found it almost unbearable to be so close to her coffin, almost impossible to look at for more than few seconds at a time. How many times afterwards had I come away from a dinner party, bridge evenings, weddings even – and broken down in the car, alone; driven home to an empty house; gone up to a lonely bed.

What happens when you write about a personal tragedy, about an experience that was so painful that my whole being became numb, I entered some kind of on-going trance that I had to maintain at any cost, some robotic state in which I knew, but only latterly acknowledged to myself, what the outcome would be – that Mary was going to die – and that, no matter how tired or distressed I might get I just had to keep on keeping on, on autopilot, driving myself, trying to appear as normal as possible, to appear in control.

Why do men have to be seen to be in control? Is it one more of the last, crumbling bastions of chauvinism? Don't let the side down, don't be seen to be crying, to be weak, put on a brave face, keep a stiff upper lip. I kept running out of brave faces and stiff upper lips. The longer you keep it up the harder you fall, come apart, almost disintegrate psychologically, sometimes publicly, but inevitably when you're alone. So why write about it? Was it a form of masochism? Why relive all the agonies, the distress?

It had to be therapy. For me it was an extension, a continuation of that period when I sat by Mary's bed in the hospice, holding her hand and talking, gently, tenderly. What did I say? Probably not enough. Is this why I had a compulsion to write, to talk to her again? Perhaps it was a guilt complex. I'm naturally taciturn – could I not find words enough for my wife as she lay dying? I'll never know. All I do know now is that this therapy, of letting my feelings wander out into words, was helping me through the grieving process.

I held Mary's arm and hand all the time as she lay in bed, usually with one of our children on her other arm; she keeping hold of me, of us, ultimately only able to acknowledge our words with a squeeze. She could do little else, heavily sedated with painkiller, and slowly dying. But she understood everything we said. As her ability to converse slowly degenerated into a nod, some kind of sound, a flicker of her eyelids, and then only the faintest squeeze of a hand, there was always an acknowledgement, right to the end.

Mary died on a Monday. The day before she died she could barely speak. But on that Sunday morning she had managed to ask how I'd slept. I then realised she knew that I'd woken during the night. In the hospice I slept with my bed pulled up beside hers, and, that night, Saturday/Sunday, I'd had a strange, unique experience. I had woken in the middle of the night because the palms of both my hands were pulsating powerfully. The flesh seemed to be lifting a full inch with each pulsation, such a powerful sensation I had to ask myself whether I was dreaming. I lay there in the darkness, holding my hands in the air, trying to determine what this not unpleasant sensation could be. Eventually I gave up and put both hands on Mary's bare arm as she slept. To do this I had to reach up between the side rails of her hospice bed – slightly higher than mine – and I lay there with both my hands surging these powerful pulses into her.

Perhaps it was a subconscious desire to transfer my body strength to her, to give her enough strength to fight back, to beat the cancer after all. I don't know how long it lasted. I fell asleep and my hands must have fallen away. I woke again briefly and the sensation had stopped. But in the morning Mary knew something special had happened and had asked. I had explained as best I could.

Through Sunday morning I kept hold of Mary, talking, thanking her for our life together, our children, our home. She seemed to be asleep, but still she acknowledged everything I said, that faint sound, a nod, a squeeze. And then suddenly she opened her eyes and looked straight at me, completely focussed, with a trace of a smile. She tried to lift her hands to my face but was too weak – she could only just raise them from the bedcover. I lifted them for her and held them up against my cheeks. Very gently, but clearly, she told me: 'I do love you so'.

Those were the last words Mary ever spoke. Some people might think it strange that I should call myself a lucky man. But if your wife is dying, what more fortunate circumstance than to be with her day and night during her last days, to know she understood everything, and that these should be her very last words.

So the experience of writing about this experience is strongly therapeutic. Perhaps it's also re-writing part of our life, recreating a love story.

I've always believed that you only remember the good things in life, unless some event was exceptionally bad. And now I only remember the good things, the funny things, the host of happy experiences we had, the experiences that Mary created for me, for us as a family. And her love for our children was so uniting, bonding, welding the family as a positive entity. And this same love carried over to our grandchildren – two little boys, my daughter's sons, who Mary worshipped. Initially this love for her grandsons surprised me with its intensity, until I remembered Mary had first revealed a ferocious bravery and determination when her cancer was initially diagnosed. Our children were then only eight and nine, and she was dogged in her resolve to see them grow up. She did – and then lived to see two gorgeous grandsons.

I sift through all the memories, mostly painful, of those last few weeks, the grievous but tranquil days in the hospice, those so few minutes after Mary had stopped breathing, as I held her wrist, the nurse holding the other arm, feeling her last moments of life ebbing away beneath our fingers, flickering ever more faintly, as a candle about to go out, and then – nothing – she'd gone; I relive the agony of the following week up to and including Mary's funeral; I know again the incredible waves of love and support that started when Mary first became seriously ill, so long ago now, and which continued through that week.

I recall my tears over my letters of thanks. I felt compelled to answer each one in longhand. And this was therapy writing of another kind, a milestone I had to get behind me, not just Thank You's to so many friends who'd written, but a positive, longhand acknowledgement of the love and affection friends had expressed for Mary, and for me and the children.

And slowly the pain eases; not so the grief, but at least I'm learning to handle it. And my philosophy that you only remember the good things in life has started to manifest itself. I still weep, sometimes uncontrollably, but no longer unaccountably. I now know why. I'm no different to any other Mr Average. But, for a while everyone must think they're unique: their pain and grief have never really been surpassed or even equalled by anybody else. However, my reactions, feelings, sensitivities, thoughts, are the same as the millions of others who've been through a similar experience. It's comforting to appreciate that you're only going through what they've already suffered – have not only come out the other side, but somehow come out a better person.

# Chapter 40

## *Friendship*

I never understood why Tricia kept in touch: just gave thanks that she did. She'd been a close friend of Mary's – the sisterhood of the dreaded cancer.

Over a number of months, Mary had slowly and courageously succumbed to the disease. Latterly Tricia had quietly lent her support, somehow managing to run her own home and keep up her magistrate's duties. She walked our dogs morning and evening and fed them, enabling me to return, as often and as long as possible, to Mary's hospital bedside. Then, finally, the hospice.

The hospice had invited me to stay and Tricia volunteered support with no time limit. I went, and returned days later, numb, on that final journey back, to a home that was now only mine. No more 'ours'. No more wife. No more life. I was 65. I was a widower.

Tricia is a born carer. She kept up her contact, phoned, visited. Never intrusive. Always solicitous about my, and my children's, well being. She continued looking after the dogs when I went back to work part time – encouraged by her. She remained a psychological prop – although I would never have admitted I needed one – much too macho, much too 'in control'. I'd manage, ride out my grief, the depth of which I never could have imagined, and then carry on – without a wife, companion, mother, homemaker.

But I didn't manage – and I was too numb, and dumb, to realise. But Tricia did. She never brought the subject up, simply kept on with her visits to what must have seemed to her a declining wreck of a man, who'd handled every emergency throughout his naval career and had been confident he could handle this: but was now blinded by his inflated sense of personal resilience.

I was accepting many casual bridge invitations and thought I was getting through them fairly well; stiff upper lip and all that! But driving back home there was no one to talk to. No one to discuss who said what, analyse that peculiar bridge hand, or the strange bidding, how someone had behaved. I had to pull over because I could no longer safely drive through the tears, thankful for the privacy of the dark, and the loneliness.

Back home to the emptiness of the cottage, only the dogs, as lonely as I was, plainly wondering why, where Mary was, so glad to see me, making me feel guilty at having left them; I wished I hadn't. I preferred their company, their unquestioning loyalty, their love. I wished I could explain to them what had happened. They knew I was crying, softly and steadily, hot tears coursing down my face in the privacy of this barren cottage, and they felt for me, offered me their paws in consolation. I would blind my way upstairs with them close at my heels, see the scratches they'd made on the doors, trying to find Mary somewhere. I tried to comfort them, and, in petting them, stroking them, hugging them, acknowledged that I was as lost and lonely as they were. Do dogs ever cry? Or are they committed always to try and comfort us: the ones who do cry? Thank God for dogs: always faithful, always loyal.

Several months after Mary died, my public stiff upper lip started to crumble. Although she never mentioned it, I think Tricia must have realised I was sliding into a serious depression. I'd taken to shaving irregularly - previously an anathema to me. Too often she watched me weep, something my generation had been brought up to believe was unmanly, and which now unmanned me completely. I'd never learned to cope with it and now it seemed that the tears repressed all the way back to my childhood just poured from me. Tricia let me cry it out for as long as it took. No hint of disapproval, only gentle, positive, unlimited support. Slowly she started rebuilding me by just being there, prompting me to talk, listening, watching me weep, letting me let myself go, just letting the grief flow, quietly reassuring me, confident I'd get back on my feet, rebuilding a self-confidence that, in hindsight, I acknowledge was in tatters.

I marvelled at her compassion and understanding. Only much later did I learn just how much personal tragedy she'd endured in her life. But she was without anger or bitterness: simply limitless compassion, and friendship.

I became wary of Tricia's visits. Partly it was because I'd not yet shed my macho 'I can hack it on my own' complex; I didn't need any more help, although I'd never forget the help and support she'd already given me so unstintingly. And partly it was because her attractiveness scared me.

Tricia was beautiful: absolutely lovely, petite, effortlessly graceful, her hair a glorious titian, the sort of woman you noticed anywhere, made me immediately conscious I was a man – and glad to be. But this appreciation of her beauty was, from the time of our first meeting until long after Mary died, purely academic, simply a natural male reaction. Latterly I assumed that a woman like her would never look twice at me: a much older man. Were I to attempt any sort of him/her association I'd be starting at too great a disadvantage. Best now to forget it. Every man must call it a day at some stage. At my age wasn't the barrenness of new widower-hood an appropriate time to bow out?

But now I found myself in a euphoric state over our friendship. This was an attractive, amusing, and compassionate companion and a she that made me all he. I returned to my former fastidiousness about my appearance – shaving once again became de rigueur. I slowly became aware that it mattered - to me, and possibly to her – how I looked. Tricia was giving me back a purpose in life, making me realise that it was there for the taking: aware also that she was the reason I wanted to pick it up.

Despite my apparent euphoria, wasn't it too soon? I'd not yet fully accepted that life has to go on and the sooner I got on with it the better. I began dimly to realise that there was little point in wallowing in reclusive widower-hood but was concerned that I shouldn't hurt Tricia. I'd come to value our friendship so much and would never have believed I was capable of bonding so strongly. How could I risk hurting her? I knew she liked me – as a friend – but couldn't imagine she could seriously be attracted to me. Would it be one-sided, bound to end in her being hurt because I was now beyond what it took to return her feelings? Or was I too afraid of committing myself? Was I on the rebound, prey to feelings I thought I could never again experience, had no wish to wrestle with again?

We trod cautiously. We visited towns new to us, neutral ground, and I was proud to have this beautiful woman on my arm. Shopkeepers were attentive, suddenly imbued with a charm not wasted on me; I was only the spectator. Tricia turned heads wherever we went, and I luxuriated in other men's envy. We were easy in each other's company, allowed each other as much space as we needed, quietly sounded each other out.

But I was still hesitant, scared to make any declaration. No fool like an old fool, especially one in a still relatively new widower-hood, albeit now several years old.

I don't remember when it dawned on me. No blinding flash of light, inspiration, understanding, but suddenly I realised I was no longer scared or uncertain. If this could be the rest of my life then I had to grab it with both hands: now. Nothing could ever undermine this friendship I valued so dearly. It was our foundation.

Just after my 70th birthday Tricia and I were married. For the first time since I'd entered the navy at age 15, I was no longer a loner – nor will ever be again.

# Chapter 41

## *Epilogue*

A passion from the past – a prayer for the future.

*HMS Ark Royal* has just been taken out of service and Great Britain no longer has a current naval fixed wing capability. By 2021 we are promised new carriers with new fixed wing aircraft to follow.

It's 45 years since I flew my last sortie from a carrier. At that time, I hoped it wouldn't be my last. I had wanted to take my next, front line, Buccaneer squadron to sea in *Ark Royal*, get some more carrier flying in – my last chance. But she was in refit and I wasn't lucky enough to stick around long enough.

All my flying gave me intense satisfaction but I've never forgotten the buzz my carrier flying gave me. The following is a little of my passion from the past.

***

My flying career largely spanned the days of catapults, arrestor wires and angled deck carriers. From *Bulwark* I flew Seahawks, from *Ark Royal* - Seahawks and Scimitars, and from *Eagle* - Seahawks and Buccaneers.

I did spend a night in *Victorious* but only 'passed through'. My squadron was due to disembark from *Eagle* but both her catapults were unserviceable. The only way we could take off was to use the full length of the deck on a free take off run, with our Seahawks defuelled down to minimum. With the ship flat out for maximum wind over the deck, we taxied as far back on the deck as we could, turned for'ard and stopped. We wound up to full throttle on the brakes, said a prayer, (none of us had ever done this before!), hoped for the best, released the brakes and started our take off run. We got airborne abreast the island, relieved, but with nails a little frayed. We landed straight on in *Vic*. After refuelling to full – kerosene for our aircraft, horses' necks for the aircrew, an enjoyable one-night pit stop with many old chums and a night's recovery - we launched from *Vic*'s catapults next morning and flew ashore.

\*\*\*

My favourite aircraft was the Buccaneer – it did what it was designed to do: low-level penetration – and it did it well. You could go places in a Bucc. at levels you'd never dare to in other aircraft. It was my first all-weather aircraft and that meant a true night flying capability, and handling on the approach to land on deck was a dream.

\*\*\*

Carrier flying enabled power projection anywhere across the oceans of the world. It gave me a lot of satisfaction being one small part of a team of hundreds of men in a ship – all working towards the efficient operation of their aircraft in pursuit of that aim.  My small contribution to the sea borne team effort was carrier flying – and I loved it.

\*\*\*

There was an aura of action and efficiency on the deck. Worked up flight deck teams were a joy to watch working aircraft, every man, in the coloured jacket denoting his team job, knowing what he had to do, when and where he had to do it. These men were fit, fast and efficient and they needed to be. Jet engine blast could blow an unwary man clean off the deck and over the side; the jet intakes could suck a man into their maw – with fatal results. Aircraft were big beasts and could be lethal – flight deck men had to be constantly 'on the ball'.  There was no room for a passenger on a flight deck in full spate.

\*\*\*

Once aircraft had started engines, for me the flight deck became a supercharged 'ballet' – orchestrated by the constant 'music' of the jet engines, although once our aircraft canopy was closed, snug in our flying helmets, we were hardly aware of the roar outside on deck.  One by one aircraft were brought out from their ship's side park into the centre of the deck where we had clearance to spread our wings. We were then marshalled forward to the catapults.

When the Buccaneer was 'tensioned' on the catapult it was pulled forward so that it sat up in the flying attitude, nose wheel off the deck. The deck officer-in-charge then gave the signal to go to full throttle: a wind up with a yellow flag above his head. A quick check of the cockpit instruments, and the pilot hand signalled 'Ready to launch'. By the time the yellow flag was dropped – the 'fire' to the catapult engineers – we, the aircrew, were settled firmly back in our ejection seats, waiting for the thrust of the catapult launch. Then we were off - into the sheer, three-dimensional elation of flying.

Maybe it was dive attacks with bombs or rockets, on the splash target towed astern of the ship, the hi-g pull out of each dive inflating g-suits around the abdomen and legs, preventing the blood draining from the upper body. Perhaps it was a long-range strike, with in-flight refuelling at altitude to extend the range. Or it could be an aerobatic display, g-suit continuously inflated in 7-g turns, vortices streaming from the wingtips. Finally there was the recovery on the carrier – for me the cherry on the top!

Flying twenty-three plus tons of aircraft back down to the deck to arrive, at the right speed (some 140 - 150 mph for a Buccaneer), into the arrestor wires, the abrupt deceleration throwing us forward against our straps, 'cleaning up' the aircraft – arrestor hook up, flaps up, folding wings was, for me, heady stuff. So was the teamwork with the flight deck marshallers after landing on, as they directed us forward into the deck park, clear for the next aircraft to land on. I found it all an exhilarating challenge and I revelled in it.

Night flying for me was almost a passion. The absolute 100% concentration, the launching from the catapult, the airborne exercise, and the recovery to land back on deck all gave me a buzz that I anticipated with relish.

To maintain good night vision, lighting on the flight deck was a subdued red - and atmospheric. Parked aircraft waited on deck for their crews, wings folded, ghostly in the gloom. Over the ship's side there was phosphorescence in the bow wave, or astern in the wake, as the carrier built up speed for launching. Beyond it was black. In the tropics that black was pure velvet.

The flight deck 'ballet' was also subdued; a flight deck by night required just a tad more care than by day. Even so, for me it was still a ballet – aircrew and ground crew working as a team – operating aircraft.

On the catapult, given the signal - a wand instead of the day flag - throttles opened to full, engine power and temperatures checked, I signal ready to launch. We settle back in our ejection seats, the wand drops, and the aircraft is fired off into the black – me straight on to instrument flying, some fifty feet above the water.

My head continuously down in the cockpit, glued to the instrument panel, we climb away, wheels up, flaps up, accelerating to optimum climbing speed, my left hand finding the switches automatically, blind.

Without looking up from my instruments I can tell when we enter cloud. In my peripheral vision I'm aware of the pulse of the navigation lights, reflecting off the cotton wool cloud surrounding our aircraft.

When the pulsing ceases we've broken the cloud tops. For the first time since we've fired down the catapult, we can look up. We have a natural horizon. By moonlight the top of the cloud layer, dropping away below us in the climb, is a sea of mother of pearl stretching off to that distant horizon, into the deep, star-studded indigo night. The beauty of this new world never fails to delight me.

Our exercise could be a climb to height, with in-flight refuelling at the top of the climb, a long range cruise to the top of the descent, and let down for a strike on a maritime target from low level.

In moonlit twilight we rendezvous with the tanker at 35,000 ft. He already has his hose streamed, its conical basket – the drogue - holding it stable in flight. We close up astern of him, flying for the lights dimly visible in the drogue's basket. Our flight-refuelling nozzle, slightly right on our aircraft nose, nuzzles and then locks into the 'basket'. We refuel to full, then ease back, and slip gently from the hose. We're on our way.

My observer already holds the target on radar and gives me a course to steer. We have a lengthy cruise to run and he keeps me advised as the range closes. At his bidding, I start our descent, to remain under the target's radar lobe. Firmly back on instruments, we penetrate the cloud layer, into the black, adjusting course regularly, directed by the observer, levelling off to run in at 200 feet, high speed. At his predetermined distance to run, the observer gives the word and I pull up to fire our illuminants. Our aim when they burst is to silhouette the target while I'm pulling round steeply on instruments, through 360°, to bring us to the top of a dive attack under the falling flares. Then get out fast.

The observer gives me the course for home as we turn in the climb back to height. It's most economical on fuel up there. We've a long way to run to mother – the carrier.

Recovering to the carrier is exacting. Descending, I settle back flying on instruments again before we enter cloud. The carrier's radar controllers now take over, marshalling all aircraft to land, spacing us out in a stream and feeding us down a descent pattern into a Carrier Controlled Approach (CCA), coming in at intervals astern of the ship, to the top of the glide path.

By this stage my observer and I are in our own exclusive world of rapport with the controller, isolated from the black velvet outside, just us and him, me locked on to my instruments, somewhere astern of the carrier.

Now level at 2,000 feet, we prepare for landing: arrestor hook down, wheels down - four green lights, flaps down, complete our remaining landing checks, and I reduce to our calculated landing speed before reaching the glidepath.

When instructed I start the descent, easing back on the throttles to give us the correct rate of descent while maintaining the right speed. Speed is also monitored by audio – a steady tone: correct, high beep: fast, low beep: slow. The controller talks us down the glidepath, advising us where we are on the slope: above, below or on it, and our line up with the centre line. Steady on instruments, I adjust accordingly.

This is intensely satisfying: carrier and successive aircraft and aircrew all working together each to bring twenty plus tons of aircraft safely down. We all know the radar controller, a shipmate, and we trust him – he is good, doing his usual professional job – talking quietly over the radio, like a Dutch uncle, as he directs us.

I am flying to his directions, relying on his expertise until the visual take over in the final stages when, as he advises, I look up from my instruments.

The only visible indications of the landing area are the flight deck centre and side line lighting, and, left and right of the landing run, deck landing projector sight lights. Each sight has a bar of green lights, one either side of the 'meatball' – a single white light. Generally pilots use the left hand sight. All lights are dimmed, including the softer 'pigtail' lights down the ship's stern.

Keep the meatball lined up between the green bars and the aircraft is on the correct glidepath. Below the greens it's low; above it's high; correct accordingly. And still our radar controller keeps talking, advising continuously until the aircraft crosses the rounddown (stern) and into the arrestor wires. From 140 -150 mph to rest in a couple of seconds, the aircraft rolling back under the elasticity of the arrestor wire system; brakes on, hook up, flaps up, fold wings, taxi forward and clear the landing area.

*** 

For me carrier flying was the ultimate. I sincerely hope it will again be – for other young naval pilots in the future.